© Copyright 2022 - All rights reserved.

You may not reproduce, duplicate or send the contents of this book without direct written permission from the author. You cannot hereby despite any circumstance blame the publisher or hold him or her to legal responsibility for any reparation, compensations, or monetary forfeiture owing to the information included herein, either in a direct or an indirect way.

Legal Notice: This book has copyright protection. You can use the book for personal purpose. You should not sell, use, alter, distribute, quote, take excerpts or paraphrase in part or whole the material contained in this book without obtaining the permission of the author first.

Disclaimer Notice: You must take note that the information in this document is for casual reading and entertainment purposes only. We have made every attempt to provide accurate, up to date and reliable information. We do not express or imply guarantees of any kind. The persons who read admit that the writer is not occupied in giving legal, financial, medical or other advice. We put this book content by sourcing various places.

Please consult a licensed professional before you try any techniques shown in this book. By going through this document, the book lover comes to an agreement that under no situation is the author accountable for any forfeiture, direct or indirect, which they may incur because of the use of material contained in this document, including, but not limited to, —errors, omissions, or inaccuracies.

WorldWide Spark Publish

ROUMANIA
PAST AND PRESENT

BY

JAMES SAMUELSON

PREFACE.

There is no country in Europe which at the present time possesses greater interest for Englishmen than does the Kingdom of Romania, and there is none with whose present state and past history, nay, with whose very geographical position, they are less familiar.

Only about nine years since Consul-General Green, the British representative there, reported to his Government as follows: 'Ignorance seems to extend even to the geographical position of Bucharest. It is not surprising that letters directed to the Romanian capital should sometimes travel to India in search of Bokhara, but there can be no excuse for the issue of a writ of summons by one of the superior law courts of the British metropolis, directed to Bucharest in the Kingdom of Egypt, as I have known to happen.' The reader may perhaps attribute such mistakes as these to our insular ignorance of geography, or to the fact that the proverbial blindness of justice prevented her from consulting the map before issuing her process; but the fact remains, that notwithstanding the occurrence of a great war subsequent to the date above specified, which completely changed the map of Europe, wherein Romania took a very prominent part and England assisted at the settlement, there are few intelligent readers in this country who could say off-hand where precisely Romania is situated.

And yet, as already remarked, the country possesses an absorbing interest for us as a nation. Placed, to a large extent through English instrumentality, as an independent kingdom, of daily increasing influence, between Russia and Turkey, for whom she served for centuries as a bone of contention, she is now a formidable barrier against the aggression of the stronger power upon her weaker neighbor, and it is satisfactory to reflect that, so far, the blood and money of England have not flowed in vain. Then, again, the question of the free navigation of the great stream that serves as her southern boundary is at present occupying the serious consideration of many leading European statesmen, and the solution of the Danubian difficulty will materially affect our trade with the whole of Eastern Europe; whilst the peaceable creation of a peasant proprietary in Romania about sixteen years since, and the advantages which have accrued to her from this social and political reform, present features of peculiar interest for those who favor the establishment of a similar class of landholders in Ireland.

In treating of these two questions, I have labored under the great disadvantage of not being able to follow current events. It is understood that the Danubian difficulty will be settled on the plan, referred to in the text, suggested by Austria for her own advantage, with certain modifications, having for their object the limitation of her preponderance. My readers will be able to judge for themselves, after reading the brief review of the question, and the references to our own commercial relations with the countries bordering on the Danube in the third and fifth chapters, whether such a settlement is likely to be final. For myself I cannot believe that any solution will be permanently satisfactory which interferes with the jurisdiction of Romania in her own waters.

As to the land question, it calls up some awkward reflections when its history is contrasted with recent and passing events in Ireland. So long as the conquerors in Romania endeavored to solve the problem, their efforts were unavailing. At the Convention of Balta-Liman between Russia and Turkey, where 'coercion' was coupled with 'remedial measures,' an ineffectual attempt was made to ameliorate the wretched condition of the peasantry on the old lines of feudalism; but it was not until the country became autonomous and the legitimate representatives of the people took the matter in hand, that an efficient remedy was applied. Then, as the reader will find detailed in the following pages, more than four hundred thousand heads of families among the peasantry came into peaceful possession of a large proportion of the land on equitable terms; and whilst the industrious agriculturist is now daily acquiring a more considerable interest in the soil, the landlords, who were merely drawing a revenue from the labor expended upon it by others, are gradually disappearing. That the prosperity and stability of the country have increased through the change is shown in many ways, but more especially by the enhanced value of Romanian Government securities, of which I have been able to append a short statement in contrast with those of Russia and Turkey.

What has occurred and is passing in Ireland the reader need not be told here. Possibly the consideration of the Romanian land question may have given a bias to my views on the whole subject, and the excited state of the public mind causes me to hesitate in the expression of an opinion which may appear to be dogmatic. Still, looking at all the circumstances—at the partial resemblance between the former condition of Romania and the present state of Ireland, at the past history of Irish reforms (such as the abolition of the Irish Church), at the rising land agitation on this side of the Channel, and at the recent recommendation of the Canadian Parliament that autonomy should be extended to Ireland—I have been able to arrive at no other conclusion than that the measures at present before Parliament may bring temporary relief to the peasantry, and temporary, nay let us hope permanent pacification, but that the question will be reopened, coupled probably with that of 'Home Rule,' and that at no distant period.

There are many other circumstances which warrant us in seeking to obtain a better knowledge of Romania, but these were the chief considerations which induced me last year to visit the country and some of its leading institutions, and to collect the materials which I now venture in the following pages to lay before my readers.

No one knows so well as I do how imperfectly my task has been performed, nor the difficulties with which it has been surrounded, and there are one or two matters of which I should like to unburden myself to the reader. He will probably inquire why I have put the cart before the horse, giving a sketch of the present condition of the country before treating of its past history. The answer is that it was not originally my intention to deal with the latter at any length; but when I came to read and study the works which have appeared on the subject in French and German (of which a tolerably full list is appended to this treatise), so many topics of interest presented themselves for the historical student that I determined to publish a connected history of the country, however imperfect it might be, from the earliest times down to the present day. And in this I was further encouraged by the fact that the attempt has not yet been made in English, excepting in a very perfunctory manner in Consul Wilkinson's work, published by Longmans in 1820, which is now quite out of date. That such a review of Romanian history, condensed as it necessarily is, was sure to be considered very dry by many readers, seemed to be certain; I therefore placed it after the description of the country as it exists to-day, and for those readers the perusal of the last chapter of that part of the work, dealing with the notabilities of the day, will probably suffice. But I believe that some matters relating to the Roman conquest of Dacia, the character and movements of the barbarians (of which I have prepared and appended a tabular statement), the subsequent history of the country, its struggles for freedom, and the condition of the inhabitants at various periods, will be new to the general student of history and sociology, and if my share has been badly done, it need not prevent him from prosecuting enquirers, for which he will find ample materials in the works of the continental writers to whom I have referred. As regards the controverted questions of the descent of the modern Romanians and the foundation of the Principalities, I would direct his attention more especially to the recent publications of Roesler and Píč, the first an Austrian and the second a Slav writer, where he will find those subjects fully and warmly debated.

The only other matter on which I desire to give an explanation is my reason for not entering more minutely into what is called 'the Eastern Question,' nor attempting, as other authors have done, to predict the future relations of Romania in regard to it. An American humorist has said, 'Never prophesy unless you know,' and many a writer on Romania must wish that he had refrained from dealing with probabilities, or from prognosticating the coining events of history. The future of the East depends upon a variety of divergent considerations: upon the relations of the Government of Russia with its people; the course of events in the newly acquired provinces of Austria, and the delicate relations between Austria and Hungary; the future action of the Prince and people of Bulgaria, the former of whom is at present under Russian influence; upon the growing power and influence of Greece; and, lastly, upon the possible, but not probable, regeneration of Turkey. And without speaking for others, I should feel it presumptuous, under the circumstances, to deal in prophecies.

As to the best policy for Great Britain, however, that is perfectly clear, and may be summed up in a short sentence. It is to facilitate, by pacific means, the solution of every difficulty and problem as it arises, and wherever it is possible, through our influence, to support and encourage constitutional government against autocracy and despotism. This we can do with great advantage in our relations with Romania, and it will be a source of much gratification to me if the information which I have here attempted to disseminate should have the slightest tendency in that direction.

CONTENTS.

PART I.
ROMANIA, TO-DAY.

CHAPTER

I. GEOGRAPHICAL AND DESCRIPTIVE

II. GEOGRAPHICAL—ARCHÆOLOGICAL

III. THE NAVIGATION OF THE DANUBE

IV. TOPOGRAPHICAL, ETC.

V. TOPOGRAPHICAL—COMMERCIAL

VI. AGRICULTURAL AND PASTORAL—THE PEASANT PROPRIETARY

VII. EDUCATIONAL—ETHNOGRAPHICAL

VIII. JUDICIAL AND PENAL

PART II.
HISTORICAL.

IX. FROM THE GETÆ (ABOUT 335 B.C.) TO THE CLOSE OF THE ROMAN DOMINATION IN DACIA (ABOUT A.D. 274)

X. FROM THE EVACUATION OF DACIA BY AURELIAN (ABOUT 274 A.D.) TO THE END OF THE BARBARIAN RULE (ABOUT THE CLOSE OF THE THIRTEENTH CENTURY)

XI. FROM THE FOUNDATION OF THE PRINCIPALITIES, BETWEEN THE MIDDLE OF THE THIRTEENTH AND OF THE FOURTEENTH CENTURIES, TO THE ACCESSION OF MICHAEL THE BRAVE, A.D. 1593

XII. THE TIMES AND CAREER OF MICHAEL THE BRAVE

XIII. FROM THE DEATH OF MICHAEL THE BRAVE (A.D. 1601) TO THE DEPOSITION OF PRINCE COUZA (A.D. 1866)

XIV. FROM THE DEPOSITION OF PRINCE COUZA (1866) TO THE CORONATION OF KING CHARLES (1881)

XV. PRESENT ROUMANIAN LEADERS AND THEIR POLICY

PART I.

CHAPTER I.

GEOGRAPHICAL AND DESCRIPTIVE.

Limits, dimensions, and population of Romania—Comparison with England—Configuration of the surface—Altitudes of towns—Mountains—Appearance of the country—The region of the plains—Plants and agricultural condition—The peasantry—Female navvies—Costumes—Wells—Subterranean dwellings—Marsh fever—Traveling, past and present—Zone of the hills—Plants, flowers, fruits, and cereals—Cheap fruits—Improved dwellings—Wages of laborers—Petroleum wells—Rock-salt—Mines—The Carpathians—Character of the scenery—Alpine trees and plants—Sinaia—The King's summer residence—The monastery—Conveniences for visitors, baths, &c.—Occupations of visitors—Beautiful scenery—The new palace—The King and Queen—Geology of Romania—Scanty details—The chief deposits and their localities—Minerals—Salt—Petroleum—Lignite—Ozokerit—Hæmatite—Undeveloped mineral wealth.

I.

The kingdom of Romania is situated between 22° 29' and 29° 42' east of Greenwich, and between 43° 37' and 48° 13' north of the equator. Its general boundaries are, on the *east* and *south*, the Pruth and the Danube, with the exception of the Dobrudscha south of the latter river, at its embouchure, and on the *west* and *north* by the Carpathian mountains, along whose heights the boundary line runs. The limit which separates it from Bulgaria, on the south-east leaves the Danube just east of Silistria, and runs irregularly in a south-easterly direction until it reaches the Black Sea, about nine miles and a half south of Mangalia. (North-east of this line runs the Romanian Railway from Cernavoda to Constanta or Kustendjie, and south-west of it the Bulgarian line from Rustchuk to Varna.) The kingdom presents the form of an irregular blunted crescent, and it is very difficult to speak of its 'length' and 'breadth;' but so far as we are able to estimate its dimensions they are as follows:—A straight line drawn from Verciorova, the boundary on the west at the 'Iron Gates' of the Danube, to the Sulina mouth of the same river on the east, is about 358 miles; and another from the boundary near Predeal in the Carpathians, on the line of railway from Ploiesti to Kronstadt, Transylvania, to the southernmost limit below Mangalia on the Black Sea, is about 188 miles.

The approximate area of Romania is 49,250 square miles, and when it is added that the area of England and Wales is nearly 51,000 square miles, the reader will be able to form an estimate of the extent of the country. But having made this comparison, let us carry it a step further. According to the latest estimates of the population there are about 5,376,000 inhabitants in Romania against 25,968,286 (according to last year's census) in England and Wales; in other words, with an area equal to that of England, Romania has about one-fifth of its population, or about the same as Ireland.

The general configuration of the surface of the country may be described as an irregular inclined plane sloping down from the summits of the Carpathians to the northern or left bank of the Danube, and it is traversed by numerous watercourses taking their rise in the mountains and falling into the great river, which render it well adapted for every kind of agricultural industry. The character of the gradients will be best understood by a reference to the map, with the aid of the following few figures. The towns of Galati and Braila or Ibrail, situated on the Danube, are fifteen meters above the sea-level, a meter being, as the reader doubtless knows, equal to 1.095, or as nearly as possible 1-1/10 yard. At Bucharest, the capital, which is thirty or forty miles inland, the land rises to a height of seventy-seven meters; still further inland, where the elevation from the plain to the hill country becomes perceptible, the town of Ploiesti is 141 meters above the sea, whilst Tirgoviste and Iasi (Jassy), each receding further into the hills, stand respectively at altitudes of 262 and 318 meters, the last-named city (the former capital of Moldavia) reaching therefore a height of over 1,000 feet above the sea-level. Or again, the plain which stretches along the whole extent of the southern part of the country may be said to occupy, roughly speaking, about a third; then comes a region of hills rising to a height of about 1,500 feet; and beyond these the Carpathian range, forming, as it were, a great rampart to the north and east, reckons among its eight or nine hundred peaks many that rise to a height of 6,000 to 9,000 feet above the sea-level. The highest of those summits is either Pionul (in Moldavia) or Caraiman, near Sinaia (Wallachia), the summer residence of the Court, which are nearly 9,000 feet high; the latter is easily accessible, even to ladies if they are fair climbers, and affords a magnificent view of the surrounding scenery. The aspect of the country, as the traveler moves inland from the Danube to the heights of the Carpathians, is very striking; and as the writer traveled at one time or another along the greater part of the river, both by land and water, and from the bank at Giurgevo to the frontier in the mountains, a brief account of his impressions and observations may be found more interesting than a mere dry geographical description of the different zones.

II.

The appearance of the plain on leaving the flat monotonous banks of the Danube is anything but prepossessing. Although the land begins to rise almost immediately, the surrounding scenery is flat and arid. The soil, which is black or dark gray, is chiefly argillo-siliceous, and the plain is overrun with coarse grass, weeds, and stunted shrubs, diversified by fields of maize, patches of yellow gourds, and kitchen vegetables. Here and there the railway runs through or skirts plantations. The chief plants in this region (and this applies to the plains generally) are willows, alders, poplars, and tamarinds, but chiefly willows and poplars among the trees and larger plants; maize, wheat, millet, and other cereals, and a variety of fruits and vegetables which will be spoken of in connection with the more elevated regions. The first impression which is made upon the traveler coming from our own beautiful hedgerows and pastures, or from the richly cultivated plains of Transylvania, is that agriculture is slovenly and neglected, and that impression is never wholly lost in whatever direction he may travel; although, as we shall see presently, the higher zones are much more carefully cultivated.

The peasantry at work in the fields present a novel and interesting appearance to the stranger, and still more striking are some of their habitations. The men generally wear a long white coarse linen blouse with trousers of the same material. The blouse is drawn in at the waist by a coil of cords or by a belt, and frequently sandals are worn, in which case the cords fastening them are wound some distance up the leg. Hats of common felt, cheap cloth, or high cylindrical caps of sheepskin, complete the external attire. In winter sheepskins take the place of the coarse linen tunic. There are two types of face to be met with among them, both of which are here depicted. The one has long mustaches and shaven face; the other type, which is said to resemble the Dacians of Trajan's Column, has the hair growing all over the face. The latter appeared to the author to resemble the generality of Russian peasants, and this view was confirmed by one or two lending observers in the country.

The women, as in many other continental countries, are the chief workers in the fields, and they are said to be much more industrious than the men. They are not alone engaged in agricultural pursuits, but perform the work of navvies, making roads, and along with the men digging railway embankments. They usually wear a kerchief rather gracefully folded over the head and under the chin; the upper part of the body is clothed in a loose-fitting jacket or bodice, sometimes white, but often of very bright showy material, and the lower limbs are covered with a skirt which is usually of a darker color than the jacket; but this is also frequently made of a bright-colored fabric. This is their every-day dress, and thus habituated the men work with square-bladed spades resembling our own, whilst those of the women have handles as long as a broomstick and bent spade-or heart-shaped blades. The gala or holiday dresses of the peasantry are very handsome, each district having its own peculiar costume, but of these we will say a few words hereafter. Sometimes, as one walks or drives through the country, he may see the peasants gossiping at the well, which is a hole dug in the ground and fenced in with planks, the bucket being raised and lowered by means of a very primitive contrivance. This consists of a horizontal tree-trunk swinging upon another tall vertical one forked at the top; a chain depends from one end of the horizontal beam or bar, to which the bucket is attached, whilst the other end is counterpoised by means of stones. Some of the wells are worked with a windlass and fly-wheel, but the one just described frequently attracts the traveler's notice.

More primitive even than the wells are some of the peasants' houses in the plains, if the hovels which serve as habitations can be so dignified. A large hole, somewhat resembling in shape an old-fashioned saw-pit, but of course of greater dimensions, is dug deep into the ground. This is lined with clay, if necessary, and from the ground or immediately above it a roof is formed of branches and twigs, in the center of which a hole is left for the issue of smoke. Sometimes a primitive doorway forms the entrance, and the people descend either by steps or an inclined plane, whilst at the opposite end a window is inserted. Occasionally, but not always, a small drain is cut round these semi-subterranean dwellings, which, as already stated, are chiefly to be found on the plains, for the purpose of carrying off surface water. It is hardly necessary to say that in these underground cells men, women, and children live together higgledy-piggledy, and that the result of such an existence is widespread disease. Marsh fever is one of the most prevalent and malignant maladies of the plains; there is hardly a family (and the families of the peasantry are very numerous) in which one or more children have not been carried off by this fever. Still there are those who maintain that the subterranean houses are not unhealthy, and they are not necessarily an indication of poverty. Such hovels, it is said, were first constructed in order that they might escape the observation of those bands of marauders, first of one nation, then of another, who have at various times overrun and pillaged the fair Danubian territory; that they were originally surrounded by trees which have been cut down for firewood; and that the spirit of conservatism, causes many peasants, otherwise well-to-do, to prefer these underground dwellings to the cottages of modern construction which constitute the villages of the higher lands. This seems a plausible explanation of their presence; but in a country which is largely cultivated, as we shall hear, by a peasant proprietary, such a primitive mode of existence, worthy of the days when the barbarians ravaged Romanian territory, is not likely long to continue.

So far as the peasantry are concerned, they are a fine healthy body of men and women, and we shall have an opportunity further on of inquiring into their habits and condition.

After traveling inland in imagination for the best part of a day—for a Romanian railway train does not emulate the 'Flying Dutchman' in rapidity, although it is a considerable advance upon the old mode of progression when a dozen horses were often requisite to drag a single carriage along the muddy roads—and having left the city of Bucharest with its many cupolas and spires behind us for the present, we approach the second, more elevated tract of country.

As the distance from the Danube increases, we enter upon a much more diversified and smiling landscape, and almost every plant growth of the sub-tropical and temperate zones is to be found there. Among trees the oak, elm, and beech are the most conspicuous; but besides these the maple, sycamore, mountain ash, lime, horse-chestnut, acacia; and of fruit trees, the walnut, hazel nut, plum, medlar, cherry, apple, pear, and vine are frequent. Fields of maize are interspersed with beds of bright yellow gourds. Wheat, oats, millet, and other cereals are common, and, in the gardens, roses, geraniums, verbenas, asters, mignonette, and a great variety of other well-known flowers of the temperate zone, add beauty and variety to the scene. Indeed, so far as natural productions are concerned, this part of Romania leaves nothing to be desired, and that these blessings of the soil are as plentiful as they are good is to be found in the cheapness of the fruits offered for sale. Little baskets containing twenty or thirty fine purple plums may be had for a penny, and beautiful peaches or large bunches of fine grapes, of natural growth of course, are purchasable at a proportionately low price. Neither of the latter fruits is equal to those forced in our houses, but they are well-flavored and tender.

And so, too, the peasantry and their habitations wear the appearance of comfort and prosperity. No more subterranean dwellings, but, in place thereof, villages consisting of habitations which resemble more or less the cottages and chalets of Switzerland and the Tyrol, although they are not generally so well built nor yet so picturesque. They are usually constructed of wood, bricks, and plaster, and are well whitewashed, their roofs consisting of little wooden or baked clay tiles or slates, and they have every convenience belonging to such dwellings. The roadside cabarets, or public-houses, are often very picturesque, the roof being frequently ornamented with festoons of vines indicative of the creature comforts dispensed within.

As we enter into the hill country, groups of peasants, men and women, may be seen on the roads and railways, keeping them in order, cutting banks and repairing bridges, and the women working with the peculiar-shaped long spades of which mention has already been made.

The wages of such laborers, it may be remarked in passing, are, for men, 2f. 50c., and for women 1f. 50c., respectively per day. Here, too, we begin to have indications of something besides agricultural industry. The smell of petroleum assails the olfactory organs, and we often see carts drawn by oxen or buffaloes, containing one or more barrels of the mineral oil; whilst on the hills are to be seen the rude wooden structures which cover the wells, and roads or tramways along which the oil is carried into the valley below. As we advance further into the mountains, evidences of another mineral treasure present themselves. This is rock-salt, of which cartloads may be seen moving to the railway stations or piled up in various places. This valuable mineral in no way resembles our rock-salt, and the large blocks might easily be mistaken for granite or rough unpolished marble. The appearance and mode of working one of the great mines of the country will be described hereafter; and the chief localities in which salt and petroleum are raised will be found on our geographical map. The principal salt mines are the *Doftana* (Prahova) near Campina, *Poiana*, and *Slanic* (Prahova), *Ocnele* Mari (Râmnicu), *Targu Ocna* (Bacau). The chief petroleum wells are also near Campina, at *Colibasu, Pacuri, Doftanet, Telega* &c., *Moineste*, &c., (Bacau). There are refineries at Tirgovistea, Peatra. Ploiesti, &c.

III.

But we must dwell no longer in this realm of fruitfulness, and must pass on to the alpine regions beyond. In so doing we change our altitude much more rapidly than heretofore, and as we travel through the ascending valleys into the pine-clad rocks and mountains it is difficult to know with what European highlands to draw a comparison. 'Is it Wales?' the English reader will naturally inquire. 'No, for the mountains are too sharp and rocky, and yet not nearly so barren as those of our principality.' 'Are we in the Pyrenees?' Certainly not; the vegetation is not so rich, few waterfalls are visible, and there is a slovenly appearance about the clayey or sandy surface, reddened here and there by ferruginous streamlets, and covered with weedy-looking brushwood which is quite at variance with the sloping gardens of the sunny south of France. Is the scenery Dolomitic? In a sense it is. The summits of the mountains are often very jagged, Rosszähne or horses' teeth, as they are called, but they are dark gray and not white or yellow as the Dolomites. The trees are the same as in other alpine lands, firs, pines, larch, and birch growing thickly to a height of about 5,000 or 6,000 feet above the sea-level; then come grass and alpine flowers, and finally the rough jagged summit. Whatever region it may resemble, and perhaps its nearest analogues are the wilder portions of the Bavarian Alps or the less rugged parts of the Tyrol, it is lovely and romantic, and needs only to be visited by a few Western tourists to become an extension of the playground of Europe; for, in combination with beautiful scenery, there are charming costumes, primitive manners, and some interesting phases of Oriental life. And should his way lead him to Sinaia, the summer residence of the Court, and the sanatorium to which the people of Bucharest resort, not as yet in too great numbers, the visitor will readily admit that there are few spots in Europe better calculated to afford rest and refreshment to the wearied mind.

Sinaia presents many attractions for the tourist. Nestling on the slopes of hills at the junction of three valleys, and immediately surrounded by mountains which vary in height from 3,000 to 8,000 or 9,000 feet above the sea-level, and are easily accessible to an ordinary mountaineer, it consists of a fine old monastery, the temporary residence of the Court, two good old-fashioned hotels, and a large number of pretty villas, the property of wealthy landed proprietors, officials, and merchants of Bucharest. There is a casino, or reading-room, and small concert hall, a beautiful bathing establishment, and a garden in which a military band discourses lively and lovely music every evening within hearing of the guests whilst they are at dinner under verandas in front of the hotels. The monastery is situated upon a high hill approached from the valley below by sloping walks and drives, and it consists of two large curtilages surrounded by low dwellings, which were formerly (and are still to some extent) occupied by monks, and now serve as the residences of the Court and its attendants. The two curtilages are really one divided across the center, and in each division is a small Byzantine church, in which the service of the Orthodox Greek faith is conducted. At the further extremity of the convent are the apartments of the King and Queen, and it is hardly necessary to add that everything is done to render this old building suitable for the abode of royalty. At the side of the monastery is a verdant plateau, from which there is a beautiful view, and whereon the peasantry, as well as many officers and ladies of the Court, may be seen, usually on Sunday afternoon, dancing the national dances of the country, and more particularly the national dance, the 'Hora,' of which some account will be given hereafter. Behind the monastery a small valley penetrates into the mountains. This valley is, in reality, an extensive wood, containing some magnificent forest trees and replete with ferns and wild flowers, whilst through the center of it a river rushes headlong, forming, as it descends, three beautiful cascades, the last or highest being surmounted by a towering rock, to ascend which, alone, is a good morning's healthful enjoyment. Behind this rock rise the Carpathian peaks, Caraiman, Verful, &c., and from the summits of these, which may be reached in two or three hours, it is said that on a clear day the distant Balkans are visible across the Danube.

But if Sinaia, with its surroundings, is beautiful to-day, what will it be in the future? Close to the railway station, on a conspicuous eminence, a magnificent hotel is in course of erection to meet the wants of the increasing number of visitors. At present the King only possesses, besides his temporary residence in the monastery, a small chalet known as the 'Pavilion de Chasse,' situated in the woods behind the monastery. Although this is externally an unassuming little villa, the interior is beautifully decorated with carved oak, and is furnished with exquisite articles of the same material, and generally with a taste for which the first lady of the land is so widely reputed. But the King is also erecting, in a favored situation close at hand, a beautiful summer palace, which will command a magnificent view of the surrounding scenery; and there he and his Queen will no doubt continue, as they do in their temporary residence, to dispense a generous hospitality to visitors, and to secure goodwill and popularity among their subjects.

But we must apologies for this digression, and return to our general survey.

IV.

In speaking of the appearance of the surface it has been mentioned that it is sandy or clayey, and it may be useful now to say a few words concerning the geological formations of the country. Little has been done by the native geologists in this direction, and the knowledge which we possess is derived from the observations of a few foreigners who have published works dealing incidentally with this region. The whole of Romania may be said to form the northern portion of the basin of the Lower Danube. In Bulgaria, on the southern side of the river, where the banks often rise to a height of 300 or 400 feet, there are distinct traces of the miocene formation; but there, as on the northern banks, before the hills are reached, there is a wide plain of loess, tertiary alluvial deposit. On the northern or Romanian bank, beginning close to the Iron Gates in the west, and extending to the eastern embouchures of the Danube, in fact over the whole zone of the plain already referred to, this alluvial deposit is found, and at the foot of the Carpathians it sometimes attains the depth of from 150 to 300 feet, and imparts to the country a neglected desert appearance where the surface is not richly wooded or agriculturally clothed in green. The second zone—that is to say, the lower hills and mountains—is chiefly of miocene formation; but beneath this, and showing itself at the surface in various parts, are strata of what Lyell calls 'a subordinate member of that vast deposit of sandstone and shale which is provincially called "flysch," and which is believed to form part of the Eocene series.' In this region, which is called by the Romanians the region of vines, are to be found marl, sandstone, chalk, and gypsum, with rock-salt, petroleum, and lignite. The last-named is an important product of the country, being used along with wood on the railways, and in brick and lime kilns.

The southern slopes of the Carpathians consist of various older strata—secondary, primary, and metamorphic—and the rocks of which they are composed are limestone, marble, schist (mica-schist and slate), and gneiss. On the summits are found conglomerates formed of quartz, limestone, and sandstone.

To this meager and superficial outline of the geological formations of the country we have only to add that the inclination of the strata is generally downwards in the direction of the Danube, and that they are often contorted in a very remarkable manner.

We have already spoken of the deposits of salt, petroleum, and lignite, and in association with the second is found the substance known as ozokerit or fossil wax. This is a brownish-yellow translucent crystalline hydrocarbon, which softens with the warmth of the hand, and burns with a bright light. It has never been industrially applied, excepting in small quantities by the peasantry, who themselves fabricate rude candles from it; but this is owing rather to want of enterprise than to scarcity of the deposit. Anthracite, too, is present in various places, but it is not worked. Of the existence of iron there is no doubt whatever. Not only are there indications of it in the ferruginous brooks and springs, but it has been found in association with coal in various parts of the country. Specimens of hematite have several times been submitted to analysis, but the results were very unsatisfactory. One sample tested by M. Hanon gave only 35.5 per cent., and another by Dr. Bernath yielded 40 per cent., of metallic iron. That gold has been found and was worked in the Carpathians as far back as the Dacian age is well known; and, according to modern writers, cobalt, sulfur, arsenic, copper, and lead are also present in different districts, but the workable minerals of Romania are at present limited to salt, petroleum, and lignite; and, looking to the importance of the subject, it is much to be regretted that the Government does not take the same means to instruct the population in practical geology and mineralogy as are employed to disseminate agricultural knowledge at the excellent institution to which reference will be made hereafter. If the people are only allowed to develop their industries in peace, it will no doubt soon become apparent that the strata are charged with considerable stores of mineral wealth.

CHAPTER II.

GEOGRAPHICAL—ARCHAEOLOGICAL.

The river system of Romania—The 'beautiful blue Danube'—Appearance of the Lower Danube comparable to the Humber or Mississippi—Floating mills—The Danube in the Kazan Pass—Grand scenery—The 'Iron Gates,' misconceptions concerning them—Their true character—Archaeological remains—Trajan's road—His tablet—His bridge at Turnu-Severin—Its construction and history—The tributaries of the Danube and towns upon them—The fishes of the Romanian rivers—Lakes—Mineral waters of Balta Alba—Roman roads—Bridge of Constantine—Roman streets, houses, temples—Statue of Commodus—Gothic and prehistoric remains—Climate—Great extremes of heat and cold—Beautiful autumn—Rainfall-Comparison with other countries—Russian winds—Sudden daily alternations—Comparison of the country generally with other European states—Resume of its productions, resources, and attractions for visitors.

I.

The river system of Romania constitutes one of the most remarkable features in its geography, has played an important part in its past history, and promises to exercise a powerful influence on its industrial and political future. This system comprises the great main artery, the Danube, with numerous confluences which take their rise in the Carpathians, and, rushing at first in torrents, then How as sluggish, often as half-dry streams, across the country before they empty themselves into the parent river.

The 'beautiful blue Danube' has been so be praised that to a traveler who visits it for its scenic attractions it is likely to prove a bitter disappointment. It is not blue, although during certain seasons it is said to have a blue tinge, but a great part of the way from Vienna to the defile of Kazan, and the whole distance from Orsova to the Black Sea, it resembles in color and appearance our river Humber, and we have heard American travelers compare it to the Mississippi. For hours and hours at a time it flows between perfectly flat banks, on which nothing is visible but reeds and willow bshes. The surface of the river is enlivened by innumerable floating water-mills, which lie at anchor either in midstream or close to the banks, and obtain their motive power from the rapidly flowing current. These are used for grinding the maize and other cereals of the country. Here and there a small town or fortification presents itself on either bank. On the Bulgarian side are the towns of Vidin, Nicopolis, Sistova, and Rustchuk, with their domes and minarets, and idle laughing crowds of gazers, either men picturesquely clad, or women sitting perched, on the rocks, and looking like so many sacks of floor all in a row. These certainly break the monotony of the great stream, but the general appearance of the river from Verciorova, where it begins to bathe the Romanian shore, to its mouth at Sulina is one long flat reach, higher, as we have already said, on the Bulgarian than on the Romanian side.

TERMINAL PIER OF TRAJAN'S BRIDGE ON ROMANIAN SHORE.
TERMINAL PIER OF TRAJAN'S BRIDGE ON ROMANIAN SHORE. (FROM A SKETCH BY THE AUTHOR.)

But although that is the stretch of the river which comes strictly within the scope of our survey, there is another portion, lying immediately above it, that well merits a passing notice, more especially as we know that it played an important part in the Roman conquest and the subsequent colonization of ancient Romania. There is perhaps no river scenery in Europe to equal, and certainly none which excels, that part of the Danube stretching for about seventy-five miles from Bazias—the terminus of a branch of the railway from Vienna to Verciorova—to the so-called 'Iron Gates.' It is here that the river cuts its way through the Carpathians, and whilst along its general course it varies in width from half a mile to three miles or more, in the Kazan Pass, a defile having on either side perpendicular rocks of 1,000 to 2,000 feet in height, it narrows in some parts to about 116 yards, and possesses a depth of thirty fathoms. The banks closely resemble those of a fine Norwegian fiord, rising more or less precipitously, and being covered with pines and other alpine trees, and occasionally, as in Norway or even in Scotland, the steamer appears to be crossing a long mountain-locked lake.

At the lower end of this reach of the Danube are what the metaphor-loving Ottomans first called the 'Iron Gates,' and they no doubt found them an insurmountable barrier to their western progress up the river. Considerable misapprehension, however—which is certainly not removed by the accounts of modern writers, who have apparently copied from one another without visiting them—exists concerning these same 'Iron Gates.' Some of the writers referred to speak of 'rocks which form cascades 140 meters' (or about 460 feet) high, 'and which present serious obstacles to navigation.' Where these cascades are we were not able to discover. The fact is that the whole descent of the river throughout this portion does not exceed twenty feet, and where it issues from the outlines of the Carpathians the banks slope more gently than higher up, and the summits are simply high hills. The 'Iron Gates' themselves consist of innumerable rocks in the bed of the river. Here and there they appear above the surface, but generally they are a little below it, and they break up the whole surface for a considerable distance into waves and eddies, through which only narrow passages admit of navigation, insomuch that in certain states of the river the passengers and cargoes of the large steamers have to be transferred to smaller boats above, and transferred to the larger class of steamers below, the 'Iron Gates.'

II.

But by far the most distinctive, and for us the most interesting, features of the Danube about here, are its historical reminiscences. Almost the whole way from Golubatz (Rom. Cuppæ) to Orsova, there are traces on the right (southern) bank of the remarkable road constructed by Trajan (and probably his predecessors) for his expedition into Dacia, and at one place opposite to Gradina is a noted tablet inserted in the rock to commemorate the completion of the road. This tablet has been the subject of much controversy, and it bears the following inscription:—

IMP. CESAR. DIVI. NERVÆ. F. NERVA. TRAJANUS. AUG. GERM. PONTIE. MAXIMUS. TRIB. POT. IIII. PATER. PATRIÆ.

The Serbian peasants, however, have little respect for heroes—at least, for ancient ones—and the barbarians of seventeen or eighteen centuries appear to have lighted their fires and cooked their 'mamaliga' against the tablet until it presents the appearance of a blackened mass. Of the road itself we shall speak hereafter at some length in connection with Trajan's expedition, but a few words concerning his bridge at Turnu-Severin may still be added. All that remains visible to the traveler to-day are the two terminal piers, of which sketches are here given; but between those piers the bridge spanned the river, and a very low state of the water discloses the tops of several other piers still standing. In speaking of one bridge we have taken rather a liberty with the facts, for it is now pretty generally admitted that there were really two structures. Further down the river is a small island which, in former times, is said to have extended to where the remains of the bridge are found, and upon this tongue of land the ends of the sections starting from either shore rested. The land is supposed either to have sunk or to have been washed away by the current. The bridge, to which further reference will be made in our historical sketch, was built after the plans of Apollodorus, the architect of Trajan's Column at Rome. It was commenced about 103 A.D., and probably consisted of twenty piers, each 150 Roman feet high and 60 feet broad, and the distance between the two terminal piers on the banks is about 3,900 English feet. The piers were of stone, but the upper part of the bridge was wood. In the northern pier the stone consists of rubble, or artificial conglomerate composed of small roundish stones and cement, and this was probably cast into blocks, but the one on the right (southern) bank is of chipped stone. On the northern side there is an old wall running up from the pier to the ruins of a tower which was evidently connected with the bridge.

TERMINAL PIER ON SERBIAN SIDE.
TERMINAL PIER ON SERBIAN SIDE. (FROM A SKETCH BY THE AUTHOR.)

But it would be better that we should reserve any further remarks concerning the archaeological relics of Romania, and also some observations of immediate interest in connection with the Danube, until we have completed a brief account of the water system of the country.

Between the 'Iron Gates' and its three embouchure, namely, the Khilia, Sulina, and St. George's mouths, of which only the second is navigable by large vessels, the Danube stretches for a distance of about 650 miles, and receives in its course numerous tributaries, whereof the following are the principal on the Romanian side. The Pruth is the most important. It forms the boundary between Romania and Bessarabia (Russia), and is navigable by small grain-carrying vessels. Next in importance historically is the *Sereth*, which divided Moldavia from Wallachia, and the remaining rivers of any moment are the *Oltu*, on which are situated the towns of Rimnic and Slatina; the *Jalomita*, watering Tirgoviste, one of the ancient capitals, and receiving as an affluent the *Prahova*, which takes its rise near Sinaia. The last-named is a very interesting river, for in the vicinity of either bank are to be found the petroleum wells or salt mines. Then there is the *Arges*, which flows past the little city of the same name and the town of Pitesti, and receives the *Dambovita*, on which the capital, Bucharest, is situated. In these rivers are to be found in their due seasons many species of fish, and as fishing is but little preserved they furnish good sport. The most important kinds used for the table in Romania are two or three varieties of sturgeon, trout (small but sweet), herrings, salmon, shad, pike, and carp, also perch, roach, barbel, tench, &c. Romania is not a lake country, and the largest lakes, called Baltas, are found in the plains near the Danube, whilst Among the inland lakes, which are few in number and importance, that of Balta Alba, in the district of Ramnicu Sarat, possesses strong mineral properties, in which chloride of sodium and carbonate and sulfate of soda preponderate. Its waters are used for baths, and are said to cure certain forms of scrofula, rheumatism, neuralgia, and other germane maladies. Besides Balta Alba, Romania possesses several other sources of mineral waters.

III.

Returning now to the 'Iron Gates' of the Danube, the portal, as it were, by which we enter the country, we find in connection with the great bridge, and also starting from other parts of the Danube, remains of Roman roads, to one or two of which reference has already been made; and in the neighborhood of these, again, evidences of permanent Roman occupation. One road, west of the Iron Gates, has been named in connection with Trajan's route. It commenced at Uj Palanka, and ran in a north-easterly direction to Temeswar (Rom. Tibiscum), and thence to the ancient capital of Dacia, Sarmizegethusa (modern Varhely), whence it is believed to have been continued to the Transylvanian slopes of the Carpathians bordering on Moldavia. This road, which, along with all the other remains here referred to, will be found in our historical map, was not situated in what is now Romania. It was joined by another starting from Orsova, which followed the valley of the Czerna, passed the modern baths of Mehadia (Rom. Ad Mediam), and joined the first road at Temeswar. A third, still more to the eastward, commenced at the Bridge of Trajan at Turnu-Severin, and traces have been found which lead to the belief that it must have crossed Wallachia in more than one direction and have passed through the 'Rothenthurm' pass in the Carpathians, whilst a fourth road, with which it was probably connected, started from the vicinity of the bridge of Constantine, near Turnu-Magurele, and is traceable in a north-westerly direction towards the Carpathians. Other roads have been distinctly made out in these mountains connecting Hermannstadt, Karlsburg, Schässburg, &c. The road on the southern bank of the lower Danube ran along the whole course of the river, and has been followed to the neighborhood of Galatz; whilst in the Dobrudscha there are still the remains of two Roman walls, one on either side of the line of railway from Cernavoda on the Danube to Constanta (formerly Kustendjie) on the Black Sea. As to the other archaeological remains, they are even more numerous and better defined than the roads. At Turnu-Magurele, close by, there are traces of a second bridge across the Danube, known as that of Constantine, and believed to have been constructed by that emperor. In the same neighborhood, at Celeiu, there have been found several interesting Roman remains, ruins of buildings in which the coloring is still visible on the walls, and a statue of Commodus with an inscription. At Recika, near the modern town of Caracal, close to the river Oltu in the district of Romanati, there are also remains of streets and houses with inscriptions; and at Slaveni, close by, are the remains of a temple of Mithras. Again, at Ciglena or Tiglina, near Galatz, there is an old Roman encampment; at Vodastra, not far from Celeiu (already referred to), still older prehistoric remains have been found, whilst at Petrosa and Buzau, on the line of railway between Bucharest and Galat, Gothic and other antiquities have been discovered.[24] Interesting but more recent relics are to be seen at Campu-Lung, the first capital of Wallachia. At Curtea d'Ardges, the second (that is subsequent) capital, is a beautiful cathedral, which will be more fully described hereafter; and Tirgoviste, the third capital, from which the seat of government was removed to Bucharest, also presents some interesting historical remains.

IV.

Before proceeding to deal with a subject in connection with the geographical position of Romania, which has special interest for Englishmen, a few words may be found interesting in regard to its exceptional and variable climate.

Both the winters and summers are very trying and severe; spring is so short as to be almost non-existent, but this is compensated for by the long autumn, a genial season which often lasts from the middle of September to the end of November. In summer the thermometer often reaches 90° to 95° Fahrenheit in the shade, whilst in winter it frequently falls to zero, but the annual average is about 57° Fahrenheit. Bain is not nearly so frequent as with us, and it seldom lasts long. Comparisons have been made between Romania and other countries which show that whilst in England we have on the average 172 rainy days in the year, there are in Western France 152, in Germany 141, and in Romania only 74. Snowstorms are not frequent, there being on the average only twelve days of snow in the year. The most trying characteristic of the climate, however, is the cold cutting easterly wind which sweeps over the steppes of Asiatic Russia, and often causes life to be almost intolerable in the Romanian plains; and another unpleasant feature is the sudden change from heat to cold between noon and evening during the later months of the year.

Looking generally at the physiography of Romania, however, it will be seen that whilst it covers an extent of country considerably in excess of some of the small but prosperous independent States of Europe, it has great advantages which they do not possess. Less rugged and mountainous than Switzerland, and not so uniformly flat as Holland, its scenery partakes of the character of both these countries. Guarded on the north and west by the Carpathian range, and commanding the whole length of the Danube in the south, its political position (to which further reference will be made presently) renders it safer than Belgium, or perhaps even than Denmark. Its soil is capable of producing, either spontaneously or with a slight expenditure of labor, every requirement of the human race, whether of necessity or of luxury. The grape, the peach, the tobacco plant thrive in the open air. Its extensive forests contain most descriptions of timber, whilst very fine salt and petroleum among its mineral treasures are already worked, and there is little doubt from the researches of chemists and metallurgists that coal, iron, sulfur, copper, and even the precious metals are safely stored beneath the surface. All these valuable natural productions may be readily conveyed down the slopes of its mountains or across the plains, by short and easy routes by land and water, to the larger watercourse which places it in communication with the outer world; and as to the obstacles offered by the 'Iron Gates' to the navigation of the upper Danube, these are soon likely to disappear in an age when dynamite effects such vast revolutions in the industrial history of nations. Add to these facts that Romania offers a rich field for the fisherman, that its alpine districts are beautiful and easy of access, and that its antiquities cannot fail to attract the attention of archaeologists; and we see already from this brief and very superficial geographical survey that it encloses within its boundaries the promise of a brilliant future. And now let us turn from the natural capacities of the country to the works and ways of man.

CHAPTER III.

THE NAVIGATION OF THE DANUBE.

The Danube—Its importance to Romania—To Great Britain—Statistics of British and foreign vessels trading there—Nature of the freight—Cereals—Our imports thence compared with those from other states—Importance of Romania as a maize-grower—Effect of the Russo-Turkish war on Danubian trade—The Danubian Commission—Its history—Austria and Romania—The Callimaki-Catargi dispatches—Alleged pretensions and designs of Austria—Necessity for the neutrality of the Danube—Pending negotiations.

There is perhaps no question of greater real moment to the newly erected kingdom than the free navigation of the Danube; for whether its possessions are limited on the southern boundary by that river, or whether at some future time they should extend beyond it, the reader cannot fail to see from what has preceded that the Danube is the great artery through which, so to speak, the industrial life-blood of the nation circulates. But if it be a matter of primary importance to Romania, it is hardly less so to ourselves. The greater part of the external trade of the countries bordering on the Danube which passes in and out of the Sulina mouth, the only navigable embouchure, is carried on in British bottoms, as the following figures will show:—

Tonnage entering and leaving the Danube in 1880.

	Steamers	Tonnage	Sailing Ships	Tonnage	Total Ships	Total Tonnage
British flag	479	408,492	15	4,214	494	412,706
All other nations	242	150,536	1,526[25]	238,312	1,768	384,848
Total	721	559,028	1,541	238,526	2,262	797,554

Thus it will be seen that the carrying trade of Great Britain to and from the Danube amounts to nearly 30,000 tons more than that of all other nations put together. And now as regards the nature of the goods carried. They consist outwards (from Romania, &c.) of cereals, and inwards of a great variety of manufactured goods. Of the former 5,394,729 quarters were exported in 1879; and it may be said generally that Romania receives in return almost every article of consumption in the way of manufactured productions, and notably from this country cottons and cotton yarn, woolens, coals, and iron.

In any year of scarcity our importations of feeding stuffs from the Danube would become a most important factor, for in 1881 the Board of Trade returns show the following comparative importations:—

Imports of Cereals in 1880.

	Cwts.
From United States	68,138,992
" Russia	12,830,851
" Canada	9,455,076
" India	6,458,100
" Romania	4,355,344

All other countries, including Egypt, which is considered by no means unimportant as a grain-producing country, sent us less cereals than Romania; and when we look at one species of grain, namely, maize, which is considered equal to what is known as American mixed, and is capable of being much more largely cultivated than at present, we find Romania third on the list; indeed, for some reason or other, her exports fell off very materially last year, for in 1879 she ranked second:—

Imports of Maize in 1880.

	Cwts.
From United States	31,087,773
" Canada	3,322,327
" Romania	1,764,482

We shall have to touch on this branch of the subject again; but if the reader wishes to satisfy himself of the great importance to this country of unrestricted trade on the Danube, he has only to refer to the annual returns of the Board of Trade, and he will find that in 1876, when the ports were closed in consequence of the last Russo-Turkish war, our trade practically ceased, and that it has hardly yet recovered from the effects of the stoppage.

Indeed, the question of Danubian navigation has been for some time past recognized as one of European importance, and after the Crimean war, when the great Powers took away from Russia a small portion of Bessarabia abutting upon the embouchure of the Danube, an International Commission was appointed, consisting of representatives of those Powers and of Romania, whose duty it was to maintain the neutrality and the free navigation of the Danube at its entrance, for which purpose they were authorized to levy tolls and construct works. Subsequently the term of this commission was renewed for twelve years from 1871 (until next year therefore), and the neutrality of works existing at the expiration of the treaty was declared permanent. By the Treaty of San Stefano (Art. xii.) and the subsequent Congress of Berlin, 1878, all fortresses on the Danube were ordered to be dismantled, and men-of-war, with the exception of guard-ships, were excluded. The rights, obligations, and prerogatives of the International Commission were maintained intact, and (at the Berlin Congress) its jurisdiction was extended to the Iron Gates.

This is everything of historical note that has, until quite recently, been published with authority on the subject, but to those who are interested either commercially or politically it has been well known that the commission was not working smoothly, and that differences had arisen between Austria and Romania concerning their respective jurisdiction. This first found public utterance in the Romanian speech from the throne last year, when the King said that his Government was prepared to defend its rights to control the navigation of the Danube in Romanian waters, or words to that effect. What followed is contemporary history. Austria, regarding this as an affront intended for herself, threatened to withdraw her ambassador, and Romania apologized. In the meantime, however, M. Callimaki-Catargi, a former Minister of Romania in Paris and London, published in an unauthorized manner a long correspondence between the Romanian Foreign Secretary and himself, which contained a statement of the Danubian difficulty that had been handed to Lord Granville. It was circulated largely in France and Romania, and is interesting in relation to future events.[26] According to M. Catargi, Austria has endeavored, almost since the establishment of the commission, to resist its action where she supposed such action trenched upon *her* interests and jurisdiction, whilst, on the other hand, she has been aggressive upon the rights of her neighbors. It appears from his statement that when it was attempted to form a 'Riverside Commission' to take the place of the original European Commission, and keep the whole course of the Danube clear (a very desirable object, as the reader will have seen from our description of the Iron Gates), Austria objected to any interference with her jurisdiction over that part of the Danube which flowed through her territory. But when more recently the commission appointed a sub-committee to study the lower Danube, and to report to it with such recommendations as would ensure the carrying out of the project in its integrity, it was found that some unseen influence had been at work to change and pervert the entire constitution and objects of the commission.

The report was made, but it was found quite inappropriate to the desired end, as it ignored the freedom of the navigation, the question of the coasting trade, &c.; whilst, on the other hand, it proposed a 'mixed commission, which was to be an executive committee, not at all contemplated by the Treaty of Berlin, and which brought to light pretensions of a new order.'

Those pretensions were an attempt on the part of one power, namely, Austria, to dominate the whole course of the river. The Executive Commission was to consist of four members, representing Austria, Servia, Romania, and Bulgaria, and the Austrian commissioner was to preside and to have a casting vote. Serbia has a very small interest in the river, as her territory extends only a few miles below the Iron Gates, and it is essential to her very existence to remain on friendly terms with her powerful neighbor, so that 'it results that Austria, who is already mistress of the upper Danube, would obtain further privileges and a veritable supremacy over the remainder of its course.'

M. Catargi goes on to tell Earl Granville 'that if Austria succeeded in securing her domination she would throw every obstacle in the way of the importation of the products of the Western nations into the great basin of the Danube in order to secure the monopoly of her own.'

This is the present condition of the Danubian question, and we have reason to believe that negotiations are proceeding which are intended to pave the way for a settlement next year. From what we know of those who represent British interests in the matter, we feel satisfied that those interests will be carefully guarded; but this must not prevent us from bearing in mind international principles and rights everywhere recognized as equitable, and which we feel confident will not be lost sight of in the negotiations. Romania is the most deeply interested; she has a perfect right to the executive control of the navigation of the Danube in her own waters, subject to her engagements with the Powers. The contention put forward more or less officially by Austria, that if this right were conceded to Romania the other riparian Powers might claim the same privilege, is answered by the simple statement that such right is theirs already, as much as it is the right of Austria to control the navigation of the Danube at Pesth or Vienna, of Germany to regulate that of the Rhine at Cologne, or Belgium at Rotterdam. So far as England is concerned, it needed not the revelations of M. Catargi to acquaint us with the fact that Austria will do as she has done, namely, attempted to limit our trade in the basin of the Danube; and our interests and those of Romania are therefore identical.

But it is to be hoped that passing events in that part of Europe will cure Austria of her aggressive tendencies, and that she will not assume the same attitude towards the Powers as she did towards her weaker neighbor. She will gain more by co-operating loyally with her to improve the navigation of the lower Danube than by striving either openly or secretly to secure a predominance which she could not permanently maintain even if her present efforts were successful.

CHAPTER IV.

TOPOGRAPHICAL, ETC.

The chief cities of Romania—The capital, Bucharest—Ignorance concerning it—Conflicting accounts—Its true character—The 'sweet waters of the Dambovitza'—Dimensions of Bucharest—External aspect—The Chaussée, the ladies' mile of Bucharest—Streets, shops, and houses—The Academy—Its collections—Coins—Dacian, Roman, and other antiquities—Excellent physical laboratory—Professor Bacologlu—The Coltza laboratory—Dr. Bernath—The Cismegiu Garden—Shabby courts of justice—Other buildings—Churches—Railway stations—Fine hospitals—Dr. Davila—The Colentina Hospital—The 'police des mœurs' and the morality of Bucarest—The 'Philanthropic' Hospital—The 'Coltza'—Its museums—Life in Bucarest—Hotels—The upper classes—Places of amusement—Cost of land and houses for different classes—Wages of artisans; of gypsies—Habits of the working-classes—Cost of living, food, clothing, &c.—Native costumes made by the peasantry—Their beauty and variety—The poorest class—Mamaliga—The gypsies—Their origin and history—Their slavery—Wilkinson's account of them in his day—Their emancipation and present condition—Laoutari or musicians—Their other occupations—Their religion—Fusion with the native Romanians—Striking contrast between gypsies and natives—Lipovans—Romanian love of bright colors—Pictorial advertisements—Amusing signboards—Absence of intellectual entertainments and occupations—Want of exchange and market buildings—Great advances since 1857—Edgar Quinet's account of Romania in his day—'The Romanian Company for erecting Public Edifices'—Funerals—Octroi duties—Their onerous character—A few words on the Jews—Bitter journalistic attacks upon them—Curtea d'Ardges—Its beautiful cathedral—The exterior—Fine tracery and ornaments—The interior—Legendary history—Negru Voda and Manole—Poem of Manole—Entombs his wife alive in the foundation—His fate—True history—Neagu Bassarab, its founder—

John Radul—Quaint and interesting tablets concerning its history down to 1804—Subsequent history and present condition—(Note: Brief history of Christianity in Romania—Atheism and indifference to religion).

I.

The chief cities or towns in Romania are Bucharest, the capital, in the district of Ilfovŭ; Jassy or Iasi, the old capital of Moldavia, in that of the same name; Galatz or Galati, in Covurluiŭ; Curtea d'Ardges, in the district of that name; Braila or Ibrail, Craiova, Botosani, Ploiestĭ, and Pitesti. We have not named them exactly in the order of their size, as it is our intention to give some details of the first four only.

PLAN OF BUCHAREST, WITH THE MAIN STREETS AND BUILDINGS.

PLAN OF BUCHAREST, WITH THE MAIN STREETS AND BUILDINGS.

(Reduced from Plan by Professor Zamphirolu.)

1. Filaret Railway Station.
2. Tirgovistea Railway Station.
3. Metropolitan Cathedral.
4. Palace.
5. National Theatre.
6. Council of Ministers.
7. Academy.
8. British Embassy.
9. Post and Telegraph Offices.
10. Church, Radu Voda.
11. Ministry of Finance.
12. Summer Palace (Cotroceni).
13. Asyle Hélène.
14. Coltza Hospital.
15. Colentina Hospital.
16. Bank of Romania.

Of the capital, Bucharest, the reader will here find a general plan, in case he should at any time visit the city. To give any lengthened account of it, however, would be a mistake; for such a description would certainly be inaccurate a few years hence, as the city is undergoing great change and improvement from day to day. Still it is the heart of Romania, the center from which all progress emanates; and whilst we shall refer to some of its more valuable institutions when we come to deal with national and social questions of general importance, we propose to dwell upon it for a brief space.

Some of the questions that are asked concerning Bucharest, even by persons who believe themselves well-informed, are highly amusing. One friend, who is really a well-read man, asked us shortly after our visit whether it was not a great continuous 'Mabille,' and he looked very incredulous when we told him that, although we had walked through and through it, and had carefully looked at all the posters announcing amusements in various places, we had no recollection of seeing a dancing-garden among them, and that we believed none existed. Another friend, a highly educated professional man, was not quite sure whether Bucharest was north or south of the Danube; but it was a place, he knew, where the chief occupation was gambling. There may be some little truth in the latter statement, but gaming-tables are forbidden, and he need not go so far from home as that to see the law evaded.

But it is no wonder that strangers are puzzled to form a correct conception of Bucharest, and their perplexity is not likely to be relieved if they read the descriptions that have been given of the city and its inhabitants from time to time. Some writers have described it as an assemblage of dilapidated houses standing in unpaved streets. Its upper classes are represented as very polite depraved ladies and gentlemen, including a large proportion of the former who have been divorced three or four times, and are in the habit of entertaining simultaneously all their *ci-devant* husbands in the presence and with the sanction of the 'man in possession.' The lower classes comprise half-naked gypsies of both sexes, with a considerable sprinkling of priests or 'popes,' eating bread and onions or mamaliga (the maize pudding of the masses), or lounging on the doorsteps of the houses, or sauntering along the unpaved streets in charge of a lean pig. According to such writers the chief occupation of the Buchareste is getting divorced or being buried in state. Then there is the romantic school of authors who represent it as a city of palaces standing in their own grounds, with numerous beautiful Byzantine churches, pleasure-gardens in which plays are performed, or where the Laoutari or minstrels (gypsy bands) play wild and stirring music all day long. There are charming Romanian belles, with flashing eyes and the sweetest of voices; dark-eyed gypsies, chaste as Diana and as fleet of foot; grave boyards, stately Turks (of whom, by the way, we never saw one whilst we were on Romanian ground, although there were plenty, very much married indeed, on the Danube steamers); reverend abbots, with long black robes and flowing white beards; and nuns in unique costumes of dark cloth, with caps and hoods resembling a crusader's helmet. The truth, as usual, lies between these two opposite extremes.

Bucharest, or Bucuresti, 'the city of joy,' as it is called by the Romanians, is a large, irregular, straggling city of about 175,000 inhabitants, situated on a dirty little stream called the Dambovita (as already stated, a tributary of the Arges), concerning which some very famous verses have been written, proclaiming its waters to be so sweet that any one who drinks of them never desires to leave Bucharest. What its retentive properties may have been in former times we are not able to say, but we can quite imagine any person who ventures to drink of the water being incapable of leaving the city for ever afterwards. However, the prosaic authorities are not greatly impressed by their national poetry in this instance. The river is being 'canalised,' or confined within stone embankments, and there is a plentiful supply of *apa dulçe* from another source, which exercises no controlling influence whatever upon the movements of the drinker. The greatest length of the city as the crow flies is about 3-1/10 miles, and its greatest breadth somewhat less, but many of the outlying parts resemble country roads rather than streets. Viewed from a distance, or from the hill upon which the metropolitan church stands, it has a most picturesque appearance, consisting of a vast number of churches, chiefly Byzantine, only a few of which are visible in our photograph, and many good-sized buildings. But what gives a peculiar charm to the city is that all these buildings appear to be placed in one vast garden, for there is hardly a single one without some trees in its immediate vicinity, and many of the larger houses really stand in gardens of considerable extent. This, too, is the cause of the city covering so large a space in proportion to the number of its inhabitants. It is built with perplexing irregularity, as will be seen even from our superficial plan, where only the main streets are given; but the intermediate spaces are filled with narrow, crooked, and ill-paved streets and lanes, their most disagreeable feature being that, in consequence of the soft yielding nature of the subsoil, the pavement gives way, and soon becomes inconveniently undulating. There are, however, several broad well-paved streets, the chief being the Podu Mogosoi, as it is still called, although after the fall of Plevna it received the more dignified appellation of the Strada Victoriei; it runs through the center of the city from an incipient boulevard—which promises one of these days to metamorphose the whole place—to a park or garden of considerable extent, where it is further continued through an alley of trees known as the Chaussée. This is the favorite drive of the Bucharesters, and at stated hours a rapid succession of vehicles pours out from various parts of the city to see and to be seen. These birjas, as the little open carriages (resembling a small *calèche*) are called, contain the moat motley assemblage of sight-seers—ambassadors, state officials, and well-to-do citizens of both sexes in European dress; ladies of more humble rank in the national costume; gypsies and poor workmen and women, who, one might imagine, would be better on foot, half-clad, and very considerably unwashed. In or about the Strada Victoriei are many of the principal buildings—the national theater, the King's palace (a very modest structure at present undergoing improvements), the Ministry of Finance, and some fine hotels. The shops, which are mostly kept by Germans and French-men, are of a fair kind, though not equal to those of Vienna, Paris, or indeed of many smaller continental capitals. The houses here, and everywhere in Bucharest, are built of brick, plastered white, and often very tastefully decorated externally with figures or foliage in terra cotta; but it is the cracking and falling off of this external coating, which occurs more readily in a place subject to great changes of temperature than in more equable temperate climes, that imparts to Bucharest the dilapidated appearance so often referred to by writers. This blemish is, however, likely soon to disappear; for the rise of a wealthy middle and trading class, and the general increase of prosperity, will lead to the substitution of stone buildings for what can only be regarded as temporary structures.

Besides the 'Victoriei,' there are several other very good streets, one of which is the Lipscanii, which derives its name from the Leipzig traders who formerly lived there, and it is still only a shop street. There are some small squares with central gardens, but the finest thoroughfare promises to be the Boulevard, which it is intended to carry round the city by connecting it with the wider roads. On this boulevard stands the Academy, a large classical building with a fine facade of columns; and in a square opposite is the bronze equestrian statue of Michael the Brave, engraved in the second part of this treatise.

II.

The Academy is the center of intellectual life in Bucharest. Temporarily the Senate meets there, but it also harbors many other institutions. First there is the National Library, with a collection of 30,000 volumes, most ably managed by M. Tocilesco, who is at the same time a well-known author, and professor of ancient history at the University. Through his acquaintance with the literature of most European nations, his own historical and ethnological attainments, and his readiness to put these as well as the treasures of the library at the disposal of strangers, this gentleman cannot fail to raise his country in the estimation of those who pay it a visit. He is also the curator of the fine Archaeological Museum in the same building, which is very valuable to historians. It contains a complete series of Romanian coins presented to the Academy by M. Stourdza; many Dacian, Roman, Greek, Egyptian, and Syrian relics; along with a smaller collection from the bronze, stone, and iron ages. Some of the Daco-Roman monuments and sarcophagi, found near the Oltu, have a special historical interest, and many of the more valuable objects, such as arms and ornaments of gold, bear runic inscriptions. Coming down to a later period, there are Albanian arms and costumes, medieval vestments and ornaments of the clergy, a magnificent carved oak screen of the seventeenth century, probably one of the finest in existence, and numerous other objects of interest to the antiquary.[31]

The natural history collection is poor, although local types are well represented; the gallery of paintings is small and good, the subjects being chiefly historical, with the addition of portraits of Heliade and other national heroes. The classes of the University meet here, but, with one exception, the appliances for higher scientific education are very inferior. That exception is the physical laboratory, which would reflect credit upon any public institution. It is contained in three or four large rooms, and comprises every modern physical appliance carefully protected from injury. Most of the instruments, which are of the first order, are made by Secretau of Paris, and a small engine and a Siemens-Halske magneto-electric machine were in course of erection during our visit. The selection of instruments and the order which pervades the whole bear practical testimony to the accomplishments of Professor M. Emanuel Bacologlu, of whose teaching power and wide-spread knowledge we heard nothing but praise on every side. The chemical laboratory is nothing more than a popular lecture hall, poor and disorderly in its arrangements, and quite unworthy of a national institution. On the other hand there is a small but perfect chemical laboratory in the Coltza Hospital close by, where the lecturers, Dr. Davila and his able assistant Dr. Bernath, give excellent instruction to the young medical students of the city. This is, however, far too small for its object, and we hope that the 'era of peace,' referred to in the speech from the throne last year, will enable the State to give greater efficiency to the instruction and appliances of the city. In any case, there is one practicable means of attaining this end which wilt be pointed out when we come to speak of the general education of the people.

III.

Under the same roof the geographical and other learned societies meet. But we have said enough of this building, and must now pass on to a few more prominent edifices in the city. Besides the Chaussée and its surroundings, there is another large park or pleasure-garden in the center of the city, called the Cismegiu, which contains ornamental waters, flower-beds, and fine alleys of trees, and is a favorite resort of the humbler classes. In the immediate vicinity of this garden stand the Courts of Justice, and the greatest service we can render to the people of Bucharest is to advise visitors to give them a wide berth, or at least to content themselves with a look at the exterior. The interior of some portions at least vies, in filth and disorder, with the meanest of our police courts. The Government buildings are of a much higher order, and that of the Ministerial Council is very spacious and well furnished. None of the numerous churches of Bucharest are really fine, excepting in their external appearance, which is often very picturesque. They are all built of brick and plastered, many roofed with metal, and the paintings in them are very inferior, however interesting some of them may be historically. The finest is the cathedral, or metropolitan church, which stands upon a commanding eminence not far from the boulevard, and beside it are two poor buildings, in one of which the metropolitan resides, whilst in the other the Chamber of Deputies meets. The church is comparatively recent, having been erected in 1656 and restored in 1859.

Bucharest has two railway stations, both situated at some distance from the center of the city. One is the terminus of the railway from Giurgevo, situated on the Danube about two hours' ride distant; the other of the lines to Verciorova, Pesth, and Vienna, westward; Predeal and Kronstadt, Transylvania, to the north; and Galatz, Jassy, and Odessa to the north-east and east. Passengers going to Constantinople travel by rail to Giurgevo, where they cross the Danube to Rustchuk, and thence proceed again by rail through Bulgaria to Varna, and on by steamer to Constantinople; but a line is in progress from Bucharest which will take them to the Black Sea through the Dobrudscha, namely, from Cernavoda to Constanta (Kustendjie), thence to the capital of Turkey by steamer.

Returning once more to the consideration of the public buildings, we have to refer to the hospitals, which are admirably managed by the 'Eforia Spitalelor,' the hospital board, as we should call it, and by its Director-General, Dr. Davila, whose work one encounters continually in Bucharest. There are seven hospitals or infirmaries, of which three at least are well worth a visit. The Colentina hospital makes up 200 beds, 130 for women and 70 for men. The wards are roomy, well ventilated and warmed, and the beds and bedding clean and comfortable. (The same cannot, however, be said of certain other arrangements.) There are ten women nurses, and we heard complaints of a want of volunteers there and elsewhere, which detracts from the humanitarian character of the work. To the hospital a dispensary is attached, where from January 1 to September 8 last year, 10,791 persons had been relieved. A very repulsive feature in this hospital is the ward containing forty or fifty unfortunate women under the surveillance of the so-called 'Police des Mœurs,' who are very solicitous about the health of a few of these miserable creatures that live in a wretched lane in the city, whilst they allow the traffic to be carried on in some places as openly as it is in the Strand or Haymarket. Another hospital, which to the uninitiated is far more attractive than the Colentina, is the Philanthropic, a beautiful building of recent construction, containing wide passages and very fine wards, and admirably fitted up with baths and all modern conveniences. The third is situated close to the academy, and is called the Coltza hospital. This was originally a monastery, at the entrance of which a statue, already referred to, has been erected to Michael Cantacuzene, the founder,[32] and it is said to have been converted into a hospital in 1715.

This may be called the students' hospital, for here is not only the little chemical laboratory of Dr. Bernath, but also dissecting rooms, amphitheater, and anatomical museum. Of the latter, indeed, there are several, osteological, physiological, &c., and they reflect great credit upon the gentlemen who have formed them under almost insuperable difficulties. There are several other important buildings in or near Bucharest. Two of these, the Agricultural College and the Asyle Helene in the outskirts, will receive a special description hereafter; but in the city itself there are, besides those already named, the National Bank, some of the monasteries devoted to philanthropic purposes, and three or four hotels, where travelers may live with great comfort and luxury at an extravagant cost.

IV.

Whilst we are speaking on this subject it may not be uninteresting to add a few words on the mode and cost of living generally. The upper classes, and such middle classes as exist, are remarkably hospitable and social; they live in great comfort, and some of them in luxury, which we fear is not always warranted by their revenues. The style of living is Franco-German, in fact pretty much the same as in St. Petersburg. Many people dine regularly at the large hotels, especially in those which have open-air conveniences for that purpose during the summer months. The theaters are well frequented, and in summer the favorite resort is an open-air theater of varieties near the St. George's Garden, where native as well as French plays are performed, and where the songs of 'Erin and Albion,' sung by natives of these shores, are well appreciated. Here may be seen grave diplomats sitting side by side with the *bourgeoisie*, and the only objectionable feature is the doubtful character of certain of the plays, which resemble some that are from time to time performed at our English theaters; both have a common origin, and would be better left in the place of their conception, that boasted center of civilization, Paris.

Whilst the upper and middle classes in Bucharest live in the style of many large continental cities, and often in great luxury, the poorer population are by no means so badly circumstanced as some writers have represented. A great many of the higher class of artisans occupy their own houses. Land is comparatively cheap, and a workman may procure a cottage with a couple of salons, a small kitchen, and a little garden, for about 3,000 francs, or 125£. The cost of a residence in the best part of the city where land is comparatively dear, with six rooms, stable, and garden, averages 80,000 francs, or 3,200£., land varying in value in the city from two to twelve francs per square yard.

Much of the rougher work is done by gypsies, but the better class of Romanian artisans, such as carpenters, joiners, painters, tin workers (who cover the roofs of buildings), receive from five to seven francs per day, working from sunrise to sunset, with two hours for meals, or on an average twelve hours per day. Italians and Germans, of whom many are employed, receive one or two francs more than natives, whilst engineers and fitters are paid eight to ten francs per day. A great deal of time is lost in Romania through feasts and holidays, of which there are, including Sundays, over a hundred in the year. During this time not only is there no production, but time spent in idleness leads to the same demoralizing waste there as elsewhere. The working classes are seen hanging about wine-shops, as they congregate about public-houses here; and, although it is a very rare thing to see people drunk in the streets, many are heavy drinkers, consuming large quantities of rachiu (grain-spirit) and sour wine.

The cost of living is moderate. Dark bread varies from 1*d.* to 1-1/2*d.* per lb., white from 1-1/2*d.* to 2*d.*, almost as dear, therefore, as with us. Romania is essentially a stock breeding country, and whilst butcher's meat varies from 4*d.* to 5*d.*, mutton costs 3*d.* to 3-1/2*d.* per lb. Common wine is 3*d.* to 4*d.* per pint; fruits of all kinds are very cheap, and afford an article of luxury to almost every class of the population. Tobacco is dear, owing to the monopoly. We believe there was an attempted revolution over the tobacco question in 1805, which, had to be put down by military force. All kinds of clothing for the poorer classes are imported, and a suit of best clothes costs about thirty francs, a pair of boots eleven to twelve francs. This does not, however, apply to the country. There the women, besides doing field work and managing the household, make *all* the clothes, the men's as well as their own; and by that is meant that they spin, weave, and make up the garments. The custom, already referred to, of wearing the national costume by ladies in the country and on state occasions in Bucharest, gives very lucrative employment to the native women, and such costumes are exposed for sale in the shops of the capital at prices varying from 6*l.* or 7*l.* to anything the wearer likes to pay. Many of these costumes testify to the exquisite taste of the females by whom they are made; for the combination of silk, wool, and thread, and the beautiful lace-work, the effect of which is heightened by diminutive spangles of gilt and silver, cannot fail to challenge admiration.

These costumes are, however, better adapted for young girls than for ladies of a maturer age.

Not only the women, but the men also, wear much livelier descriptions of dress than we are accustomed to in the west of Europe; and whilst the frilled unmentionables of some of them would excite ridicule among our hardy operatives, the brocaded vests of others would perhaps be regarded by them with envy.

The preceding remarks concerning the working classes do not, however, apply to common laborers. These are chiefly gypsies, hundreds of whom, men, women, and children, may be seen carrying bricks and mortar, and performing every kind of drudgery, for which they receive about one or two francs per day. If they are engaged upon the erection of a building, they work, cook, and sleep in it; otherwise they find shelter where they are able. They are frequently half-naked, the children sometimes completely so; and their chief, if not their only food, which they eat in common with all the poorest classes, is mamaliga, or maize-meal boiled and flavored with a little salt. This is sold at about 2*d.* for 3 lbs., but its price depends upon the maize crop.

V.

As to the gypsies themselves, concerning whom our readers will no doubt have heard a great deal in connection with this country, they formed, until recently, a nation within a nation, and even now they speak a language of their own, and to some extent stand aloof from the remaining population. They are the same people variously named Bohemians by the French, Zigenner by the Germans, Gitanos in Spain, Tschinghenneh by the Turks, and Tsigani by the Romanians, who look upon them pretty much as the white man regards the negro, between whose nature and that of the Romanian gypsy there is much that is analogous. That they are of Hindoo origin few doubt, for their language has great affinity to the Sanscrit; and when they first entered Romania, probably early in the fifteenth century, they were simply a race of wandering barbarians, a later arrival, who were soon enslaved by the boyards. Many of them followed the occupation of gold-washers in the Carpathians, and part if not all the product of their labor fell to the portion of the wives of the Voivodes; indeed, according to some writers, a considerable number were slaves, whom the princess or her officials did not hesitate to sell, maltreat, or even put to death with impunity.

Wilkinson has given us anything but a flattering description of them in his day (1820). The Principalities, he says, contained about 150,000 of them, and 'they make a more profitable use of them than other countries do by keeping them in a state of regular slavery.' They were able to undergo constant exposure to the rigors of the weather, and were fit for any labor or fatigue, but their natural indolence caused them to prefer all the miseries of indigence to the enjoyment of comforts that are to be reaped from industry. They were thieves from choice, but 'not with a view of enriching themselves, and their thefts never extend beyond trifles.' The women were well-shaped before they began to have children; both sexes slovenly and dirty in the extreme. An account of their habits in the coarse language of the historian would be unfit for our readers' perusal. There was no regular traffic in them, 'both purchases and sales being conducted in private, and the usual price for one of either sex was from five to six hundred piasters.' He says the Government owned 80,000, consequently more than one-half of them, and they were 'suffered to stroll about the country, provided they bound themselves not to leave it, and to pay an annual tribute of the value of forty piasters each man above the age of fifteen.' They lived in tents near the large towns, and seem only to have worked as much as was requisite to keep body and soul together. But, he adds, 'they possess a natural facility and quickness in acquiring the knowledge of the arts,' and musical performance was their forte. They were also employed as slaves in the households of the boyards, especially in the kitchens, which they made 'not less disgusting than the receptacles of swine.' They were bastinadoed, often in the presence of the master or mistress, and 'the ladies of quality, however young and beautiful, do not show much delicate reluctance in similar instances of authority.' Other punishments, some very inhuman, were inflicted; and although the owners had no power of life or death over them, if the latter were the result of too severe beating 'neither the Government nor the public took notice of the circumstance.' Not only was it 'under the care of these depraved servants that the boyards were brought up,' but as the women of the higher classes were not in the habit of nursing their infants, they placed them in the hands of gypsy wet-nurses, who imparted to them their diseases, and no doubt influenced the morals of their after-life.[36] Although the gypsies were nominally freed in 1848, their condition remained unchanged after the revolution was suppressed, and it was not until 1854 that they were permanently liberated. To-day there are nominally 200,000 of them in Romania, and until recently they were divided, or divided themselves, into distinct castes following various occupations. The highest of these were the Laoutari, or musicians, who generally perform in bands consisting of four or five men each. These usually play upon one or two violins, a mandoline, and the Pandean pipes. Their music is wild and plaintive, giving the impression from a distance that two or three bagpipes are being played. They have the credit of being very good musicians, and of being able to perform national airs from the ear alone. Some of them have risen to the position of acknowledged composers, and indeed, for that matter, many individuals among the gypsy race occupy comparatively high posts in other departments of human intelligence.

Another section are workers in metal, such as tinkers and brass-founders; a third work in wood, and perform various duties connected with the building trade; but a large proportion are still vagabonds and thieves, who infest the country, and are a nuisance to the honest peasants and laborers. The last-named class profess no religion and obey no law, excepting the criminal law when they are forced. The settled part of the gypsy community belong to the national Church; the women are chaste as against the Romanians, but their morality is said to be very lax among themselves. It is, however, hardly fair to speak in these general terms of the gypsy race at present. As already stated, many of them occupy very honorable positions in society; and some years since a German writer predicted what is now taking place, namely, a fusion of the gypsies with the Romanians. We were informed by a learned philologist in Bucharest that this process is rapidly going on; the castes are not so clearly defined; intermarriages with Romanians are of daily occurrence; many of the gypsies do not even know their own language; and their number is rapidly diminishing. Intellectually they are talented, but lazy. Many of the men, and still more of the women, are very handsome. Although every gradation of shade is to be found among their faces, pretty much as one sees in the negro race in the United States, the features of the Romanian gypsies are generally well-formed Indo-European. Nothing is more striking than to see two women pass each other, or walking side by side: the one a Romanian, fair, florid, and blue-eyed, the other a gypsy with a skin as black as a sloe, jet-black hair, and black eyes, and yet the features similar in both cases, and each woman in her way handsome.

Many stories have been related concerning the gypsies, and their character has often been invested with romance; but we cannot afford them more space, and we are loth to give *any* to another class of beings whom one sees in Romania, namely, the self-mutilated sect of Lipovans, well known to persons who are, or rather were formerly, acquainted with Russia, out of which country they were driven when they took up their abode in Romania. They are chiefly hackney-carriage drivers, and wear the Russian dress, consisting of a long cloth coat bound at the waist by a belt, and a round peaked cap. We were informed that the police are making efforts to get hold of the leaders of this sect, which is undoubtedly a blot upon the civilization of any country in which its members are to be found.

VI.

The Romanians are very fond of bright colors, and one of the peculiarities which strike the visitor to Bucharest is the hues of the women's dresses, sometimes, but not always, as tasteful as they are brilliant. Another feature is the love of the pictorial art in connection with the advertisements of tradespeople. Among many examples of this, in various vocations, is the frequent recurrence of signboards, representing a lady reposing in her bed after an interesting event, whilst the nurse (who thus advertises her profession) is holding up a beautiful infant in her arms for the admiration of its parent and the general public. The amusements of the working classes, and for that matter of all classes, are by no means of the highest order. The Romanians love music, and many are accomplished musicians. The national theater is well attended by the middle classes during the season, so are the *cafés chantants* by the lower orders; but there is no intellectual enjoyment as in Western countries, no popular lectures nor entertainments, no societies for mutual improvement for any class of the community. If one enquires what learned societies there are, he may probably receive, as we did, a long list of them, bearing imposing names, and many said to publish 'Transactions' (*Zeitschrift*); but enquire a little further, and you will find that this society has been defunct for so many years, and that one never met—that this 'Zeitschrift' was published once, but not a second time, and so on. The Geographical Society has done some good work. In 1875 they published a report through their secretary, M. Cantacuzeno, which contains a great deal of valuable information concerning Romania; but unfortunately, as in the case of all Romanian statistical records, this differs in many cases from the statements of other 'authorities,' and cannot be accepted as entirely trustworthy.

These remarks, however, are not applicable to the researches and publications, in transactions and reviews, by savants such as Hasdeu, Aurelian, Tocilesco, Bacologlu, Prince Jon Ghika, Cogalniceanu, and many others. These are, however, entirely out of the reach of the multitude, who stand greatly in need of popular instruction, a fact which has been recognized by the Queen, who is not only doing all in her power to popularize information by means of simple publications, but we believe made an effort, hitherto ineffectual, to introduce a system of popular lectures.

In another respect the city is behind the age, and that is in its commercial arrangements. Although there are large transactions in raw produce, in the manufactures of all nations, in stocks and shares, there is no public Exchange, no Stock Market, no Corn Exchange, all the business being transacted by ambulating brokers. But if the reader knew in what condition the country was before the Crimean war, he would marvel, not at the absence of such institutions, but that there should be any need of them. In his work on the Romanians published in 1857, Edgar Quinet suggests as the means of their regeneration after so many years of oppression 'a bank,' 'an institution of credit,' and railways, of which there were at that time none in existence. Now there are banks, credit institutions, railways between most of the important centers, and others in progress. In fact, it is no exaggeration to say that the progress which has been effected in this country in twenty-five years has in other European States necessitated one or two centuries; and this is a circumstance of which most writers on the country have lost sight in their criticisms. For the purpose of erecting suitable buildings for trade, and for public bodies generally, a corporation has recently been started which calls itself the 'Romanian Company for building Public Works.' Its capital is ten millions of francs, and Prince Demetrius Ghika, President of the Senate, is the chairman, with an unexceptionable board of directors, and no doubt the next five or ten years will witness changes and improvements as rapid as those which have occurred in the immediate past.

Much, perhaps too much, has been written concerning Romanian funerals. That they are showy, almost to irreverence, and that the exposure of the face of the corpse in its glazed coffin is repulsive, there can be no doubt, but they are not one whit worse than the lugubrious processions with their 'arrangements' in black and feathers which are still to be seen in England; and there, as here, it is to be hoped that with improving national taste these exhibitions will be discontinued.

Very different, however, is the old-fashioned system of octroi, of which the poorer classes complain bitterly, still in vogue not only in Bucharest but in all the other large towns of Romania, and the still more iniquitous poll-tax. The latter amounts to eighteen francs per head, and is levied on rich and poor alike. It is, however, needless to say more on that subject; for the 'Romanul,' a daily journal, owned by M. Rosetti, and published by him whilst he was Home Secretary (August 27, 1881), contained a most effective leading article against the tax, from which it is clear that its injustice is recognized in the highest quarters. As to the octroi system, it is bad beyond all conception. A municipal tax, sometimes of so much per 100 kilos (4 to 44 francs), at others *ad valorem*, or again upon each article, is levied upon almost everything required by the inhabitants as it is brought into the city, from food, clothing, and the necessaries of life, to such luxuries as wine, artificial flowers, and carriages. And what aggravates the evils of the system is that the municipality farms these duties to men (usually Jews) who evade the authorized schedule by giving credit to needy persons and then compelling them to pay exorbitant rates of interest (if it can be so called) for the accommodation they receive. It is for such practices as these, resulting in part from the want of good government combined with the improvidence of the people, and from the readiness of the Jews to turn these and similar circumstances to favorable account, that the latter have been subjected to persecution which formerly took the shape of violence and outrage, and which is now confined to bitter invective and national ill-will.

The Jews, said 'Romania Libera' (a very inappropriate title for the exponent of such views), are masters of the trade of the country and poison everything economically. Joint-stock establishments are recommended by it for the sale of clothes, shoes, and linen. The Government must regard it as its sacred duty to foster this movement with all its influence. 'The Jews need have no apprehensions. We will not pitch them into the Danube, nor requite them with a Sicilian Vesper as they deserve. Preventive economical regulations are much more effective than the above-named measures.'[40] It is needless to remark what a pernicious influence such an article as this would have upon an excitable people who had been the victims of usury and oppression; and whilst no language is sufficiently strong to apply to the perpetrators of such outrages upon the Jews as have disgraced the Eastern nations who have been guilty of them, Englishmen should hesitate before they fix the blame upon the government of any country in which they occur. The Jews are the chief traders in Romania, and if they are exorbitant and usurious the way to meet them is by competition and enterprise on the part of the native traders, not by invective and abuse.

VII.

Before passing to the consideration of one or two other Romanian towns which will necessitate a reference to the trade of the country, we will devote a few pages to the description of one of the most interesting localities, or rather of a building therein, which is generally considered its most noteworthy historical relic, and that is the church or cathedral of Curtea d'Ardges.

The small city of Curtea d'Ardges, which contains one or two good old churches, is situated on the river of the same name, a few hours' drive from the station of Pitesti on the Bucharest and Verciorova (Vienna) Railway; it is the seat of a bishop, and is one of the oldest towns in Romania. It is said to have been founded by Radu Negru, which is tantamount to saying that its foundation is lost in obscurity. In its immediate vicinity is a monastery containing a most beautiful cathedral, around which cluster many interesting historical associations, and whereof we propose to give a brief description. It is of the Byzantine order, but the architect has employed in its decoration a large amount of Moorish or arabesque ornament, and the whole building resembles a beautiful large mausoleum. The stone with which the cathedral is faced has usually been called marble, but it is a whitish gray limestone somewhat resembling lithographic stone,[42] which is very easily workable with the chisel, but hardens on exposure to the air. We have said it is faced with this stone, that is externally, for the internal face of the building is of brick plastered for the reception of paintings. The church is of an irregular form, being composed of a square block, behind which is a large polygonal annex; the whole is raised upon a pediment seven feet in height, and the portal, which is Moorish, is approached by twelve marble steps, said to symbolize the twelve tribes of Israel. From the square main portion of the church a large dome rises in the center, and two smaller cupolas in front, whilst a secondary dome which is larger and higher than the central one surmounts the annex behind. The domes and cupolas constitute the summits of what are called by architects 'tambours;' the tambours of the cupolas are round, that of the central dome octagonal, and that of the hinder secondary one pentagonal. From all the domes alike there spring inverted pear-shaped stones, each bearing a cross which consists of an upright rod traversed horizontally by three smaller ones; the crosses bear balls and chains, and symbolize the Trinity. On the ground, opposite the portal, and within the stone balustrade which surrounds the church, there is an exquisite little open structure resembling a shrine. This consists of four plain Arabic pillars supporting a series of moldings which form a square cornice, and crowned with a dome, pear-shaped ornament, and cross, precisely as in the cupolas of the church itself. The windows in the body of the church and on the tambours of the domes are very narrow, and those on the tambours or cylinders of the smaller cupolas are curved and slope obliquely at an angle of seventy degrees, which gives the spectator the impression that they are leaning, somewhat in the same manner as the well-known spire at Chesterfield. The ornamentation on the outside surpasses all powers of description. It comprises a large corded molding, about halfway between the pediment and the cornice, passing right round the main building; and circular shields above this molding, which, along with the windows, are decorated with the most exquisite tracery, wherein flowers (chiefly lilies), leaves, and convoluted bands play a conspicuous part. Everywhere, on the cornices, tambours, and balconies, chaste wreaths and crowns of lilies add beauty and lightness to the fabric, and give to the whole the appearance of a fairy structure.

TRACERY ON EXTERNAL SHIELD.
TRACERY ON EXTERNAL SHIELD.

Within, the building is less interesting; it is dimly lighted by the narrow windows, artificial light being furnished by means of numerous candelabra during divine service. The secondary dome is supported by twelve Arabic pillars, and the walls and domes are decorated with frescoes of the orthodox kind—the Saviour, Virgin, and Apostles, with scenes from the Old and New Testament, also with portraits of princes and bishops of the See. The length of the building inside is about 76 Vienna feet, the greatest breadth 41 feet. The height of the two domes is 86 feet and 81 feet respectively, and of the smaller cupolas 66 feet.

If the architecture and ornamentation of the cathedral are beautiful, the historical records which it contains are even more interesting. It is true that great uncertainty hangs over these, as over all other Romanian chronicles, but certain facts in connection with the building and its history are well established.

TRACERY ON EXTERNAL SHIELD.
TRACERY ON EXTERNAL SHIELD.

Its archives have been carried off by the invaders who, from time to time, sacked and plundered its valuable treasures; but several inscriptions inside and outside of the church, some of which are in the Serbian and old

Slavonian language, and others in Romanian, throw light upon its history and construction.

First, however, we must inflict upon our readers a little legendary lore, which, although it illustrates the uncertainty of the early history of the country, will give them a glimpse of the national thought and feeling in the past. According to tradition the cathedral was founded by 'Neagu Voda,' of whom we shall speak hereafter; and it is said that whilst he was a hostage at Constantinople he built a magnificent mosque for the Sultan, who allowed him to take away to his own country the surplus materials, and that from these he constructed the cathedral after his own designs. A still wilder legend makes one Manoll or Manole the architect, and it is said that he had several master-masons associated with him in the work, but that the efforts of the combined masons failed to raise the building. Neagu Voda had commanded them on pain of death to proceed with it, when Manole, to save their lives, proposed that they should follow the old custom (legendary let us hope) of building up a woman in the foundation; and it was decided that the woman who first made her appearance with the provisions for her husband on the following day should be the victim. They all swore to keep the fact secret from their wives; but Manole was the only one who kept his word, and consequently his wife Utza was the first to appear.

'He took her by the hand at once
And led her to the building,
Then pointed out where she should stand,
And he began to build:
"Be, my beloved, without fear."
She did not interrupt his discourse.

'The other masons in astonishment
All look at him with terror,
And all stand at a distance,
For they dare not venture near;
When he softly speaks to her,
And with haste builds her up.

'"This joke is not good,
Manole, my beloved;
Reflect that I am a mother,
And that I am bringing up your son."
But Manole still jokes
And hastens as much as he can.

'Up to her breast he had built up,
And she sweetly sings to him;
The strong wall bruised her,
And she swims in tears,
But when he had finished,
The wall more than over topped her.

'This was the remedy:
And the wall was able to stand;
And after this the monastery
Ceased to fall any more;
The wind, the earthquake do not shake it.
Utza within the wall upholds it.'

Thus far the poet; but the legend does not end there. The boasts of the masons were so arrogant after the cathedral was completed that Radul, or

Neagu (for he is called by both names), gave orders for the scaffolding to be removed, and left them to die of hunger on the roof. Manole and his companions sought to save themselves by constructing parachutes of light wood, but as each attempted to descend he was dashed to the ground and turned into stone. Manole himself was the last to make the attempt, but when he approached the parapet he was horror-struck at hearing the plaint of his wife as he had heard it when he was building her up in the foundation, and, losing all sense and power, he fell to the ground. From the spot where he fell dead a spring of clear water gushed forth, and a fountain which was erected there is still known as Manoll's.

And now to pass from fiction to fact. According to the inscription upon a tablet outside of the church, it was founded by Neagu Bassarab, a prince of Wallachia, to whom we shall refer hereafter in our historical sketch. He is reported to have been very pious and patriotic, to have founded many monasteries and restored the cathedral of Tirgovistea. He died about A.D. 1520, and was buried in the church at Ardges. He did not, however, live to complete the cathedral, for another tablet within the church says that John Radul, or Radul d'Affumaz, to whom reference will also be made in our historical summary, caused the paintings to be executed in 1526.

During the sixteenth and seventeenth centuries the church was desecrated and plundered by ruthless invaders, Christians (Hungarians) as well as Mohammedans, who carried off its treasures, which are said to have been of great value. In 1681, however, Prince Serban Cantacuzene, of whose good deeds we shall speak hereafter, completely restored the cathedral, as appears from the Romanian inscription on a tablet outside near the portal. This inscription is quaint and interesting, and deserves a place in any work professing to deal with the history of the country. After a number of deeply pious and moral reflections it goes on to say:—

> 'Therefore Nyagoe Voivode Beserab, of happy memory, the great grandfather of my wife on the mother's side, who was a pious and God-fearing man, when he was invested with the government of Wallachia, did, among many other good deeds, cause to be erected a large and splendid monastery in this town of Argesia, along with the other cloister buildings in the vicinity, for the worship of God and in honor of his sainted mother;

which monastery, as it may readily lie imagined from the high wages paid to the workmen engaged in its erection, must have been a very costly undertaking. After a considerable period the foundation and steps began to give way, either through some error of the builders or owing to the damp caused by long-continued rains which loosened the stones. About that time I, Johann Scherban Kantakosino Beserab Voivode, in the name of God, was entrusted with the government of my ancestors. As soon as I became acquainted with the dilapidation of the monastery, I at once resolved to restore the building of my ancestors in order that the memory of that famous prince (Nyagoe) might not be forgotten, and I sent our boyard Dona Pepano as superintendent with numerous workmen, and thereupon restored the whole building where it had suffered damage, and bolted with iron the stones which had loosened, that they might thus continue to hold together, and then I further determined to endow the sacred monastery with the income from the hill of Menesti, near Ardges, to hold and enjoy its entire revenues. These shall be in support of the holy monastery and in eternal remembrance of us and our ancestors.

'In the year 7190, the 26th August.

'This happened under the Metropolitan Kyr Theodosius.'

At the close of the eighteenth century Ardges was constituted a bishopric, and at the beginning of the present, Bishop Joseph was at great pains to renew and restore several portions of the cathedral. The inscription commemorating this event is brief:—

'To the glory of the Holy Trinity, to the glory and praise of the Holy Virgin Mary the Mother of God, this church was restored where it was injured by the rain. Where, however, the color was only obliterated, it was repainted; at the instigation of Joseph the first Bishop of Ardges, in whose time also other work was done, under the Metropolitan Dositheos and Prince Constantine Ypsilanti. The superintendent of the work was Meletin (of the Monastery). In the year 1804, 25th October.'

Besides having suffered at the hands of barbarians of various nations, this beautiful fabric has from time to time been injured by earthquakes; but it has survived all these calamities, and has been frequently repaired, restored, and beautified since the beginning of this century. The property and incomes of monasteries have been largely applied to secular purposes, and among those whose resources have been much curtailed is that of Ardges.

It is to be hoped, however, that, either through State support or private benevolence, this beautiful monument of medieval art and valuable historical record may not again be allowed to fall into decay, but may long remain what it is at present, undoubtedly the gem of Romania.

CHAPTER V.

TOPOGRAPHICAL—COMMERCIAL.

Tramways in Bucharest—Other efforts at improvement—Galatz—Its position on the Danube—Quays, streets, buildings, &c.—Importance as a seaport—Languages requisite for trading there—Almost entire absence of English firms—Reports of the Consul-General, Mr. Percy Sanderson—The quality of British manufactures—(Note: The author's experience)—Causes of preference for foreign over British manufactures—Commercial treaties—Austrian pressure to the detriment of Great Britain—Statistics of our import and export trade with Romania—Infancy of her manufacturing industries—Difficulties hitherto existing—War and uncertainty of investments—The new port of Constanta (Kustendjie)—Other Romanian towns—Jassy—Its position and institutions—(Note: Conflicting estimates of its population)—Ibrail, Craiova, Ploiesti, &c.

If many of the streets of Bucharest are badly paved and the city imperfectly sewered, it is at least striving hard to keep pace with other European towns in regard to modern conveniences. Its main streets are well lighted with gas, and it boasts a good line of tramways round and through various parts of the city. But when we come to consider what is now the second town of importance in Romania, Galatz, we have to step back a few decades before we can realise its condition. It is situated on the left bank of the Danube about ninety miles from the Sulina mouth, and to the east of it is Lake Bratish, which is only separated from the great river by a strip of marshy land. On the whole it is more regularly built than Bucharest, and for about a mile along the river's bank the business portion extends, with its quays for ships discharging, ships loading, foreign agencies, timber yards, and railway loading and discharging berths. In the town itself there is nothing of interest to strangers. The streets are in a condition alternating between mud over your knees and dust over your ankles, imperfectly if at all drained, and lighted with oil lamps, of which one in every three is usually put into requisition. There are some good-sized public buildings, including the Prefecture, some hospitals, two of which, one called St. Spiridion, and another built during the Russo-Turkish war, were a great boon to the wounded of all the armies. There is also a cathedral, such as it is, and several Greek churches, one of which is said to contain the remains of Mazeppa; a synagogue or two, and a few other places of worship. Then there is a 'park' and a garden, and altogether Galatz resembles Buchareston a small scale, and without its improvements. The chief boast of the place seems to be a constant water-supply, which is, however, so regulated that whilst one householder is watering his garden his neighbor cannot perform the same operation, but must wait patiently until he has finished; and finally there are, as a matter of course, a good many brick houses, some of one story and some of two, in which dwell a very kindly and hospitable set of inmates.

The importance of Galatz as a seaport is, however, quite another matter. Although this country transacts a very considerable trade with it, there are very few English houses or agencies there, the chief business being carried on by German, Italian, Greek, and French firms; and not only those languages, but also Turkish and Bulgarian, are requisite for trading purposes.

The chief commodities exported to England are, as already stated, maize and barley, and the chief importations from this country are cotton yarn, cottons, woolens, machinery, hardware, cutlery, dry stuffs, spices, tea and sugar, but besides those there is hardly an article used by a civilized community which is not supplied to Romania from this country. In two admirable reports published in 1877 and 1878, our Consul-General in Romania, Mr. Percy Sanderson, has reviewed the trade between the two nations, and he gives some rather significant hints to 'fair traders,' that is to say not in the refined sense in which the term has been recently employed, but in its good old-fashioned signification of honest dealers. 'It cannot be said,' he remarks, 'that the bulk of the goods imported from Great Britain forms by any means a fair sample of its produce and manufactures,' and 'there is already a tendency among the well-to-do classes to purchase French or Austrian manufactures when they are prepared to pay a high price for a really good article, although the same goods might possibly be furnished them from Great Britain at a lower rate.'[48] But Consul Sanderson gives another reason for the preference shown for foreign as distinguished from English manufactures. It is that the local trade is chiefly carried on by natives of those countries from which the articles preferred are imported, 'whilst there is not a single shop in Galatz kept by an Englishman—it seems doubtful whether there be one in the whole of Romania.' And there is still a third reason, to which he only refers incidentally, but we question whether it is not the most cogent of all. Whilst continental states, and especially Austria, have shown little delicacy in exacting favorable treaties of commerce from the Romanian Government, England has been at a disadvantage in that respect. We may be told that we are placed on the most favored nation footing, but we were informed at Bucharest by persons occupying high positions, and whose statements may be trusted implicitly, that, although this is apparently and nominally the case, it is not so in reality, as the commercial treaties have been initiated by Austria, and so framed as to give a preference to her manufactures.

Notwithstanding these drawbacks, however, our exports to Romania are on the whole increasing, as witness the following statistics (Board of Trade, 1881), although there has been a slight falling off in cotton stuffs on which the tariff is high, and in manufactured iron.

Total Exports from Great Britain to Romania.

	1878.	1879.	1880.
British manufactures	£887,488	£997,078	£1,112,761
Foreign and colonial produce and manufactures	112,987	100,354	86,501
Total	£1,000,475	£1,097,432	£1,199,262

Total Imports into Great Britain from Romania.

	1878.	1879.	1880.
Maize	£587,635	£805,788	£558,745
Barley	316,402	462,622	796,808
Other produce	66,518	104,592	106,283
Total	£970,555	£1,373,002	£1,461,836

The manufacturing industries of Romania generally are hardly in their infancy, but at Galatz are to be found a wood factory and sawmills of a very superior order, owned by Messrs. P. Goetz & Co. They are lighted with the electric light, and are doing a large and increasing export trade; indeed last year (1881), as we are informed, a cargo of deals &c. was shipped from this factory to the Panama Canal Works. There is a very large flour mill, and also the 'Galatz Soap and Candle Company;' but this last has not proved a success, inasmuch as the raw products, including stearine (which is found in Romania as ozokerit), are all imported at a cost which interferes with their profitable employment. Whilst we are dealing with the question of manufactures, we may mention that besides the petroleum refineries referred to in a former chapter, there are in Romania sugar factories at Chitilla and Jassy, match factories in Bucharest and Jassy, and one cloth factory. Steam mills for grinding flour abound, and there are water mills for assisting in the preparation of flannel.

This seems a small beginning, but there is much hope in the future. The same causes that militated against the prosperity of Romania in other respects have rendered the prosecution of national industries an absolute impossibility. Wilkinson referred at considerable length to this matter sixty years since. Who would have ventured to invest capital in mills and factories which were liable to be burned or plundered by Turks or Russians for strategical or other warlike purposes, or would be taxed beyond endurance by a suzerain master for the maintenance of his Constantinople harem and of his needy officials? The soil indeed could not be carried off, or there would not have been even an agricultural industry. But the time is not far distant when the advantages of Romania as a manufacturing country will become apparent, and when her native products, coupled with her proximity to the Danube and Black Sea, will enable her to compete successfully with other nations, especially with those near neighbors from whom she is at present compelled to draw her supplies of manufactured commodities.

Her statesmen already recognize these facts, and they are taking steps accordingly. A new seaport is in course of formation at Constanta (Kustendjie), which will be connected with Bucharest and the whole of Romania through the existing line to Cernavoda, and one in progress to Bucharest. Besides being useful as a defensive maritime station, this new port will give an impetus to trade, which will be further stimulated by the establishment of *entrepôts*, hitherto confined to the seaports, at Bucharest and elsewhere.

But we have devoted sufficient space to Galatz and the nascent commercial and manufacturing industries of the country, and before treating of what is by far the most important source of her wealth, namely, her agricultural resources, we must say a word or two about the old Moldavian capital, Jassy. This is picturesquely situated at an altitude of more than 1,000 feet above the sea-level, on the railway from Pascani (Galatz-Cernowitz) to Kischeneff in Russia. The number of its inhabitants is uncertain, probably about 75,000, and includes a very large proportion of Jews, who monopolise the trade and banking business of the place. It stands upon three eminences, and its principal streets have been paved by contract with a London firm at a cost of 200,000£. It is lighted with petroleum lamps, and is badly drained and sewered, but possesses some important buildings, and contains many fine residences belonging to the landed gentry. Besides a university where there are some men of considerable attainments, it has a museum, school of art, various secondary educational establishments, and law courts, including a court of appeal. A noteworthy circumstance connected with the inhabitants of Jassy, and which applies equally to the whole of Romania, is that the death-rate is persistently lower and the birth-rate higher among the Jews than the Christians, and in fact there have been periods when the Jewish population was increasing whilst the remainder was at a standstill. When Jassy ceased to be the capital of Moldavia, it claimed and was awarded compensation by the legislature; but, according to the authority just quoted, 'no payment has ever been or appears likely to be made.'

Next in importance to Galatz as a port is Ibrail, or Braila, also near the mouth of the Danube; indeed, according to Consul Sanderson, the exports of the latter exceed those of the former, whilst Galatz imports much more largely owing to its nearer proximity to the embouchure and to the fact that the steamers first touch there. The same writer believes it probable that some day Ibrail will be a more considerable port than Galatz, but both are likely to be interfered with by the new port of Constana. The other large towns, Craiova, the former capital of Little Wallachia; Ploiesti, a considerable town, with many picturesque churches, on the line from

Bucharest to Kronstadt, and the junction from whence the railway branches off to Galatz, &c.; Tirgovistea, a former capital of Wallachia, not situated on the railway; Pitesti, &c., are all interesting in their way, but not sufficiently so to detain us, and we must now direct our attention to other phases of Romanian progress.

AT THE CABARET ON A HOLIDAY.
AT THE CABARET ON A HOLIDAY.

CHAPTER VI.

AGRICULTURAL AND PASTORAL—THE PEASANT PROPRIETARY OF Romania.

Cultivated acreage of Romania—Comparative estimates of agricultural products; waste lands, &c.—Nature of soil—Rotation of crops—Agricultural implements—Old-fashioned ploughs—Improved machinery—Yield of cereals—Maize, wheat, rye, barley, &c.—(Note: Report of M. Jooris)—Uncertainty as to yield per acre—Estimates—Quality and value of Romanian cereals—Slovenly cultivation—Cost of raising cereals—Uncertainty of estimates—Present position of agriculture—Discouragement of immigration—Competition of the United States—Cattle—Oxen and buffaloes—Sheep—Wool—Cheese, butter, &c.—Capabilities of the soil—Tobacco—Cotton—Agricultural education—The Agricultural and Sylvicultural College of Ferestreu—M. Aurelian—The grounds and buildings—External arrangements—Experimental growth of trees, fruits, cereals, &c.—Number of professors and pupils—Internal arrangements for board—Cost of education—Laboratory and excellent collections—History of the plough illustrated by models—'École des Arts et Métiers'—Manufacture of farm requisites—School of design—The peasantry—Their history—Varieties of tenure prior to 1864—Creation of a peasant proprietary by forced sales of land—Success of the reform—Subsequent allotment of state lands—The 'obligations rurales'—The dark side—Fate of improvident peasants—Forced to sell their labor—Quasi-servitude—The boyards or landed gentry—Improvidence and involved condition of many—Pledged estates—'Fermage'—Purchase of their lands by industrious peasants and others—Decline of the boyards—Excellent qualities of the peasantry—Great endurance—Industry of women—Education in progress—Bright future for the peasantry—Importance of their prosperity to the State—(Note: Comparative numbers of agricultural and other classes).

I.

The area of Romania, as already stated elsewhere, is about 49,252 square miles, and estimates have been made of the cultivated and uncultivated acreage, which approximate sufficiently to give us a fair idea of the agricultural condition of the country. According to those estimates, which were probably made at the period (1864) when the peasant proprietary was created, about one-fifth is employed for the growth of cereals, garden products, and vines; rather under one-third is pasturage and hay; one-sixth forest; and the remaining nine-thirtieths, or nearly a third of the whole, still remains uncultivated.

The soil of the country is rarely less than three to four feet in depth, is easily turned, and, as already stated, it is usually a dark argillo-siliceous earth, which is so greatly charged with humus (decaying organic matter) that manure is rarely found necessary. The rotation of crops is largely practiced, usually maize, wheat, then fallow; but very poor soil, capable of producing only rye, is often allowed to lie fallow for many years together. Much of the cultivation is performed with very primitive implements, the ordinary old-fashioned plough being furnished with a share resembling the broad flattened lance-head of a harpoon, which penetrates the earth horizontally. Of late years, however, a constantly increasing number of improved ploughs, reaping, mowing, and steam threshing machines have come into use. In 1873, according to Consul Vivian's report, there were about 185,000 native ploughs against about 38,000 imported ones; but even then already there were nearly three times as many steam as there were horse threshing machines in use, and since that time the employment of all kinds of improved machinery has been greatly on the increase, and several large English and American implement makers have agencies in Romania.

There is little doubt that in the course of a few years the old-fashioned agricultural implements will disappear altogether; for the configuration of the surface, which in the plains somewhat resembles the rolling prairie of the far West, is peculiarly adapted for the use of modern machinery of every description.

The agricultural industry of the country may be said at present to be practically confined to the growth of cereals, especially maize, barley, and wheat, and the rearing of sheep and cattle. The total yield of cereals of all kinds has been roughly estimated at 15,000,000 quarters, which is but a very small part of what might be produced; and when we seek for information concerning the proportions of the different species of grain, we find nothing but statistics long out of date, and at variance with each other. The probable proportions are, however (subject to annual variations), one-half maize, one-third wheat, and the remaining sixth barley, rye, and millet, whereof the last named is increasing rapidly. As to the yield per acre, although we have gathered together all the information that could be obtained, we find it impossible to fix anything definite; nor is this to be wondered at if we look at the great differences which exist even in the United States of America, where the people are ravenous for statistics. On some farms in Romania the yield is as low as eight bushels per acre, and if it were not that the peasants own the soil and perform their own labor, it would not pay for cultivation; but, on the other hand, we hear of very large yields on good farms, and notwithstanding these remarks, which might lead to the opposite conclusion, we are told on good authority that since the creation of the peasant proprietary the average yield per acre has considerably increased.

> (Although it is impossible to fix anything like a definite yield, the following figures may serve as a basis of calculation, and they will at least allow how material has been the general increase in the production of cereals:—In 1869-70, Vivian gives the yield (which exceeds that of following years) as 31,264,953 hectolitres. In 1881 M. Jooris gives it as 45,000,000 hectolitres (one hectolitre = 2.75 bushels). Taking M. Jooris's estimate as 15-1/2 million quarters and the quantity of land under cultivation *for cereals* only as 6,000,000 acres, this would make the average yield of *all* cereals a little over twenty bushels per acre; and, looking at the very large preponderance of maize, barley, oats, and rye over wheat, that does not appear to be an unreasonable estimate. Beyond this we shall not venture to go, and if the reader desires to prosecute the inquiry further he will find ample materials in the consular reports, the works of

various writers on Romania, and a series of letters which appeared in the 'Times' last year from the pen of their Bucharest correspondent; but we must give him the very judicious and needful counsel which we ourselves received from a leading statesman of the country who favored us with statistics: 'Il faut contrôler'—check everything.)

Owing to the rough and ready system of cultivation in Romania, the maize, which needs no special care, is far better and more highly prized in this country than the wheat. The latter is worth, on the average, 5s. per quarter less than Western States spring wheat, and this is owing largely to the dirty condition of the seed-wheat used in Romania; whilst, on the other hand, the maize is quite equal in quality and value to American mixed.

If it be difficult to calculate the yield per acre, it is impossible to give a trustworthy estimate of the cost of raising the various cereals. Attempts have been made to do so, and so far as they go they are no doubt accurate. For example, in an article on 'Farming in Romania,' which appeared in the 'Times' of July 14, 1881, from the pen of its able correspondent, there are estimates of the cost of raising and carrying to market wheat, barley, oats, maize, &c.; but when we state that the yield of wheat is put down at 18.8 bushels, maize at 22.6 bushels, and barley at 37.7 bushels per acre, it will be seen by anyone acquainted with the agriculture of the country that this cannot be used to estimate the average cost per quarter. However, as it stands, the calculation of the total cost per *acre* is as follows:—Wheat, 66.35 francs, or (at 25.10 per 1*l*.) 52*s*. 10*d*.; barley, 59.70 francs, or 47*s*. 7*d*.; oats, 55.09 francs, or 44*s*. 4*d*.; maize, 59.29 francs, or 47*s*. 2*d*.; and the farmer, who is a large landed proprietor and employs labor, had evidently devoted more attention to the production of wheat than to maize, which is not usually the case. We obtained several estimates whilst in the country, but they differed so widely that it would not have been fair to strike an average, and all that can be safely said on the subject is that the conditions of cultivation are such as to point to constantly increasing production at a diminished cost per quarter for some time to come, inasmuch as the introduction of improved machinery will more than compensate for the gradual application of manure to the soil. There are, however, many obstacles to progress. For political reasons the Government discourages immigration from other countries, and therefore the untilled lands will have to be idle until there is a sufficiently large population to cultivate them. The Romanian peasant is very conservative and slow to move, but improved communication, modern implements, the encouragement given to agricultural training, and last, but not least, the competition of the Western States of America, cannot fail to act as impulses to spur him on to increased exertions.

Next in importance to the growth of cereals comes the rearing of sheep and cattle; but this is of consequence to the country itself rather than to Western nations, as the export is comparatively small. The number of cattle bred in the country does not appear to increase materially. There are three varieties of oxen, and one peculiar kind of buffalo, of which there appear to be about one hundred thousand in the country. The buffaloes are very dark, almost black, with horns lying back upon the animal's neck, but in other respects they are hardly distinguishable from ordinary horned cattle. The value of cattle naturally varies in different parts; oxen are worth from 3*l.* to 10*l.* each, according to their size and capacity for draught, the greater part of the field labor being performed by those animals or by buffaloes. Sheep, goats, and pigs are also reared in large quantities. The wool of the first-named is used for spinning and weaving, and sheepskins with the wool left on are worn as winter garments. Cheese is also manufactured from sheep's milk, and a curious custom in Romania is to make the cheese in the form of a long thin cylinder, wrapping bark tightly round it in the manufacture. From this slices are cut, bark and all, and served to the guest; this gives the cheese a slight, but not disagreeable, flavour of bark. Of cheese, wool, butter, and lard, considerable quantities are exported annually to Transylvania, Bulgaria, and Turkey. So far as England is concerned, the only other products besides cereals, which we receive, are small quantities of linseed and rapeseed; but Romania produces millet, which is coming into increased consumption, rye, beans, beetroot, which is converted into sugar in two existing factories, flax, hemp, and, as we have already said, vines and every kind of fruit and garden produce. Her soil is capable of growing, and formerly did produce, very good tobacco; but in this matter she has shared the fate of Ireland, for the necessity of levying a tax on the article led to the suppression of its growth in the country; and, lastly, we were assured by able agriculturists that there is no reason why there should not also be raised in Romania a plant which, of all others, ministers most largely to the comfort of man and the prosperity of the land of its production, namely, cotton.

II.

No doubt the recent appointment of a Minister of Agriculture in Romania will impart a considerable stimulus to the most important branch of national industry, but that is a question of the future. At present the only important aids to progress are the agricultural schools; for although there are small autumnal shows of grain and farm products, there has been only one agricultural exhibition, and that, we believe, was far from being a success. Committees are, however, formed in fifteen different districts on a somewhat similar basis to those of our science and art classes, to provide instruction in farming, and the fountain-head and center of those is now the Agricultural and Sylvicultural College at Ferestreu, about two miles from Bucharest. This institution is well worth a visit, and the stranger is sure of a cordial reception from the director, M. Aurelian, to whose published works we have already made frequent reference. The work is carried on in a handsome building, which stands in extensive grounds not far from the termination of the Chaussée, or promenade, mentioned in our description of Bucharest, and the arrangements and appliances are admirable.

First as to the grounds. These are divided into sections, in which experiments are proceeding in the growth of every tree or plant which the Romanian soil is capable, or is believed to be capable, of supporting. Besides extensive plots for all kinds of cereals there are small beds and plantations for named plants, flowers, and vegetables. Considerable space is devoted to vine-culture, where, besides many other kinds, we found Californian grapes flourishing; and in addition there are numerous orchards and collections of fruit trees, the variety of which testifies to the richness and productiveness of the soil. Apiaries are not wanting, but no cattle is reared on the grounds.

In the building instruction is given to about 120 pupils living on the premises, of whom one half devote their time to the study of practical farming, and the other to the manufacture of implements, for which there are workshops (*ateliers*) close at hand. There are ten teachers, of whom six rank as professors. The pupils are nearly all peasants and *bourgeois*; instruction is gratuitous, and the cost to the State is about 450 francs per head annually. The admission is by competitive examination, and for twenty vacancies in the agricultural section there were last year sixty applicants, whilst in the mechanical school the number of applications is still greater.

The arrangements for tuition in the interior of the building are quite on a par with the external ones. There are collections of dried plants, seeds, sections of wood, &c., and a smaller collection of geological and zoological examples. In one place the history of the plough is illustrated by means of models, beginning with the Egyptian, 2000 years B.C., and going through a long succession; the Greek, 490 B.C., the Roman, the Gallic, the Chinese, the Siamese, the primitive Romanian (already noticed), with many others of ancient or medieval times, and ending with a great variety of improved modern construction. Models of fruits, various products of hemp, and other vegetable fibers and tissues, and many other objects of interest to tho agriculturist, are to be found there. The laboratory is good, and the instruction imparted is of a useful and practical kind. In the 'École des Arts et Métiers,' the neighboring workshops, everything is taught that is requisite for conducting the mechanical part of farm labor. Implements, wine and cheese presses, maize-separating machines, carts, and even tables and chairs for the homestead are made by the students with the aid of excellent machinery. Nor is theoretical training neglected. Besides being instructed in chemistry, plans and elevations of stables, granaries, cottages, &c., have to be drawn by the students, and their work is very ably executed. In fact the parent institution and its branches are exercising a most important influence on the agriculture of the country, and no one who has visited the college of Ferestreu will for a moment feel any doubt as to the great future in store for Romania. The only matter of regret is that the funds of the institution do not fully suffice to meet its requirements; but it is to be hoped that these will be more liberally supplied than they have been hitherto by wealthy members of the community, such as the larger landed proprietors, and that dependence will not have to be placed on State aid alone. It is through the medium of these institutions that the peasant will have to acquire such instruction in improved agricultural methods as shall cause him to discard his old-fashioned notions, and enable him to secure an adequate return for his labor.

III.

When we come to consider the past history of Romania, we shall find that in the earlier periods the peasants were first independent tillers of the soil; that later on they were enslaved by the boyards, or sold themselves and their families to secure sustenance; that they were nominally emancipated from the ownership of the native boyards, only to be transferred as *scutelnici* to officials and other favored nobles; and that eventually a democratic government and the increasing power of the people secured for them not only actual liberty but a real ownership of the soil which they had for centuries tilled for landlords who lived in idleness.

It will be interesting, especially during the present attempted land reforms in Great Britain and Ireland, to state here what has occurred in Romania during the last few years, and to consider what further changes are likely to result from the conversion there of a large portion of the soil into peasant holdings. Previous to the year 1864 there were three kinds of tenure in Romania in which the peasantry were interested. The soil of the country was practically divided between the boyards and the State, the former holding by far the larger share. The peasants owned a small patch of land contiguous to their huts or hovels (many of which are, as we have already stated, to this day semi-subterranean), and so much was their undoubted property. But they cultivated the soil on three different conditions or principles. In Moldavia the boyard allotted a certain portion of the estate to his peasants for cultivation for their own use, and in return the latter rendered stipulated services to their landlord. In Wallachia a portion of the fruits of the soil was given to the boyard for the right to cultivate a definite quantity of land; and in the neighborhood of Bucharest a kind of mixed system prevailed. In 1864, however, the Government practically said to the boyards, 'The peasantry have been deprived of their right to the soil, but you, having inherited it, have also a vested interest in it, and your respective ownership must now be equitably adjusted.' The peasantry were therefore put in possession of about one-third of the landed estates at prices, fixed by the Government, to be paid to the landlords. Those prices were not always equitable. Table-land which was cultivable was assessed at the same value as hill-country to the disadvantage of the former. However, such as it was, the arrangement was carried out. The peasants of course had no money; therefore the Government paid the boyards, taking the titles of the land in pledge, and the peasants were bound to repay the amount to the State in annual installments. The Government in turn created a loan, the 'Obligations Rurales,' which were to have been paid off in 1880, but they were not quite extinguished a year after they should have been, and a portion of the remaining debt was converted into a new loan which will expire in 1924. It was, however, only a small proportion of the original debt, and this fact speaks volumes for the industry of the peasants. The change did not, however, end there. About five or six years since *State* lands were allotted to about 50,000 of the peasants who were too young in 1864 to profit by the emancipation; and this was done on still more favorable terms, the land being sold at the old prices of 1864, although it had risen greatly in value, and the purchase-money repayable in fifteen years. Now, to all intents and purposes, every peasant is the proprietor of his holding, and one of the wisest things done by the Romanian Government was to pass an act before the expiration of the 'obligations rurales,' which prevented the alienation of their holdings by the peasantry for a period of thirty years; otherwise a portion of the land would have fallen to usurers and harpies who were speculating on being able to secure it when it came into possession of the nominal proprietor, by advancing loans upon it, as they do upon that of the improvident landlords.

But this leads us to the dark side of the picture. The industrious peasantry, who form the large majority, have paid for their allotted lands, and a great many continue to buy from the indigent boyards. Many are, however, still embarrassed, and some even in virtual servitude, this being the result of their own indolence and misconduct. For a large number of idle or destitute peasant holders, being unable to pledge their land in consequence of the act just named, are forced to sell their labor for one, two, or more years in consideration of money payments by their landlords, such contracts being permitted by the State and enforced by the local authorities and by custom and public opinion; that is to say, the breach by a peasant would reduce him to starvation, as no one would supply him with the necessaries of life. As nearly as we have been able to ascertain, about one-third of the whole peasantry are owners of their holdings without hypothecation, are doing well, and buying up additional land; about the same proportion are in possession of their holdings, but find it necessary to pledge their labor for one year, or perhaps a somewhat longer period, whilst the remaining third are practically serfs on their own farms.

IV.

Now as to the boyards, or old landed aristocracy. There are many wealthy landowners, and those who manage their own estates are the most prosperous. A large proportion, however, contract with sub-tenants to farm the land for a fixed sum (*fermage*). Among these many are poor and involved. When we were at Bucharest the 'Crédit Foncier' held titles of land to the extent of fifty millions of francs, and that probably represented about one-third of the whole known mortgages of the country. Since about 1870, when the rate of wages began to rise in consequence of the formation of railways and the resulting increase in the demand for labor, a momentous change has taken place. Improvidence and *fermage* have sounded the knell of the old landed gentry. Their estates have in many cases been bought up by the *fermiers*, their sub-tenants; the peasantry have purchased considerable quantities of land in addition to that allotted them by the State, and merchants and traders have also obtained possession of a portion by purchase, thus laying the foundation of an influential middle class, which at the present time can hardly be said to exist in the country. The consequences of this change cannot fail to be the development of agriculture, provident landowners, and the general prosperity of the entire nation.

We hesitate somewhat to draw any further comparisons between the past land reforms of Romania and those in progress in Ireland or impending in Great Britain; but certain striking contrasts force themselves upon our attention. In Romania a *portion* of the soil was taken from the boyard at a fixed price and sold to the peasant, without delay or litigation: the results being, first, an immediate improvement in the condition of the peasant, and his ultimate independence and prosperity; secondly, an exposure of the uselessness and helplessness of the indolent boyard landlord so soon as he was forced to attend to his duties and pay for his labor; in many cases his rapid decadence and extinction. For Ireland, under similar conditions, an Act is passed by which, to some extent in the direct interest of the Irish landlords, and indirectly for the protection of those in Great Britain, the old conditions of landlord and tenant are sought to be retained and amended, or the land to be transferred by sale, involving what are practically lawsuits with their appeals and all their delays, or an interminable period (about thirty-five years as against fifteen) for repayment. In Romania the *people*, through their parliament, fixed the conditions of transfer, and the boyards were forced to submit after centuries of exaction and tyranny; in Britain the Parliament, consisting largely of landowners and persons opposed to all reforms, and from which the representatives of the aggrieved parties were almost entirely excluded, has groped about for a remedy, thwarted and threatened at every step by an irresponsible body of legislators, who have for the time being resolved themselves into a trades union of landowners; and masses of the peasantry have been driven into the roads. What the future result of the Irish land reform will be it is impossible to predict. We can only hope for the best.

We have already said that the Romanian peasant is old-fashioned and slow to move, but he has also excellent qualities. He possesses great hardihood and endurance, and will work, not very constantly it is true, during the hottest weather from five a.m. to eight p.m. with a couple of hours for meals and rest during the heat of the day. On the other hand he will face the keenest cold with a bared breast, and is satisfied with mamaliga as his daily food. As we have already said, the women work harder even than the men, besides doing a great deal of work at home, which only Romanian women are able to perform. The children work also, beginning often at five years of age, but they attend school during the winter from October to April. As we shall see presently, the progress of education is slow; for although there is supposed to be a school in every village, many of them are closed, and there is a great want of teachers. Education is, however, progressing steadily, but it will be a generation or two before every peasant is able to read and write. As in the town, so in the country, there are a great many fast days, which the peasants do not, however, always observe. During the week days they are abstemious, but, although they do not get drunk, they spend their Sunday in drinking, and one of the greatest curses of the country has been the substitution of alcohol prepared from grain for the old plum-spirit which was formerly drunk and which was much less injurious in its after-effects. All things considered, however, the future of the peasant is not dark. If he is at all industrious, he owns his farm, and by sobriety and diligence his possessions are increasing annually; the gradual spread of elementary and technical instruction, of which the foundations are firmly laid in the country, will open his eyes to the advantages which he enjoys; and soon he will appreciate the fact, already known to all enlightened persons in Romania, that upon the labors and exertions of the peasantry depend not only their own fortunes, but the future progress and prosperity of the fatherland.

CHAPTER VII.

EDUCATIONAL—ETHNOGRAPHIC.

Educational laws—Statistics—Cost of instruction to the State—(Note: Comparison with Great Britain)— Backward condition of education—Imperfect state of university instruction—Romanian youth in Paris and elsewhere—Impolicy of the system—Pecuniary loss to the country—Moral drawbacks—Edgar Quinet's views—Conflicting opinions in Romania—Need for the encouragement of home instruction—The Asyle Hélène—A remarkable institution for girls—Its foundation and history—Dr. Davila again—Princess Elena—Constitution of the school—Classes and subjects taught—High standard for the training of teachers—Proficiency of the higher pupils—Marriages from the Asyle—How negotiated—Wretched payment of state teachers—Other schools and institutions—A few ethnographic considerations—Descent illustrated philological—Latin roots in the Romanian language—Examples—Their significance—Magyar roots, indicative of foreign domination—Examples—Romanian music, perpetuates the old days of oppression—Dances—Gerando's description of an historical dance—(Note: Reference to works on the subject).

I.

Theoretically education in Romania is everything that can be desired; practically it is still far otherwise. The Constitution of 1866, article 23, declares that primary instruction shall be compulsory and gratuitous, and that primary schools shall, by degrees, be established in every commune.

In 1877-8 there were two universities (Bucharest and Jassy), 96 private schools, 55 secondary and normal, 26 technical and special; 1,242 boys', 265 girls', and 628 mixed primary schools. The total number of scholars set down as attending all these institutions was 119,015 (95,765 boys and 23,250 girls), and the total number of teachers 4,486. The whole amount of money expended on education in that year, from State, religious, municipal, district, and commercial sources, was rather over 260,000*l*. In 1881 the total amount set aside by the State for all purposes of education and *public worship* during 1882 was 450,000*l*. These figures show, in a population exceeding five millions, 2,412 schools with an average attendance of nearly 50 scholars each, who were being educated at a cost of about 2*l*. 3*s*. per head, including those in universities, training, and all schools of every description; but the actual cost of the children taught in primary schools only was about 1*l*. 8*s*. per head.

We refrain from criticizing these figures, for they do not represent the present state of education. Many of the village schools, we were told on undoubted authority, are closed, and the attendance at others is largely increased. Besides collecting the most authentic information, we visited schools of every kind, some more than once, sometimes alone and unexpectedly, at others accompanied by persons in authority, normal, primary, secondary, commercial, and district schools, and the conclusion arrived at was by no means favorable to the *present* general state of education, although there is no doubt that there are many schools, well conducted by able and zealous teachers, and that the system will become developed and improved in the course of time. A few facts will suffice to confirm this statement. In regard to higher education, there are said to have been in 1878 in the two universities 61 teachers and 508 students. The Romanian youth do not, however, as a rule receive their higher education in their own country, and it is computed that from seven hundred to a thousand of them are always being educated abroad, and chiefly in Paris. This is not to be wondered at, for there are no suitable facilities at home, and among thoughtful men it is a source of great anxiety for the future welfare of the country. Looking at the matter first in a pecuniary light, and taking the lowest estimate, the cost of educating seven hundred young men such as those who are sent abroad must be at the least 80,000*l*. or 90,000*l*. annually—we are sure this is considerably below the mark—whilst the total expenditure of the two universities in Romania was, in 1878, about 22,000*l*.! If, instead of sending this large sum of money to Paris and other educational centers, it were expended at home, it would be the means of attracting to Romania a class of teachers very different from many of those who are at present dignified with the title of professors. This was the opinion expressed to us by men of sound judgment and discrimination in the country, and we are not prepared to differ from them. But there is another and a still graver danger to the country arising out of the system. To send a youth from home, withdrawing him from the watchful care of his parents at the most dangerous period of his life, namely, between the ages of seventeen and twenty-one, is of itself a doubtful proceeding; to send him to Paris is in many cases certain ruin. This is not a mere hastily formed opinion, and probably the expression of it may not find a welcome in every quarter. But it is historically true. No one has written a more flattering account of the Romanians than Edgar Quinet. Writing in 1857, he touches with as much delicacy as possible upon their defects and shortcomings, and hints that their vices are copied from the French; and he goes on to say: 'The sons of the boyards come to complete their education with us.... The danger for these young minds, which are exposed without control to so great a fascination, is that even our vices appear to them to be sanctioned' (*consacrés*). It is true he does not discountenance a system which brings grist to the mill of the French academical institutions, but warning them against the pitfalls of Paris life he says: 'Let them continue to visit us.' Well, they have continued to visit them for twenty-five years longer, and if the reader would know the result he must inquire of the Romanians themselves. No doubt opinions differ. There are persons whose views are entitled to great respect, and who approve of this sending of the youth abroad in preference to letting them obtain an imperfect education at home, speaking with satisfaction of sacrifices which are made by persons with straitened means to secure a polite education for their children. On the other hand the views of professional men and of men of the world largely predominate in the opposite direction. Omitting what were doubtless exaggerations, such as that 80 per cent. of the youths who go to Paris return with a perfect acquaintance with the French language, the *cancan*, and nothing more, we are assured that a large proportion fail to derive such an amount of benefit as to justify the outlay; that they acquire French vices and luxurious habits; and that on their return they do not hesitate to express their distaste for home and home occupations. Education abroad, we were told, is incompatible with true patriotism. As already stated, these views may be exaggerated; but when the drain upon the country which necessarily results from the system is borne in mind, and the way in which it militates against the engagement of suitable instructors in Romania, it is well worth the consideration of all true patriots (and the Romanians pride themselves upon being so) whether they should not in future encourage their own educational institutions in preference to those of other countries; and this we say, notwithstanding the fact that of late years youths have in some cases been sent to our English universities and public schools rather than to those of the gay city. In England these considerations weigh so seriously with the heads of families that the movement is progressing rapidly for bringing the highest form of education as closely as possible to the doors of the parents, as witness the recent establishment of universities and colleges in Manchester, Leeds, Liverpool, and Wales. And should there be any doubt as to the feasibility of such a reform, it can be solved without going beyond the limits of the Romanian capital, where there is an educational establishment for girls which is as unique as it is well conducted.

II.

The 'Asyle Hélène' at Bucarest, although it is nominally a foundling institution, really presents many educational advantages which are only to be found in the ladies' colleges of England and the United States. A large proportion of the scholars are foundlings or orphans; but many pay for their instruction, and some of the girls are the daughters of parents of acknowledged position in society. The school was originally what it still professes to be, an asylum for foundlings, which was conducted in a private house belonging to Dr. Davila, who is still the active spirit in the institution. At that time only forty children were educated in it. In 1862 the Princess Elene Cuza, a lady of great virtue and benevolence, placed herself at the head of the institution, and in 1869 the present building was erected. If the Agricultural College with its grounds is to be admired, much more so is the Asyle Hélène. It is a palatial building which stands upon an eminence, is surrounded by beautiful plantations, and approached by fine avenues, whilst its educational arrangements are as excellent as the institution is beneficent. The Queen is its patroness, and she takes great interest in its success. It accommodates 230 girls from nine to nineteen years of age, most if not all of whom live in the institution, and twenty little children who are educated on the 'Froebel system.' The pupils attend four primary classes, and then proceed either to the five higher girls' classes, or to a technical school (*atelier*), also in the same building, whilst a good many are trained as teachers. The ordinary course of instruction lasts five years, to which one year is added for the last-named class of scholars. The subjects taught in the four primary classes are Romanian language and history, writing, arithmetic, drawing, music, the elements of physical science, sewing, and embroidery, whilst the instruction advances further and further until in the fifth girls' class (the ninth in the school) the girls are taught Romanian, French and German literature, universal history and geography, drawing from nature and models, designs for embroidery, geometry and perspective, natural history, mineralogy, chemistry, vocal music, needlework, bookkeeping, &c., and in the highest class of all (that for teachers) there are added geology, physiology, cosmography, and Italian, in addition to French and German. The collections and appliances to facilitate instruction in these subjects are excellent, consisting of chemical and physical laboratories, a small museum of natural history, geology, &c., a library, workrooms, an artists' studio, a theater where the children give performances and recitations, and a simple gymnastic apparatus. No doubt many of the pupils limit the range of subjects in which they try to excel, but what we can vouch for after twice visiting the school with Dr. Davila, and seeing the pupils at the Asyle as well as in their summer quarters, a convent in the Carpathians, is that they are well taught, and that some of them would be a credit to the most advanced students in any school we have visited. The readiness with which they answer all questions, whether of a practical or theoretical nature, in a language which is not their own, is as surprising as it is creditable. Many of course belong to a humble rank in life, and their limited intelligence renders them fit only to become domestic servants, the avocation for which therefore they are trained; others go out as teachers in State and other schools, whilst several already referred to become ornaments to the society in which they afterwards move. All are well fed and clothed, and appeared to be happy and grateful for their benefits. Many of the girls are married from the institution, the mode of proceeding being one which is not quite consonant with our English notions on the subject. A teacher or some other young man applies to the committee for an introduction to a suitable girl, and if they are satisfied with his respectability and his means of maintaining a wife, they ascertain which of the girls desires to be married, and after the young couple have met twice or three times, if they like each other a marriage is negotiated (just as in the case of the royal families of Europe)! The marriage takes place in the Asyle, the bride receiving her trousseau and a very respectable little dowry, and the event is always the occasion of great rejoicing, in which Dr. Davila does not fail to take a prominent part. These marriages, he told us, have in nearly every case turned out happy ones, far more frequently in proportion to their number than similar events outside of the institution.

The teachers in the Asyle Hélène are fairly well paid, the higher class receiving about 50*l.* per annum, board and lodging; but this is by no means the case with school-teachers generally in Romania. We closed our ears to a great many things that savored of scandal during our visit to the country, but this was one thing which it was impossible to ignore. So wretched indeed is the pay of the State teachers that they push on the children of those parents who give them employment as private tutors in order to eke out a livelihood, to the neglect of the other scholars.

The Asyle Hélène is supported partly by endowments and partly by State aid, and is managed by a committee. In connection therewith is also a boys' school at Penteleimon, founded by the Ghika family, and remodeled by King Charles in 1868, to which a hospital of invalids is attached.

The girls' training school of the State at Bucharest is an admirable institution, presided over by an accomplished and energetic lady, who expressed great regret that the want of sufficient funds prevented them from competing with the Asyle Hélène, which is acknowledged to be of a higher order.

There is also a German 'Realschule' in Bucharest, founded by a benevolent German, at which the teaching is all that can be desired; but as to the State normal school for young men intended as country teachers—well, we refrain from expressing any opinion of our own. A learned friend hinted something about the application of dynamite to the whole concern; and if it could be done without injury to human life, perhaps that would be the best course to adopt.

The one fact in connection with the state of education in Romania, however, which forces itself upon our notice, is the question of teaching the youth of the country at home.

Primary instruction is sure to progress; it rests to a large extent with the Government, and in the course of time teachers will be forthcoming to carry out the excellent system in its integrity; but as to applied science and higher education generally, that depends upon parents themselves; and, modifying a well-known saying, it resolves itself into the question of 'Romanians for Romania, or Romanians for France?'

III.

And this reminds us of a matter to which we must make a brief reference, though it will be more fully treated hereafter, namely, the ethnographic character of the people of Romania; for whilst it is unfortunate that in practical everyday life and in politics they do not at present rely sufficiently upon their own internal resources, there is no doubt that theoretically they are very sensitive and proud of their nationality. To a stranger visiting the country for a brief period this is the most perplexing question of all; but the perusal of its history, and a careful consideration of the opinions of well-known writers, bring into prominence certain facts which cannot fail to be interesting. From the number of tribes and nationalities by which the country has at various times been overrun, it is impossible for an unprejudiced thinker to come to any other conclusion than that, like ourselves, the Romanians are a mixed race, although the Latin undoubtedly predominates; and to the evidence of history may be added that of the language and customs of the country. The language not only presents a variety arising out of the domination of the various races, but in some respects indicates the nature of that domination, and the customs have a like significance. As a general rule the Romanian language is derived from the Latin, but there are many words of Turkish, modern Greek, Polish, and Hungarian or Magyar origin. Among the Latin words are the names of many localities and towns which have evidently existed since the Roman period, as witness:—

Latin	Romanian	English
Danubius	Dunărea	Danube
Porata	Prutu	Pruth
Ardiscus	Argesu	Ardges
Alutus	Oltu	Olto
Turris Severi	Turnu-Severinu	Turn Severin
Nicopolis	Nicopolu	Nicopolis
Caracalla	Caracalu	Caracal
Dravus	Drava	Drave
Carpates	Carpati	Carpathians

Then, again, among common names of things and qualities there are objects which could not change, such as parts of the body, well-known animals of all ages, &c., as for example:—

Latin	Romanian	English[67]
Aqua	Apa	Water
Aurum	Auru	Gold
Ferrum	Fer	Iron
Barbatus	Bărbatu	A (bearded) man
Caput	Cap	Head
Manus	Mână	Hand
Nasus	Nas	Nose
Vena	Vina	Vein
Os	Os	Bone
Oculus	Ochiu	Eye
Digitus	Deget	Finger
Pes	Picior	Foot
Pectus	Pept	Breast
Canis	Câne	Dog
Piscis	Pesce	Fish
Dominus	Domnu	Lord
Umbra	Umbră	Shade

Frigidus	Frigu	Cold
Calidus	Caldu	Warm
Albus	Alb	White
Niger	Negru	Black
Casa	Casa	A cottage

and so on through the whole vocabulary of common things and attributes.

On the other hand, when we come to examine the words of barbarian origin, we find that they relate to the character of the dominant race and their rule over the natives. If we take, for example, the words of Magyar or Hungarian origin, we find them to denote war, conquest, mining, taxation, punishment, &c., such as *baia*, mine; *bănui*, repent, rue; *bereŭ*, a wood; *bicao*, fetters (on the feet); *bir, poll-tax; *birâu*, a judge; *bitangu*, wandering about; *bucni*, to strike; *buzdugány*, war-club; *cătănie*, soldiers, soldiers' habits; *cheltúi*, to give or spend lavishly; *făgădău*, drink-shop; *giulus*, the Reichstag, or national assembly; *hodnogiŭ*, lieutenant (from *had*, war); *hotar*, boundary; *lanțĭŭ, chain; *odorbireu*, headsman; *tábără, camp, war, army; *varda*, watch-house; and so on.

Besides these words and phrases derived from the Latin and barbarian languages, there are others relating to ecclesiastical matters imported from the Greek; indeed, an examination of the language is itself an interesting historical study, and if now we turn to the arts and customs of the Romanians, we find the same interesting relations with her past history.

Of the music of the Laoutari we have already spoken. It is weird and plaintive, and no one who has listened attentively to the airs played by some of those bands can have failed to be struck with their 'telling' character, how they give vent alternately to feelings of joy and sorrow, of mourning and rejoicing, and, like the music of Poland, &c., call to mind the conquered condition of the people in the past. As with the music, so with the dances. A writer, to whom we shall refer later on, M. Opitz, described the 'Hora,' the national dance of the Romanians, as being illustrative of their conquered condition, and a recent acute observer has left us his impressions on the same subject.

'I remember one dance (says he) of which I forget the name, but which pleased me exceedingly. After the dancers had gone one or two paces in pairs in a circle, the men separated from the women. The latter moved singly round the men, as though they were seeking some object dear to them. The men then drew together and moved their feet like marching soldiers; next using their long sticks, they made irregular springs and uttered loud cries, as though they were engaged in battle. The women wandered about like shadows. At last the men with joyful gestures rushed towards them as though they had found them after great danger, led them back into the circle, and danced with joy and animation. Here we see how mighty is tradition. This dance is a complete poem! Who knows of what long-forgotten incursion of the barbarians it is a reminiscence?'

From those few illustrations it will be seen how the language and customs of Romania are interwoven with her past history. We have but touched the fringe of the subject; but that it is a fertile source of interesting study and research we are convinced, and therefore recommend those who are able to follow it up to give it their attention.

CHAPTER VIII.

JUDICIAL AND PENAL.

The jurisprudence of the Constitution—Romanian courts—The Code Napoléon—Complaints of patronage—The penal system—Capital punishment abolished—History and effect of the abolition—Statistics—The prison system—Abuses—Enumeration of prisons—Employment of convicts—Ornamental art among them—Objects made by them—Absence of educational measures—Criminal statistics (and note)—Visit to the 'intermediate' prison of Vakareschti—An old monastery—Description of the prison—Scene in the court-yard—Untried prisoners in fetters—Promiscuous intercourse of prisoners—Mischievous effects—Views of a 'juge d'instruction' concerning the system—Various classes of prisoners—Lenient treatment of them—Partial employment—Safeguards against mutiny—Visit to the penal salt mine of Doftana (or Telega)—Former treatment of prisoners—A lingering death—Present treatment—Conditions of penal servitude—Compared with work of our colliers—Abuses—Descent into the mine—Its condition—Unearthly sounds and sights—Enormous salt cave—Floor of the cave—Convicts at work in chains—Mode of excavating and raising salt—Lighting the mine for visitors—Return to the surface—Visit to the penitentiary—Its discreditable condition—Alleged frauds upon convicts—General mild treatment of criminals in Romania—Utilisation of convict labor—Comparison of cost and results of systems in Romania and England—Favorable to Romania.

I.

As in the case of education, so, too, in regard to its judicial and penal system, the Constitution of Romania contains many admirable provisions (articles 13, 18, 104, 105, &c.) for the maintenance of right and the suppression of wrong-doing. Equal rights, ordinary tribunals, speedy trial by jury, abolition of death punishment, these are the excellent principles upon which the judicial system is based; but neither there, nor for that matter in any country, are they completely put into practice. There is one Court of Cassation with sections, and a Court of Accounts at Bucharest. Courts of Appeal at Bucharest, Jassy, Craiova, and Focsany, and minor tribunals in the chief town of each district. The French Code of Jurisprudence is adopted, with modifications which would not interest our readers; but the penal system is somewhat unique, and is well worthy of a closer study and consideration. Of the miserable accommodation for the exercise of judicial authority in Bucharest we have already spoken in describing the capital. Lawsuits are very tedious; whether more so than in England we are unable to say. Great complaint exists of patronage in the appointment of judges, most of whom are comparatively young men and political partisans. This it is proposed to remedy by what would practically be popular election; whether the cure would be any better than the disease is questionable. The penal system, as we found it carried out in Romania, is mild, utilitarian, and slovenly; and if all that was told us be true, we fear we must add that it is by no means free from corruption.

The chief points of interest to Englishmen are the absence of capital punishment and the substitution of forced labor for life, or for a long term of years, and the utilisation of penal labor in the salt mines and elsewhere. Capital punishment ceased *de facto* in 1852; for although it was not legally abolished, neither the then ruler, Prince Stirbey, nor his successor, Prince Couza, who governed the joint Principalities, would sign a death-warrant. It was legally abrogated in 1865, and the Constitution of 1866 declares that it cannot be re-established, excepting for military offenses. No increase, but rather a diminution, of capital crimes has taken place since the change was effected; for although the population has doubled in the towns, where homicidal crime is most frequent, the number of offenses has not materially increased. The following figures prove this statement:—

Total Committals and Convictions for Homicide.

Year	Committals	Convictions
1869	248	185
1870	249	154
1871	267	140

1872	327	204
1873	455	258
1874	258	167
1875	236	169
1876	386	250
1877	307	187

The punishment for murder with malice aforethought is now penal servitude for life, other phases of homicide five to twenty years, in both cases mine labor. In cases of infanticide, if the offspring is illegitimate it ranks as manslaughter. The following is a condensed summary, with brief comments of our own in parenthesis, of a report on the prison system which was kindly furnished to us by the Romanian Inspector of Prisons, a zealous, well-meaning, and most courteous official, as are all Romanian officials.

II.

The penitentiaries are divided into two classes, 'preventive' and 'central.' In the central prisons three kinds of punishment exist, forced labor, confinement called 'reclusion,' and correction. The men condemned to forced labor work in the mines (in what manner we shall see presently) during the daytime, and at night they sleep above ground in the prison. On Sundays and fête-days they do no work. The product of the labor of the convicts belongs of right to the State, but in order to encourage the prisoners three-tenths is given to them. (We may at once say that this is not faithfully carried into practice, as we know from personal inquiry that many of them are compelled to expend their earning to secure the common necessaries of life.) Aged and feeble persons are transferred to the prison of Cozia, where they weave, &c. The prisoners condemned to 'reclusion' work in tanneries and rope walks, as for example in the prison of Margineni, and they are entitled to four-tenths of the products of their labor. In the correctional prisons the convicts cultivate the soil, make bricks, &c., and are entitled to half their wages. In all the prisons the convicts are permitted to employ their leisure time in making articles of use or ornament from materials furnished to them by the authorities, which are sold to visitors, and the State gives them a proportion of the fruits of their industry. (These articles we found to be beautifully made. They consist of egg-cups, paper-knives, forks, spoons, &c., carved in wood and resembling similar objects made in Switzerland and the Black Forest. One prisoner had made a tobacco-box of dough, painted and decorated it with artificial flowers of the same material, so that it was not distinguishable from porcelain; another had forged an axe-blade of steel, etched the surface and fixed it upon a polished ebony rod with a terminal spike, forming a miniature ice-axe, and so forth.)

Religious service is provided for the convicts, but so far as we could learn no educational means whatever, although, according to various reports which were handed to us, by far the larger proportion of the prisoners are Romanians who can neither read nor write.[72]

The total number of persons, men and women, confined in the sixteen State prisons in Romania in 1880, *including untried offenders*, was 5,252, or about one per thousand of the whole population. Of these 850 were undergoing forced labor in the mines, and 2,491 were imprisoned for less serious offenses. Only 265 were minors, and about 100 or 150 women. A strange contrast to our criminal statistics. Besides the inmates of State prisons there were 1,665 persons confined in the district prisons on January 1, 1881, who had been convicted of minor offenses.

III.

One of the most remarkable phenomena in the eyes of a stranger visiting Romania is the application of monastic edifices to lay uses. The monastery of Sinaia is, for the present at least, a royal palace; the Coltza Hospital at Bucharest is an old convent. At Brebu(or Bredu), near Campina, is a monastery apportioned to the Asyle Hélène as a holiday residence for the girls; the State archives are deposited in the monastery of Prince Michael in Bucharest, which has been set aside as the residence of the learned philologist Professor Hasdeu, in whose charge they are placed; and so, too, the 'intermediate' prison of Vakareschti is a large monastery close to Bucharest, of which the towers are conspicuously visible as one enters the city by rail from Giurgevo. On approaching this building, which stands upon a considerable eminence, by road from the capital, the only feature which attracts attention, and shows that it is not an ordinary monastery, is the sentinel pacing to and fro outside, but the moment you enter through the portal its real character becomes apparent. You find yourself in a large square curtilage, or, more correctly speaking, an extensive quadrilateral, in the center of which stands a church of the usual Byzantine order, the four sides of the quadrilateral being the old monastery buildings, two stories high, converted into prisoners' cells and dormitories, kitchen, a workshop for making paper-backed books (*cartons*), and the quarters of the prison officials. The scene as one enters the place is a strange one indeed, and resembles what the Fleet Prison must have been in its palmy days, with certain very significant modifications. It is the receptacle of various kinds of prisoners, men and women awaiting trial and others undergoing short sentences. All those were, on the occasion of our visit, at large in the court, and some of the first-named who were accused of homicide were chained at the ankles by order of the 'Juge d'Instruction.' There were about a dozen of them so manacled, and before we left (the Chief Inspector of Prisons being our guide) these men complained bitterly of the hardship of being chained when, as they asserted, they were innocent. All classes of prisoners seemed to associate without restraint, and although perfect order prevailed, this freedom of association and conversation must be, and indeed is, most inexpedient and injurious. Young men new to crime herd together with hardened criminals, and we were told by a Juge d'Instruction, to whom we subsequently spoke on the matter, that the free intercourse is greatly provocative of crime. 'Young fellows,' he said, 'who, when they are first arraigned, are disposed to admit their guilt and repent, come before us, after a temporary adjournment of their cases, with quite another story, evidently prompted by some hardened criminal whom they have met in the intermediate prison.'

Every class was represented there, from the comparatively well-dressed swindler and forger to the peasant and half-naked gypsy. The prisoners appear to be leniently treated, and those who are unconvinced are permitted to purchase such food as they please. The cells and dormitories are not very clean, but they are comfortable compared with those in another prison, to be referred to presently; the ventilation within doors is good, and the open court has all the advantages of a healthy convalescent institution. The food appeared very good; certainly the soup was so, and altogether there could be no complaint on the score of harsh treatment, although some men were, on sufficient grounds, placed in solitary confinement. The chief defects are free intercourse among the prisoners, want of cleanliness, the absence of educational means, and only partial employment of the prisoners, some of whom are engaged in the book manufactory, whilst the greater proportion lounge about in idleness. Our guide, the Chief Inspector, expressed great anxiety for an improved system, and pleaded, as usual, the want of necessary funds. Although there appeared to be an amount of liberty inconsistent, as it seemed to us, with prison discipline, all attempts at mutiny would be easily suppressed if they should arise; for there are always about ninety soldiers in the barracks, attached to the prison, and the prisoners are well aware that insubordination would be immediately quelled and punished. But we have said enough of this rough and ready mode of dealing with the lighter forms of crime, and must now ask our readers to accompany us on a somewhat unpleasant though interesting excursion to one of the establishments where the worst class of convicts expiate their offenses against society—a penal salt mine.

IV.

There are five salt mines in Romania,[73] two of which are worked by convicts, and the one we propose to visit is that of Doftana, generally known as the Telega mine, which is situated at a short distance from Campina, a station on the railway line, about halfway between Ploiesti and Sinaia. Before descending into the mine, however, a few particulars concerning the treatment of the prisoners maybe of interest. These are men (never women nor young persons) sentenced to penal servitude for a period of ten years or more, and until the year 1848 they lived, or rather died a slow death, entirely in the mine. They were compelled to sleep in their clothes on the floor of rock salt; never saw the light of day after they had once entered the mine; and whatever might have been the nominal term of their sentence, disease and their unnatural surroundings invariably cut short their miserable existence after about four years' confinement. Now they work in the mine from 8 A.M. to 4 P.M. in winter, and from 6 A.M. to 6.30 P.M. in summer, and then leaving it, they march to the penitentiary, about a mile distant. They work in gangs of about six or seven, and each man is obliged to raise at least 700 kilograms (about 14 cwt.) of salt per day. For that quantity they receive, or at least *they are credited* with, 30 per cent, of their wages, which are fixed by tariff, and for all above 700 kilos they get half their wages. These are reckoned at fourteen centimes per 100 kilos up to 600, and eighteen centimes per 100 for all above. So far as the actual labor is concerned, we have no hesitation in saying that it is not nearly so exhaustive nor painful as that of thousands of our English colliers, besides being free from the dangers which constantly impend over our poor miners, but there are some serious and quite unnecessary hardships inflicted upon the men. One of these is that they get nothing to eat until noon, and therefore, unless they buy food with their earnings, they must walk to and from their work and labor for several hours upon an empty stomach; another is that the benevolent intentions of the State in regard to the stimulus of remuneration are defeated by the neglect or dishonesty of certain of the officials. The prisoners now rarely work out their term. Either their sentences are shortened for good conduct, or on some special occasions a certain number are pardoned by royal grace, and we were informed that they rarely die in penal servitude. And now let us descend into the mine, a proceeding which will be facilitated in the reader's thoughts if he will kindly take before him our little plan, which is reduced from the engineer's drawing of a section actually in use on the spot.

The descent is effected on foot through a vertical cylindrical shaft used for that purpose only, and divided at intervals by platforms which communicate with one another by good broad wooden staircases. The visitor is provided with a lighted candle attached to the end of a stick, which serves at the same time as an excellent test of the purity or impurity of the air in the mine, for the lower he descends, the more frequently he will find his light to be extinguished by carbonic acid gas, arising chiefly from the exhalations of the convicts. There are no inflammable gases in the mine, and the men work with naked lights. As he descends ladder or staircase after staircase, the visitor becomes conscious of the presence of human beings in the mine, for strange unearthly sounds greet his ear more and more plainly as he approaches the long gallery which traverses the mine at about 110 feet below the surface; and this effect is rendered still more weird through the surrounding darkness, relieved only by the faint light of his candle and those of his companions. From moment to moment he hears hollow echoes of the human voice uttered in snatches and accompanied by a continuous clanking of chains, which makes his blood creep until he has become to some extent accustomed to the sound. The shaft through which he is descending is cut and rounded with great precision, first through a mixture of clay and rock-salt, and then in the solid rock-salt itself. To render it impervious to water he will find the wall here and there lined with buffalo hides.

Arrived at the horizontal gallery the visitor passes along it until he comes to a platform guarded by a fence or railing, and then he finds himself near the roof of an enormous cave which is probably unlike anything to be seen elsewhere.

We have been in a good many strange localities, and have witnessed many impressive scenes both on and under the earth's surface, but we confess that none has ever been comparable to this one. All is dark excepting where our candles cast a faint glimmer about our immediate neighborhood, and far below we now hear the voices, as well as the rattling of the convicts' chains, more continuously and distinctly, and see numerous lights dancing about fitfully in small clusters. Those are the candles of the convicts who are cutting rock-salt in gangs on the floor of the cave. Continuing our descent down another flight, or rather series of flights, of stairs, we at length arrive at that floor which is about 200 feet from the surface, and there we find ourselves surrounded by homicides, burglars, and the very dregs of the criminal ranks of Romania. There is no guard with us; and, indeed, of what use would even a small escort be against about two hundred and fifty desperate ruffians armed with pickaxes if they thought fit to unite in an assault upon our little party? They have no such intention, however, and the feeling of the visitor is rather one of pain and sorrow to see so many able-bodied fellows manacled than of fear in their presence. The mode in which they get the salt is by cutting an oblong figure in the floor, deepening this until it resembles a mound, and then cutting the block thus formed transversely into smaller ones and breaking the salt out in lumps.

Their work, which is little if at all impeded by their light chains, is performed with pickaxes; and, as already stated, they raise in this manner from 700 to 1,400 kilos (14 to 28 cwt.) per day, which is conveyed to the surface through a special shaft.

The cave is 80 feet high and 400 feet long, and there is another smaller one at right angles with it, shown by a dotted line upon the plan, and every part of it, floor, roof, and walls, is of solid rock-salt. A curious effect is produced by the officials of the mine causing a mass of lighted tow to be dropped through the shaft used for raising the salt, whilst the visitors stand below; this partially illuminates the cave in its descent, and shows its vast proportions. But there is nothing further to detain us in this great chamber of crime, so we will again mount the ladders and seek the genial air and sunshine above ground. The penitentiary in which the convicts are confined after they leave the mine is about a mile distant, and as we drive thither we pass small bodies of them trudging along in the same direction and manacled at their feet. It is a large barrack-like structure, with dirty dormitories, where the men lie in long rows upon wretched pallets. The air of these dormitories is foul, and burning resin is used to fumigate them. One of our companions, a young Romanian, remarked that during the day the convicts breathe an atmosphere vitiated by their own exhalations, whilst at night they are suffocated by the fumes of resin. Their food is wholesome enough, consisting of mamaliga and soup. For making the latter the prisoners receive, *theoretically*, meat at the rate of 100 grams (3-1/2 ounces) per head; but when we instituted a diligent search for some, bones only were the result, and one of the gentlemen observed that the meat was consumed a mile off, meaning at the quarters of certain officials, whilst the bones fell to the prisoners' share. However this may be, one fact was admitted, namely, that by some process of conversion, known only to the initiated, the convict rarely sees his share of his wages, and certainly receives no more nourishment than is necessary to keep body and soul together. It is said that they spend their earnings in luxuries, and probably some may do so; but that the officials are poorly paid, and that it is difficult to find an honest one, these are statements we heard on authority which it was impossible to discredit.

As we have said, however, the rules of the prison are framed with a view to the welfare of the convicts, with the exception that nothing is done to educate them. But there are no harsh punishments; if a man misbehaves himself, his chains are shortened, and very bad conduct is punished with solitary confinement. The prisoners, we were told, are never whipped nor otherwise ill-treated; and if it be true that men who are sent there for robbery are themselves often the victims of plunder at the hands of officials, the minister who is at the head of the department involved will no doubt take measures to prevent the continuance of such an iniquitous example.

And after all there is another phase of this question which must not be lost sight of when we criticize the institutions of a young nation which has only just achieved its independence, and whose first step was to abolish the vindictive capital sentence of 'a life for a life.' The first law of nature is self-preservation, and Romania is still obliged to economize in all departments of the State in order to place her national police—her army—on a sound footing. It is wonderful how she is able to conduct her department of justice even as she does. Her convict labor is so well utilized that it leaves her a handsome profit. Her total expenditure on all judicial and penal matters in 1880 was under 170,000*l.* with a population of 5,000,000, whilst with only seven times that number of inhabitants the Government outlay of Great Britain in the same year amounted to the enormous sum of 5,922,443*l.*, without reckoning the heavy local burdens for the protection of life and property. And yet both life and property are certainly as secure in Romania as in England, without the halter or the cat, two of the barbarous expedients for the prevention of crime which are still employed in our boasted Western civilization.

PART II.

HISTORICAL.

                    And now
The arena swims around him; he is gone
Ere ceased the inhuman shout which hailed the wretch who
    won.

    He heard it, but he heeded not; his eyes
Were with his heart, and that was far away:
He admitted not of the life he lost nor prize,
But where his rude hut by the Danube lay,
There were his young barbarians all at play,
There was their Dacian mother—be their sire,
Butchered to make a Roman holiday.
    All this rushed with his blood. Shall he expire,
And unavenged? Arise, ye Goths, and glut your ire!

CHILDE HAROLD'S PILGRIMAGE, iv. 140.

                    He was more
Than a mere Alexander, and, unstained
    With household blood and wine, serenely wore
His sovereign virtues—still we Trajan's name adore.

CHILDE HAROLD'S PILGRIMAGE, iv. 111.

CHAPTER IX.

FROM THE GETÆ (ABOUT 335 B.C.) TO THE CLOSE OF THE ROMAN DOMINATION IN DACIA TRAJANA (ABOUT A.D. 274).

The Getæ; their supposed origin and history—The Dacians; their origin and migrations—Their incursions into the Roman provinces—Their King, 'Decebalus'—His contests with Cornelius Fuscus and Tertius Julianus—Legends regarding him—Domitian pays him tribute—Trajan—His first expedition against the Dacians—His supposed route—The engineering works of the Romans—Defeat and submission of Decebalus—Trajan's triumphal return to Rome—The bas-reliefs on Trajan's Column—Description of the first expedition therefrom—Decebalus breaks the treaty—Trajan's second expedition—Capture and suicide of Longinus—Defeats of the Dacians—Arrival of the Romans before Sarmizegethusa and its destruction by the Dacians—Suicide of Decebalus and his chiefs—Dacia a Roman province—Approximate boundaries—Carra's opinion of the colonists—Hadrian destroys Trajan's bridge—Duration and decline of the Roman power in Dacia—The Goths and Vandals defeat the Emperor Decius—They are beaten by Marcus Aurelius Claudius (called Gothicus)—Permanent withdrawal from Dacia by Aurelian—Conflicting opinions of historians regarding the evacuation—Gibbon's views probably correct—Character of the colonists who remained in Dacia.

I.

A

though the earliest authentic records of Romania or, more correctly speaking, of Dacia, the Roman province which embraced Romania, Transylvania, and some adjoining territories of to-day, do not reach further back than about the century immediately preceding the Christian era, a good deal of information is to be gathered from the writings of Herodotus, Dion Cassius, and other early historians regarding the *Getæ*, the race from whom the Dacians sprang. The Getæ were in all probability a branch of the Thracians, who were among the earliest immigrants from the East; and for some time before they appeared in Dacia, which was situated on the northern side of the Danube (or Ister, as it was called by the Romans), they had settled between the south bank of that river and the Balkans (Mount Hæmus of the Romans). About the fourth century B.C., however, the Getæ had crossed the river, either driven north by an inimical neighbouring tribe, the Triballi, or in consequence of the growth of the nation itself. When they were first encountered by the Greeks, they occupied the eastern part of Dacia, reaching probably to one portion of the Black Sea; and some account of them is given by Ovid, who was exiled to their vicinity, but little is known of them until they came in contact with the Roman armies. The Getæ have little direct interest for us, but as we find associated with them the names of Philip of Macedon, Alexander the Great, and Lysimachus, a few words concerning their connection with those heroes may not be out of place, and will at least serve to fix a period in the history of the people. Whilst they were still seated on the southern side of the Danube, they are said to have been the allies of Philip in his expedition against the Scythians, and in his contest with the Triballi; but Alexander the Great found them on the northern bank of the river when he undertook the conquest of the Thracian tribes prior to his expedition into Persia. He is said to have crossed the Danube at a place not clearly defined (B.C. 335), and to have defeated about 10,000 foot and 4,000 horsemen. These took refuge with their families in a wooden town, from which they were also dislodged, and fleeing to the steppes they escaped from the victorious Greeks. Now it is that we find the name Getæ changed into that of Dacians, and in the events which followed during the reign of Lysimachus they are known by both designations. After the death of Alexander the Great, Lysimachus inherited Thrace, and subsequently acquired Macedonia and Asia Minor; but in order to secure the first-named territory he found it necessary to cope with barbarian tribes, who formed a coalition against him. These he defeated; but inasmuch as the Getæ or Dacians, under their king (hellenised) Dromichætes, had co-operated with the barbarians, he undertook an expedition into their country north of the Danube shortly afterwards. Penetrating to their barren plains, he sustained a defeat, and was captured along with his whole army. According to certain Greek writers he was treated with great magnanimity by the Dacian king; but all are agreed that the latter only liberated him for a ransom of some kind, either in money or territory. Paget thinks he secured a large treasure, as many thousands of gold coins have been found, some of them bearing the name of Lysimachus. 'I am in possession of some of these coins,' he says, 'and though many were melted down by the Jews in Wallachia, to whom they were conveyed across the frontier in loaves of bread, they are still [1850] very common, and are frequently used by the Transylvanians for signet rings and other ornaments.'

From the time of Lysimachus until about that of Augustus Cæsar we hear little or nothing of the Getæ or Dacians, and we will therefore pass on to what may be called the Roman period.

II.

Some modern writers are of opinion that when the Romans first became acquainted with the country north of the Danube, they found two allied or germane tribes, the Getæ in the eastern, and the Dacians in the western part of the territory; but according to Dion Cassius the Romans called all the inhabitants north of the Ister '*Dacians*,' no matter whether they were Thracians, Getæ, or Dacians, and the probability is that the Getæ had spread themselves gradually over the plains westward, then acquired possession of the Carpathian mountains, and descended into the plains of Transylvania.
 Their fastnesses, called forts or cities, were built of wood, and were situated in the mountains, and there it was that their fiercest contests with the Roman arms took place previous to their complete subjugation.

The first we hear of them is that under a powerful chief Burvista or Boerebestes, they conquered their neighbors, the Boii, Jasyges, and probably other tribes, at the eastern boundary of their territory, driving them from their possessions, and from that time they appear as a distinct nation constantly threatening the safety of the Roman provinces in their vicinity. Julius Cæsar, it is said, proposed to attack them shortly before his death, as they made periodical inroads into the Empire, more especially into Mœsia, the country lying between the Danube and the Balkan mountains, of which the Romans had secured the possession. Every winter, as soon as the Danube was frozen over or blocked with ice, they descended from their mountain fastnesses, crossed the broad stream, and carried fire and sword into the Roman territory. Before the latter people had time to gather their forces, their barbarous enemy had retreated, and, the river being once more open, the Dacians endeavored to prevent the landing of the Roman troops, or, failing that, they made good their retreat to the mountains, whither the Romans feared to follow them. Nor were the Dacians by any means despicable opponents. Although many of them fought bareheaded and clothed in a light tunic, they were well acquainted with the use of armour, and possessed standards, shields, helmets, breast-plates, and even chain and plate mail, fighting with bows and arrows, spears, javelins, and a short curved sword somewhat resembling a sickle.

They fought on horseback as well as on foot, and it is said that they sent showers of poisoned arrows into the ranks of their enemies. Of their further proceedings in war as well as in peace we shall have occasion to speak hereafter. About the year 10 B.C. the Emperor Augustus sent one of his generals, Cn. Lentulus, to punish them for having entered and devastated Pannonia under a chief Kotiso, but the expedition was ineffectual, and for a long series of years they continued to harass the Empire, often threatening to overrun whole provinces. One such enterprise is mentioned by Tacitus:—

> 'Commotions about the same time broke out among the Dacians, a people never to be relied on, and since the legions were withdrawn from Mœsia there was no force to awe them. They, however, watched in silence the first movements of affairs. But when they heard that Italy was in a blaze of war, and that all the inhabitants were in arms against each other, they stormed the winter quarters of the cohorts and the cavalry, and made themselves masters of both banks of the Danube. They then prepared to raze the camp of the legions, when Mucianus sent the sixth legion to check them, having heard of the victory at Cremona, and lest a formidable foreign force should invade Italy on both sides, the Dacians and the Germans making irruptions in opposite quarters. On this, as on many other occasions, fortune favored the Romans in bringing Mucianus

and the forces of the East into that quarter, and also in that we had settled matters at Cremona in the very nick of time.'[81]

It was in the reign of the Emperor Domitian, however, that the inroads of the Dacians assumed their most formidable proportions. About this time it is probable that the Dacians were divided into several tribes, and that one leader more powerful than the rest had secured the chieftainship of the whole nation. Thia chief is known to historians as 'Decebalus,' although there is great difference of opinion as to whether that was his name or his title.[82] In the year 86 A.D., he gathered together a great host, and, crossing the Danube into Mœsia, defeated and killed the prætor Oppius or Appius Sabinus, seizing several of the Roman fortresses and driving their army to the foot of Mount Hæmus. As soon as the defeat and the position of the Roman forces became known, Domitian collected an army in Illyria and placed it under the command of Cornelius Fuscus, a general of more bravery than experience, who entered Mœsia, and, finding that Decebalus, according to precedent, had retired across the Danube, followed him into his own country, only, however, in his turn to be defeated and slain. Upon this the Romans again recrossed the river, leaving behind them their baggage and many prisoners. Tacitus writes in great indignation concerning these reverses:—

> 'So many armies in Mœsia, Dacia, Germany, and Pannonia, lost through the temerity or cowardice of their generals; so many men of military character with numerous cohorts defeated and taken prisoners; whilst a dubious contest was maintained, not for the boundaries of the Empire and the banks of the bordering rivers, but for the winter quarters of the legions and the possession of our territories.'[83]

Whilst these events were occurring, Domitian is said to have been making progresses and indulging in all kinds of excesses, but; fortunately for him and for the honor of the Roman arms, another general succeeded in stemming the tide of invasion, and eventually (A.D. 89) in assuming the offensive. This was Tertius Julianus, who had already distinguished himself in Mœsia under Otho and Vespasian. Following Decebalus into his own dominions, he was not content to remain in the plains, but pursued him into his mountain retreats, where he completely overthrew him in a pitched battle and compelled him to sue for peace. It is in the accounts of this expedition that mention is first made of regular roads in Dacia, and two passes, the Vulcan and Rothenthurm (or Red Tower), are referred to. A place called Tapæ is also named, near to which Julianus is said to have overthrown Decebalus, and where subsequently Trajan obtained a victory over the same prince; but so much doubt attaches to the movements of Julianus that it will be better for the present to defer any reference to those localities. The whole account of Julianus's campaign in Dacia is mixed up with legendary tradition. It is said that he threatened the capital of Dacia, Sarmizegethusa, and that he would have succeeded in capturing it and in reducing the whole country but for a stratagem of Decebalus, who caused trees to be cut down to a man's height in the woods through which the Romans had to pass, and clothed them in armor, which so terrified the soldiers as to stay their progress. According to another account he cut the trees through their trunks but allowed them to stand, and when the Romans attempted to force their way through with their engines of war, the trees fell on them and killed them. Whether it was the difficulty encountered by the Roman general in attempting to cope with his warlike enemy in his mountains and forests, where the arts of war as practiced by the former were not so readily applicable as in the plains, or the more probable circumstance that Domitian had been unsuccessful in an expedition against two other tribes, the Quadi and Marcomanni, and needed the support of Julianus, certain it is that the overtures of Decebalus were at length received favorably, and a peace was concluded with him in the year 90, which was less favorable to the victors than to the conquered. Decebalus refused to treat in person with the Roman general, but sent one of his chiefs (some historians say his brother), with whom the conditions were arranged. According to Roman accounts Decebalus restored the Roman prisoners, acknowledged the supremacy of Domitian, and accepted sovereignty at his hands. It subsequently transpired, however, that this was not the whole treaty, and that Domitian agreed to pay the Dacian king an annual tribute, and to send him a number of skilled artificers to teach him the art of constructing works and fabricating arms upon the Roman model. Domitian then celebrated a triumph, which was however made a subject of ridicule by those who were aware of the actual result of the expedition.

We now approach a crisis in the history of Dacia. During the short reign of Nerva nothing was undertaken against the country, and Decebalus continued to harass and annoy the Romans in Mœsia until Trajan (who had been adopted by Nerva) ascended the throne (A.D. 98).

This emperor at once began preparations for putting an end to his humiliating relations with Decebalus and his people, and although there have been many conjectures concerning his motives and intentions, there can be little doubt that his object was eventually, if not immediately, to incorporate Dacia with his empire. Already in the reign of some of his predecessors the construction of a military road along the right or south bank of the Danube had been proceeding, and the first operation of Trajan was to hasten the completion of this road for the passage of his troops.

With this object he is said to have reconnoitred in 98 and 99, and the road probably attained completion as far as the bank opposite Orsova, about A.D. 100, as the tablet at Gradina, to which reference has already been made, indicates. It is impossible for us to estimate the difficulties which must have attended this undertaking. Possessing as we do explosives and rock-borers with which to break a passage through mountains and to blast rocky embankments, we can hardly understand how a people, with such limited mechanical appliances as then existed, can have surmounted the obstacles that presented themselves to their progress. In one place the way was a plank road resting on beams, which were driven into the perpendicular face of the solid rock a few feet above the water's edge, whilst a little further on it is seen to wind along terraces cut artificially, high up on the hillsides. Hundreds if not thousands of lives must have been sacrificed in the work, for it must be remembered that the Roman generals and artificers had not only to combat natural difficulties, and to overcome the same obstacles as those which our modern engineers have to face, but that they were harassed by the savage but skilled enemy from the heights above, or from the opposite bank of the river, which here and there narrows itself into defiles 150 or 200 yards wide.

As soon as the road was sufficiently advanced for the passage of his army, A.D. 101, Trajan commenced his first expedition into Dacia. The constitution and number of his forces are not accurately known. They varied, according to different accounts, from 60,000 to 80,000 Romans, with a considerable number of allies, Germans, Sarmatians, Mauritanian cavalry, &c., the last-named under Lucius Quietus; and these Trajan is said to have assembled at a place somewhere south of Viminacium, which subsequently served as the base of his operations.

Pages upon pages have been devoted by ancient and modern historians to surmises concerning the routes taken by Trajan in his expedition and the localities where his encounters with the Dacians took place, but in every case the ascertained facts have been few in number. The best history of the campaigns is delineated in the bas-reliefs on Trajan's Column at Rome, and many details have been collected from fragmentary writings of Dion Cassius and other old historians.

For the convenience of crossing the Danube the army was divided into two parts, and the river was crossed by bridges of boats at two points, one near Viminacium and the other opposite Orsova. The first section then skirted the western slopes of the Carpathians through the valley of the Theiss, and so entered the Dacian highlands; the other marched up the valley of the Tierna (Czerna), past the baths of Mehadia, which already existed in the Roman period, and the two divisions of the army formed a junction at Karansebes, or at Tibiscum close by, where two Roman roads met;
Trajan is known to have accompanied and led the eastern division until the junction was completed. It is probable that in that year (101 A.D.) no serious encounter took place between Trajan and Decebalus, who had been occupied for some time in preparing for his defense, and had now received reinforcements from many of the neighboring tribes. One of these in the name of the allied tribes sent a threatening message to Trajan, written or scratched upon a fungus, warning him to withdraw his troops, but he heeded neither this admonition nor overtures of peace proceeding from Decebalus himself. His army went into winter quarters, and early in 102 A.D. he commenced operations by forcing the Iron Gate pass in the Carpathians, and encountered the enemy, it is said, at the same place where Julianus had previously defeated Decebalus, namely, Tapæ. Here the Dacians again met with a sanguinary defeat, but the Romans also sustained severe losses, and Trajan secured himself in the affections of his soldiers by tearing up his garments to make bandages for the wounded.
After this reverse Decebalus sought to reopen negotiations with Trajan, but on his refusal to receive the emissaries of the emperor, who declined to

meet him in person, hostilities were renewed, and the war was prosecuted by the Dacians with great fierceness and barbarity. The discipline and warlike resources of Rome, however, maintained the ascendancy for her arms. Decebalus was pressed from stronghold to stronghold, and defeated in one encounter after another, until at length his capital Sarmizegethusa was threatened by his triumphant enemy. Then it was that he sued earnestly for peace, and accepted the unfavorable conditions offered him by Trajan.

He was compelled to give up all his war material and artificers, to raze his fortresses, to deliver up all Roman prisoners and deserters, to conclude a treaty defensive and offensive with Rome, and to appear before and do homage to the emperor. Dacia thus became a vassal but autonomous province of the Empire, and, content with his victory, Trajan returned to the capital, taking with him certain Dacian chiefs, who repeated the act of homage in the senate. He then celebrated a triumph, and received the distinctive title of 'Dacicus.'

As we have already stated, the story of Trajan's expeditions into Dacia is recorded in the bas-reliefs of the column bearing his name and still existing in Rome. These bas-reliefs have been subject to various readings and interpretations, but we have so far avoided referring to them under the impression that they can only be taken in a general sense to represent the exploits of Trajan, and that any attempt to extract from them the names of localities is at best a hazardous experiment. With these reservations, however, it is safe to say that they vividly represent incidents of the campaign and bring us face to face with the warlike character and customs of the contending nations. The progress of the expedition, as shown on the column, is divided into sections, placed one above another, and separated by stems of trees which coil round the column; in the first of these sections we see the passage of the army across the Danube over two bridges of boats. The Roman soldiers are chiefly bareheaded, carrying their shields and helmets, and many bearing standards with eagles, images of the gods, and other devices. Some of the objects carried are supposed to be lanterns, from which it is inferred that the passage took place at night. In advance are the trumpeters bearing long curved horns, and the led horses of Trajan and his generals. The last-named have already crossed the river, and Trajan is seated on a platform surrounded by his officers, haranguing his men. Next we find ourselves in the enemy's country, although there are no signs as yet of the Dacians, and the two succeeding sections of the column are occupied by the progress of the Roman arms. The soldiers are felling timber, removing obstructions, and building forts and bridges, over all of which operations Trajan is seen to preside in person. In the fourth division the Dacians appear, suing for peace; the emissaries are clad in long robes, and Trajan meets them outside a fort. Then follow further incidents in the campaign; encounters take place between the opposing forces, in which the Dacians are defeated and their dead lie scattered on the ground. They are then seen retreating with their women and children, devastating the country and slaying their cattle which are heaped up in piles. Trajan is again present, sparing the old men, women, and children, and making prisoners. Now the Dacians are the attacking party, and the Romans defend themselves behind forts; and then again the army is in motion with Trajan at its head, crossing rivers, and erecting fortifications. In the next section the Dacians have made a stand, and the scene represents a pitched battle in which they are again defeated with great slaughter. All the incidents of the fight are vividly depicted: Romans fighting from their chariots, Dacians and their allies mounted and on foot, prisoners brought in, and a man, apparently a spy, bound before Trajan himself. Then follows a further advance, which occupies some of the succeeding scenes of the panorama. Here the Romans fall into an ambuscade, from which they extricate themselves; there they pass a post of danger, apparently a wooden stronghold of the Dacians, under cover of a wall of shields held aloft by the soldiers; and at length they arrive before a fortified town, where Trajan is again seen seated upon a platform, surrounded by his generals, whilst the Dacians, one of whom is supposed to be Decebalus himself, kneel round about, suing for peace. In this scene the attire, emblems, and accouterments of the two contending nations are presented in marked contrast. The Roman standards and eagles have already been mentioned; those of the Dacians generally represent serpentine monsters at the end of a long pole. Whilst the Romans carry their tall, curved, oblong shield, the oval ones of the Dacians ornamented with floral devices lie heaped in confusion. Most of the Dacians are bareheaded, but some, supposed to be chiefs, wear a head-dress resembling a cap of liberty. Another section completes the panorama of the first expedition, representing the embarkation and landing of Trajan; the sacrifices, triumph, and rejoicings in the capital.

But Decebalus had no more intention of abiding by the terms of his treaty with the Roman emperor than had Trajan with that of his predecessor. The Dacian king had no sooner seen his enemy's back than he repaired his fortresses, armed his people afresh, sought new alliances with his neighbors, and commenced depredations upon the territories of Rome and her allies. Then it was that Trajan prepared to chastise the barbarians, and this time he determined to crush the Dacian power completely, and to annex the conquered country as a Roman province. Although he is said to have been in Mœsia in A.D. 104, the actual movements against Dacia only commenced the following year, and in this as in the preceding expedition the routes pursued by the Roman army have not been clearly defined. The bridge across the Danube from Gladowa to Turnu-Severin was most likely completed, and part, if not the whole, of Trajan's army crossed there. Those writers who believe that in the first expedition a portion of the forces entered from Pannonia, say that, knowing the geography of the country better, Trajan now sent a division up the valley of the Theiss, crossing the Danube at Viminacium; whilst there is little doubt that a portion of the army continued the march eastward along the Mœsian bank of the Danube, crossed at a station opposite the mouth of the Alutus (now Oltu), landed near the modern Celeiu, and, crossing the plain, entered the mountain fastnesses through the Rothenthurm pass.

By whatever routes Trajan's army invaded the dominions of the doomed king, it is known that his advance was prompt and successful, and that this time the fame of the Roman arms prevented Decebalus from securing many allies. He once more sued for peace; but Trajan's terms being a virtual relinquishment of his independence, he prepared himself for a supreme and desperate effort for the defense of his kingdom. At first it is said that he attempted to remove Trajan by assassination, but that his emissaries were detected and put to death. Another expedient seems to have been temporarily successful. He managed to decoy into his power Longinus, a Roman general, said to have been a great favorite of Trajan, and, holding him as a hostage, Decebalus demanded extravagant terms of peace. To this proposal Trajan gave an evasive reply, in order, if possible, to save the life of his officer. The last-named, however, with true Roman patriotism, had a message conveyed to Trajan by his freedman, advising him to proceed with his operations, and at the same time he himself took a dose of poison in order to relieve his master from further perplexity on his account. Decebalus then offered to give up the body of the Roman general and certain other captives in return for the escaped freedman, but Trajan returned no answer to his proposal. Very little is known of the incidents of this campaign, excepting that Trajan forced the passes of the Carpathians, and, taking one defended post after another, drove the enemy into the vicinity of his capital; that the tribes who had allied themselves with the Dacians, amongwhom the Sarmatians, Jasyges, and Burri are named, deserted them one by one, and that the Romans at length laid siege to Sarmizegethusa, where Decebalus had taken refuge. After a brave but ineffectual defence the king, rather than yield himself a prisoner, committed suicide with his sword; whilst his followers, after setting fire to the town, imitated the example of their leader by taking poison. The head of

Decebalus was cut off and sent to Rome by Trajan, who discovered and divided among his soldiers vast spoils and treasures which the Dacians had endeavored to conceal, and then returned to Rome, where (A.D. 106) a triumph was celebrated on even a grander scale than after the conclusion of his first expedition.

Before drawing to a close this hasty survey of the rise and fall of the Dacian monarchy, let us turn again for a moment to the bas-reliefs upon Trajan's Column, the indelible and, after all, the most trustworthy record of his second expedition. Passing hastily over the first scenes, which comprise tho landing of his troops, the assault and capture of a fortified place, the defeat of the Dacians, and what appears to be a refusal on the part of Trajan to grant them peace, we have a very faithful and circumstantial picture of a halt, where the emperor is present at the offering of a bull as sacrifice. Then there is a continuance of the march inland, followed by fierce contests between the two armies. At length the Romans arrive before a walled city (probably Sarmizegethusa) where all the incidents of a siege, including personal adventures, are portrayed. A Roman soldier, standing at the top of a scaling ladder, has struck off the head of one of the Dacians on the wall, whilst the latter are seen hurling stones and other missiles at those engaged in the assault. Then comes another application for peace, a Dacian prince kneeling at the feet of Trajan; whilst in the same section, separated only by a couple of thin trees, we have the scene of the Dacians setting fire to their city, and in close contiguity is their dying leader. The remaining scenes depict the Roman soldiers dividing the spoil. Trajan is addressing them, distributing rewards, and bidding them adieu. Then follow secondary incidents; the building of fortresses by the Romans; one or two more contests in which Trajan's generals defeat the Dacians, driving them into the mountains, whither they are seen fleeing with their flocks, women, and children. One of the last scenes represents the second triumph of Trajan, with soldiers who arrive bearing the head of Decebalus. Some of the minor incidents in the panorama are intended to exhibit the barbarity of the Dacians, one being the exhibition of a row of heads stuck upon spears on the walls of a town or fortress; another the burning and torturing of naked Roman prisoners by Dacian women. Altogether these bas-reliefs, which are said to be the work of several artists, present anything but an edifying spectacle of the ancient mode of warfare.

III.

Whatever uncertainty attaches to the details of Trajan's expeditions, there is none as to their ultimate result, nor concerning the chief operations of the conqueror and his successors in the newly-acquired territory, which was formally annexed as a province of the Empire. Some historians have attempted to define with great minuteness the boundaries of the new province, but more cautious writers content themselves with naming approximate limits; and these have done wisely, as there is no doubt that the movements of the neighboring tribes and even of the conquered Dacians (for it is a mistake to suppose, as some do, that they went out of existence) prevented any strict line of demarcation. The nominal boundaries of Roman Dacia were the river Theiss on the west, the Pruth on the east, 'barbarians' on the north, and the river Danube on the south. The country actually colonized embraced the Banate of Temesvar, Transylvania (Siebenbürgen), and Romania as they exist to-day. There were several centers of colonization, of which the chief was Ulpia Trajana, including the old capital of Decebalus, Sarmizegethusa (now Varhely), and other important centers were Apulum and Cerna or Tierna.

Trajan and his successors built fortifications, walls, and towns; and, attracted partly by the fertility of the plains and partly by the gold mines of the Carpathians, the Roman colonies soon swelled in numbers and importance. Different opinions have been expressed concerning the character of these colonists. One modern writer, Carra, who is considered an authority in Romanian history, says that the Romans regarded Dacia as the French, Cayenne, and sent thither a colony consisting of the scum of the principal towns of Greece and the Roman Empire. Their descendants, he adds, who inherited their vices and cowardice, were turn by turn conquered and enslaved by the Sarmatians, Huns, and Tartars. This is a statement which rather affects the feelings of modern Romanians than the current of historical events, and it brings us face to face with an inquiry which we shall have to handle with great circumspection, namely, the descent of the modern Romanians from the old Daco-Roman colonists, lest we find ourselves involved in a controversy that would fill volumes. So far as the records of Roman history enable us to judge, Carra has done great injustice to the colonists of Dacia. It is true that the Romans banished some of their malefactors, and especially political offenders, to their colonies, as Ovid was expatriated; and that Trajan colonized Dacia from various parts of the Empire; but the custom of the Roman generals, which Trajan would doubtless have followed, was to divide the most fertile districts amoungst their veteran soldiers, and therefore, if the charges of cowardice and debauchery made by Carra were true, they would apply to the bravest in the legions who had conquered the almost indomitable Decebalus. But Carra lived and wrote at a time (A.D. 1777) when cool judgment could hardly be expected in a writer on Romania, and if he were alive to-day he would be surprised to hear that there is a school of modern historians who, using his very authorities, deny that the descendants of the Daco-Roman colonists were ever to be found on Dacian ground during the incursions of the eastern barbarians. But of that more hereafter.

The history of the Roman occupation of Dacia, which lasted from the time of Trajan until it was evacuated by Aurelian, affords little to interest the reader. Dacia was, so to speak, the outwork of the Empire which served to hold the barbarians at bay during its 'decline and fall;' and the country was more prosperous than during the period of its independence, when the tribes were constantly at war with one another and there was no settled government. That the attitude of the barbarians was threatening even a few years after the death of Trajan is, however, more than probable, for his immediate successor, Hadrian, contemplated withdrawing his legions, and destroyed the bridge across the Danube, 118 or 120 A.D. Some writers, indeed, attribute this act to his jealousy of Trajan, others to his hatred of Apollodorus, the architect; but most probably the cause assigned by Dion Cassius, that it was to prevent its being used by the barbarians for making inroads into Mœsia, was the true one. During the reigns of Antoninus Pius and Marcus Aurelius for about half a century, the barbarians were kept in check, although even during that period they had managed to encroach upon the Roman territory.

At the beginning of the third century, however, the Roman hold on Dacia began to be very precarious, and we approach the time when the dark veil of the so-called barbarian ages is drawn over the history of Europe. That the Roman emperors had to contend, with very varying fortunes, with barbarous tribes is certain, and that their arms were still frequently successful is proved by the erection of fortresses and towns, named after their emperors, on the borders of their possessions. For example, Caracalla defeated certain barbarous hordes about A.D. 212, and assumed the name of 'Geticus,' but whether the conquered tribes were Dacians or Goths is uncertain.

A few years later the Quadi and Marcomanni made inroads into Western Dacia, but they were held in check by the proconsul Varus, who built a tower or fort in close proximity to Trajan's bridge, of which the ruins are still visible to travelers on the Danube, and which has given its name to the modern town of Turnu-Severin. But the Goths, a people of Scandinavian origin, had been for some time previously drawing nearer to the borders of the Roman Empire. Between the beginning of our era and the end of the second century they had spread themselves, associated with the Vandals, in the direction of the Carpathians and the Ukraine, and in the reign of the Emperor Philip (243-249) they made irruptions into Mœsia. In that of Decius they invaded the Roman territory a second time under a chief, Cniva, and, after defeating the Romans and compelling the emperor to flee, they took and sacked Philippopolis. Shortly afterwards Decius met them again, but he was again defeated and slain. The barbarians then retired with their plunder.

The next event of importance was the defeat of the Goths (about 268 or 269) by Marcus Aurelius Claudius. They had once more entered Roman territory, had overrun Mœsia and Illyria, and were approaching the capital; it was therefore found necessary to raise a powerful army and drive them over the frontier. This time they were defeated with great slaughter at Naissos in the Balkans and elsewhere, and were then driven across the Danube. Marcus Aurelius, who took the name of 'Gothicus,' describes the fate of the enemy in these terms: 'We have annihilated 320,000 Goths, and have sunk two thousand of their ships. Everywhere rivers are covered with their shields, all the banks with their swords and spears, whilst the fields are sown with their bones. The roads are indistinguishable; much baggage is taken. We have captured so many women that every soldier is able to possess two or three of them.' And yet, notwithstanding this decisive victory of Marcus Aurelius, his successor Aurelian found himself very shortly afterwards in deadly conflict with these same Goths, and his contests were so doubtful in their results that he was glad to make a treaty of peace with them and leave them in undisturbed possession of Trajan's Dacia. That he decided to withdraw the Roman legions (about 270 or 275 A.D.) from Dacian territory, that he offered protection to all colonists who were prepared to follow them across the Danube, and that a new colony, called Dacia Aureliani, was founded along the south bank of the Danube: these are contradicted facts. But when we come to inquire into the details of the withdrawal and the composition of the remaining population, we find such a conflict of authorities that it is impossible to come to a definite conclusion. Nay, not only do the historians differ from one another in regard to the conditions under which Aurelian evacuated Dacia Trajana, or Dacia north of the Danube, but in some cases they even contradict themselves, and, after a careful perusal and comparison of the statements of many of them, we are quite disposed to accept the opinion expressed by our own historian Gibbon, who, after saying that Aurelian withdrew the Roman legions from Dacia and offered the alternative of leaving to those colonists who were disposed to follow him, adds:—

> 'The old country of that name (Dacia) detained, however, a considerable number of its inhabitants who dreaded exile more than a Gothic master. These degenerate Romana continued to serve the Empire whose allegiance they had renounced by introducing among their conquerors the first notions of agriculture, the useful arts, and the convenience of civilization. An intercourse of commerce and language was gradually established between the opposite banks of the Danube, and after Dacia became an independent State it often proved the firmest barrier of the Empire against the invasions of the savages of the north. A sense of interest attached these more settled barbarians to the alliance of Rome, and a permanent interest very frequently ripens into sincere and useful friendship.'

And Gibbon, who had read and studied the works of Eutropius and his successor Vopiscus, as well as other more recent historians, gives us further details of the negotiations that took place between Aurelian and the Goths, which remove any doubts as to the accuracy of his views. Aurelian treated with the barbarians after a battle had been fought which was by no means adverse to the Roman arms, and he stipulated with the Goths that they should contribute an auxiliary force of 2,000 men to the Roman army. He moreover secured a large number of hostages, being the sons and daughters of Gothic chiefs, whom he sent to Rome to be educated. He adds, concerning the constitution of the province north of the Danube: 'This various colony which filled the ancient province, and was insensibly blended into one great nation, still acknowledged the superior renown and authority of the Gothic tribe, and claimed the fancied honor of Scandinavian origin.'

But this is not all. The great historian, whose views can only be rejected on what we may call a political or partisan theory, believed the Roman colonists to have been industrious agriculturists; for when he speaks, in another place, of the temptations which led the wandering Goths in the first instance to cast longing eyes upon Dacia, he says: 'But the prospects of the Roman territory were far more alluring, and the fields of Dacia were covered with a rich harvest, sown by the hands of an *industrious*, and exposed to be gathered by a warlike people.'

In bringing the history of the Roman occupation of Dacia to a close, we have therefore to acknowledge that, far from being inhabited by the scum of the earth as Carra supposed, the country was at first in the hands of an industrious, though probably a sparse peasantry, and, as Gibbon has said, 'only those who had nothing to lose accompanied the Roman army,' leaving the remainder, a large body of industrious Daco-Roman agriculturists, ruled over by a tribe of warlike barbarians. What these and their posterity suffered, will be seen from the narrative in our next chapter.

CHAPTER X.

FROM THE EVACUATION OF DACIA BY AURELIAN (ABOUT 274 A.D.) TO THE END OF THE BARBARIAN RULE (ABOUT THE CLOSE OF THE THIRTEENTH CENTURY).

The 'Barbarians'—Brief mention of them by Romanian historians—The Goths—Their settlement in Dacia—Defeat by Theodosius and disappearance—The Huns—Their ferocity—Attila—His successes—Deserted and overthrown by the Gepidæ—His death, and expulsion of the Huns—The Sarmatians—The Gepidæ ally themselves with the Byzantines—Defeated by the Lombards under Alboin—The Avari—Settle in Dacia—Are defeated and dispersed by Priscus and Heraclius—The Bulgari—Their origin and that of the Slavonians—Their cruelty—Warlike habits—Severe punishment of criminals—Superstitions—Their 'Chagan,' or chief rider—Conversion to Christianity—Their chieftains—Improved habits—Curious superstitions—Career of the Bulgari—Invasion of the Eastern Empire and defeat by Belisarius—Supreme in Dacia, Mœsia, and Serbia—Vicissitudes—Story of Krumus—Daco-Roman princes—The Bulgarian territories annexed by Basilius to the Greek Empire—The Ungri, or Hungarians—Their supposed origin—Their cruelty and ferocity—Hallam's description of them—German account of their savage mode of warfare—Ravage Europe—Settle in Hungary and found a kingdom—Are driven over the Carpathians by the Bulgari—(Note: Story of their contests with the chiefs Gellius, Gladius, Mariotus, &c.,—The anonymous notary of King Bela)—The Patzinakitai—Scanty records concerning them—The Wallachs—Controversy regarding their origin—Daco-Roman descendants—Mediæval accounts of their origin and character—Anna Comnena—Bonfinius—Æneas Sylvius—M. Opitz—Their career in the Danubian territories—Revolt in alliance with the Bulgari—Foundation of the Wallacho-Bulgarian Empire by Peter, Asan, and John—The historical *soufflet*—Recognition of the new empire—Its duration—The

Kumani—Their domination—The Teutonic Knights and Knights of St. John—Interesting correspondence between King Joannitz and Pope Innocent III.—Temporary conversion of the Bulgarians to Rome—Downfall of the Wallacho-Bulgarian Empire—Irruptions and retirement of the Tartars—End of the barbarian age.

I.

If the reader will imagine a country somewhat larger than the United Kingdom situated in a part of the European continent which renders it accessible from almost every side, and can conceive of eight or nine great hordes of armed savages tens or hundreds of thousands strong, with many smaller ones, pouring intermittently, and even simultaneously in some instances, into that devoted territory, and there alternately burning and plundering or making slaves of each other or of the original settlers, during a continuous period of more than a thousand years, then he will have formed some idea of poor Romania (or perhaps it would be more correct to say of the territories north and south of the lower Danube) as it existed between the end of the third and of the thirteenth centuries.

It is not surprising that some of the historians of Romania, who have managed to fill volumes, should have slurred over what really constitutes half the period of her national existence in a few pages, nay even in some instances in a few lines; and that they should have substituted what one writer has called 'brilliant declamatory evolutions' for the conclusions of careful research. For the last method sometimes leads to the discovery of discrepancies between standard authors of fifty or a hundred years in the chronicle of events. For us the history of the so-called dark ages in that part of Europe is full of interest, inasmuch as the Danubian plains constituted the highway over which the barbarians wandered who were the ancestors of a large proportion of the existing population of Europe; and we have sought, in the table appended to this work, to bring some kind of order out of the chaos of events narrated by historians. Beyond this, it is true, we cannot do much to serve the student of history, and it is a matter of regret that the character of this work necessitates our treating the subject with such inconvenient brevity; but we must appeal to the patience and good nature of our readers whilst we seek to give as much interest as possible to a necessarily dry and tedious narrative.

For about a century after the withdrawal of the Roman legions, the *Goths*, a people of whose origin and exploits we have already spoken, ruled in Trajan's Dacia, except during a brief interval (327 A.D.) when Constantine, having built a bridge across the Danube at or near Nicopolis on the southern, and Turnu-Magurele on the northern bank, overran the country and once more incorporated it with the Empire. This occupation was, however, of short duration. Finding that he could not maintain his supremacy north of the Danube, and that the Goths were even settling on the right bank, Constantine is said to have established Roman colonies south of the Balkans, and, according to some historians, it was from those settlers that the country has derived its present name of Roumelia. That the Goths must have founded permanent settlements in various parts of Dacia is obvious from the traces they have loft behind them, notably in the neighborhood of Buseu. Moreover, in the middle of the century (361 A.D.) they are said to have embraced Christianity, although we hear shortly afterwards (370 A.D.) that their king Athanaric subjected the Christians to the most cruel persecutions. At that time they were probably on more neighbourly terms with the Romans, for when a new enemy, the Huns, appeared in the east and threatened them with annihilation, many of them were allowed by the Emperor Valens to cross the Danube and settle peaceably on the right or southern bank. Shortly afterwards, however, we find them first defeating and slaying Valens and then fighting in alliance with the Huns (378) against the Emperor Theodosius, who attacked them in Dacia. This is the last we hear of the Goths as such, but a branch, the Gepidæ, afterwards rose again and for a considerable period dominated in Dacia.

II.

The *Huns* who drove out the Goths and followed them in the occupation of the country, are supposed by some to be of Scythian, by others even of Chinese origin, and Gibbon has very graphically described their first appearance and movements. 'The numbers,' he says, 'the strength, the rapid motions, and the implacable cruelty of the Huns were felt, and dreaded and magnified by the astonished Goths, who beheld their fields and villages consumed with flames and deluged with indiscriminate slaughter. To these real terrors were added the surprise and abhorrence which were excited by the shrill voice, the uncouth gestures, and the strange deformity of the Huns. These savages of Scythia were compared (and the picture had some resemblance) to the animals who walked very awkwardly on two legs, and to the misshapen figures, the Termini, which were often placed on the bridges of antiquity. They were distinguished from the rest of the human species by their broad shoulders, flat noses, and small black eyes deeply buried in the head, and as they were almost destitute of beards they never enjoyed either the manly graces of youth or the venerable aspect of age.'

These were the beings who devastated and dominated in Dacia for three-fourths of a century (375 to about 453 A.D.), and others such as these, we may add, were still harrying the peacefully disposed population six or seven hundred years subsequently, when the ultra-barbarian *régime* was about drawing to a close.

But the rule of the Huns was not uninterrupted. Shortly after they obtained possession of the Gothic kingdom in Dacia they were defeated by the Emperor Theodosius I. (about 378), but from that time until the reign of their King Attila ('the scourge of God') nothing of importance is noted in their history. This monarch not only brought the whole of Dacia under the yoke, but (about 443) he conquered Mœsia, and pressed the Romans so hard that Theodosius II. (408-450), as well as the Eastern Emperor, were glad to make peace with him, by which he retained the greater part of his conquests north of the Danube. It is impossible, nor would it be legitimate here, to follow Attila through his victorious career. All we need to mention is that when the tide was turning against him, the vassal tribes, whom he had dragged through Europe as allies, deserted him, and the Gepidæ, a branch of the great Gothic nation, helped to hasten his downfall; for, revolting under their chief Ardaric, they not only defeated his army, but became masters of the whole of Dacia. At the conclusion of the reign of Attila, who died or was murdered about A.D. 453, the Huns were driven back into Asia, whence they once more invaded Europe a few years later; but, although we hear of them casually, in union with other tribes, more than a century afterwards (about 564), they never recovered their power in Dacia, and are of no further interest to us in this connection.

III.

The reader will remember that even in the wars between the Romans and Dacians other barbarian tribes took part. Of these the Quadi, Marcomanni, and Sarmatians continued to harass the successors of the first-named, and even to make irruptions into the Empire. The *Sarmatians* especially were very formidable, and from time to time they settled in Dacia during the occupation of the Goths, giving both them and the Romans much trouble. They were encountered by more than one Roman army, and were driven back into and through Dacian territory; but at length, about A.D. 375 Valentinian defeated them with great slaughter, and we cease to hear of them in connection with Romanian history.

With the *Gepidæ*, that branch of the Goths who defeated Attila, it was otherwise. After the withdrawal of the Huns they took possession of Northern Dacia, and managed to obtain such a firm hold on the country, that it was actually known to some of the older historians as 'Gepidia.' There is, however, nothing of interest in their history. Sometimes they were at war with their more powerful southern neighbors; anon they formed alliances with them on advantageous terms, and aided them to keep other tribes in check. The Roman Empire was now split into its Eastern and Western divisions, and it was with the Byzantines that the Gepidæ made their treaties. These, however, were capable of rendering them little effectual service at periods of grave danger, and when (about 550 A.D.) the Lombards, a warlike tribe who are believed to have migrated southwards from the shores of the Baltic, in combination with an Asiatic horde, the Avari, made inroads into their territory, the Gepidæ were quite incapable of making head against them. We have said that the latter nation contracted treaties, offensive and defensive, with the Eastern Empire, but it must not be supposed that either the emperors or the barbarians were very constant in their attachments. At one time we find some particular tribe in alliance with the emperors of the East, assisting them to keep back new assailants; at another they entered the armies of the Eastern emperors, to help them in their attacks upon their Western rivals; then, again, it is two tribes associated to root out and exterminate a horde in possession; and shortly afterwards it may be that the tribes who were allied are arrayed against each other. About the time named, the *Lombards* and Avari, as we have said, made inroads into the territories of the Gepidæ, the first-named being under the lead of a brave and fierce leader, Alboin, and in a very short period (between 550 and 567 A.D.) they managed not only to defeat the Gepidæ, but so completely to break their power, that some writers speak of them as being annihilated. Then it was that the Emperor Justinian (527-565), fearing them as opponents, and desiring them as allies, tempted the Lombards to enter his service; and, bent upon conquest rather than upon becoming settlers in the land which they had already acquired, these crossed over the Danube and left their associates, the Avari, in undisturbed possession. The *Avari* ruled intermittently in Dacia from about A.D. 564 to 610-640, when, venturing to cope with the Byzantine power, they were first encountered and defeated by Priscus, a Greek general, and later on by the Emperor Heraclius (610-641), and from that time their nation was gradually dispersed.

IV.

But now we arrive at a period when there was some little interval in the successive inroads of barbarians, and a breathing time for the peaceably disposed inhabitants of Dacia; for the next race of wanderers who entered upon the fertile plains of the Danube succeeded in holding their ground almost as undisputed masters for three centuries. Later on, as we shall find, they founded a second dynasty in combination with the Wallachs; and, although their rule was troubled by the incursions of other barbarians, and by wars first with the Byzantines and afterwards with the Hungarians or Magyars, yet they managed with some intermission to remain the governing power, and their descendants have ruled in various localities even down to the present day.

But what makes the history of this tribe, the *Bulgari*, so interesting, is not so much the domination which they exercised in the Danubian provinces, as the insight which it gives us into the condition of the people during the dark ages; and although we must content ourselves with a brief sketch of their career and a few incidents selected from it, we can confidently recommend our readers to prosecute the inquiry for themselves, with the certainty of being repaid for their labor and research. The origin of the Bulgari, or Bulgarians, like that of most of the so-called barbarians, is more or less clouded in mystery. According to some writers they were of Scythian origin, and comprised numerous tribes, among whom the Wallachs, the Croats, and the Moravians are the best known. Gibbon says that the Bulgarians and Slavonians were a wild people who dwelt, or rather wandered, on the plains of Russia, Lithuania, and Poland. They were bold and dexterous archers, who drank the milk and feasted on the flesh of their indefatigable horses. Their flocks followed, or rather guided, their movements, as it was in search of pasture for these that they roamed about from place to place. They were practiced in flight and incapable of fear. Roesler is of opinion that they were an offshoot of the Huns, and in the earlier period of their career, he says, they adopted the costume of all the Ural races, and notably of the Avari. The hair of the head was shorn off with the exception of a tuft. Their war-standards were horses' tails; before a battle there was a muster, at which arms and horses were inspected, and if any defects were discovered, the warrior who was guilty was at once put to death. The day and hour of combat were fixed by soothsayers, propitious signs were sought, and war-ditties chanted. It was a custom to make a drinking-vessel of the skull of some famous chieftain among the enemy when he was killed in battle. (We shall have a notable example of this presently.) Any freeman or slave who strayed beyond the boundaries of the territory was killed by the border-guard if he was detected. Dogs and even human beings were offered as sacrifices. Their sentences for the expiation of crime were as barbarous as the people themselves. Noses and ears were cut off as the most ordinary punishment. Polygamy was practiced, and eunuchs protected the harem. The ruler, who was called the 'Chagan,' had power of life and death over his subjects. He alone sat at table during his meals; his 'court,' including even his spouse, squatted around and fed upon the floor. In the seventh century their religion was a mixture of heathenism and Mohammedanism, and they were only converted to Christianity by slow degrees after they had settled on the Danube and come into close contact with the Eastern Empire. Even then we find (about the middle of the ninth century) that although the kings embraced Christianity, the great mass of the people remained unconverted, and even resented the change of religion in their rulers.

There is much more that is interesting in the customs of the Bulgarians, especially when they had come under something like a settled government.

The nobles seem to have resembled our 'ealdormen' in the very earliest phase of our history, and to have exercised considerable influence, notwithstanding the absolutism of the ruling head. From living only in tents of skins, a practice still adhered to in the warmer months, they built wooden huts in winter. They clothed themselves in long robes, and wore caps which were doffed reverentially in the presence of their rulers. They fed on millet and on horseflesh, and drank mead and a liquor extracted from the birch tree. Their punishments continued to be most barbarous, quartering alive being a common practice. Their superstitions were interesting. Serpents were 'taboo,' so was a hut which had been struck by lightning, whilst the howlings of dogs and wolves were good omens, significant of success or plenty.

We first hear of the Bulgari towards the close of the fifth century when they were situated near the mouth of the Volga, from whence they moved into Dacia. Meeting with little opposition and joined by other tribes, they soon became formidable invaders of the Eastern Empire, and are said to have carried their arms time after time through Thrace, Epirus, Thessaly, as far as Peloponnesus in Europe, and into Asia Minor, until at length they were met by Belisarius, one of the generals of Justinian, probably about 538-540 A.D., who defeated and drove them back over the Danube. Meantime they had come under the yoke of the Avari, and it was not until the middle of the seventh century (about 678-680), when that warlike tribe had been broken up by Heraclius, that the Bulgari, under the leadership of a powerful chief Kuvrat, obtained the ascendancy in Dacia. This chieftain formed an alliance with Heraclius, and he and his successor Asparich succeeded by their prowess in bringing not only Trajan's Dacia, but also Mœsia, and what is now Serbia, under the Bulgarian rule, and in founding a State which subsisted to the beginning of the eleventh century.

Of the condition of the people under this *régime* we have already spoken, and there is too much similarity between its incidents and those which preceded and followed, to justify our dwelling upon it at any length. It consists of a series of victories over, or defeats by, the Byzantine emperors. At one time we find the Bulgarians losing battle after battle and their power on the wane; then we hear of a Bulgarian chief going to Constantinople, embracing Christianity, and forming a marriage alliance with a niece of the empress (Irene, 780-802). Next a powerful and savage king, Krum or

Krumus, comes to the throne (probably reigning 807 to 820 A.D.), and commences hostilities against the Emperor Nicephorus (802-811). Having defeated and slain him, he is said to have illustrated the custom already referred to by making a goblet of his skull. The succeeding emperor (Michael, 811-813) fared little better, having suffered an ignominious defeat at the hands of Krum, who pressed forward to the very gates of Constantinople. Thence, after dictating terms of peace, he withdrew into his own territories, taking with him, it is said, 50,000 Daco-Romans who had been made slaves by the Byzantines, and settling them on the north bank of the Danube. Krum died A.D. 820 or thereabouts.

Another feature in the history of the country, to which we shall refer more fully hereafter, is the part taken by the dominant race for the time being in the obstruction or promotion of Christianity, and in the schism in the Catholic Church. At first we hear of little else than persecution of Christians, and the successor of Krum is said to have martyred one Bishop Emanuel, who was preaching the Gospel in his dominions. Other Bulgarian chiefs or kings, however, courted the favor of the Christian emperors and adopted their creed, until the country was annexed to the Greek Empire in 1014 A.D.

A word or two more concerning the prominent events preceding the first fall of the Bulgarians. About the end of the ninth century the descendants of the Daco-Romans, recovering from the repeated blows they had received by the successive barbarian irruptions and conquests, are said once more to have rallied to power; and several chiefs or kings are believed to have been of Daco-Roman origin. Of these Simeon (about 887), Peter (? A.D.), and Samuel (about 976 A.D.), are conspicuous. The first-named we find at war, first with the Grecian Emperor Leo (893 A.D.), whom he defeated; then with the same ruler and his allies the Ungri, under Arpad, their king. Finding himself hard pressed, Simeon made peace with Leo, and turned his arms against the Ungri, whom he defeated with great bloodshed and drove out of his territories. (To the Ungri and their career we shall return presently.) These feuds continued for a long period, and about 970 A.D. the Bulgarians crossed the Balkans, but were beaten by the Greeks, whilst two or three years afterwards the Greek emperor (or rather one of them, for there were several pretenders to the throne), John Zimisces (? 972), attacked Marcianopolis, the Bulgarian capital, and took the king, Boris, prisoner.

Before the end of the century another Bulgarian king, Simeon, had fought the Greeks with varying success, but ultimately the Emperor Basilius II. (1014 A.D.) completely annihilated the Bulgarian army, and annexed the whole country as a province of the Greek Empire. Thus ended the first rule of the Bulgarians.

V.

Of all the tribes or hordes of the East who made the devoted plains of the Danube their highway into Europe, there were none who have earned a character so notorious for rapine and cruelty as the *Ungri*, or Hungarians. Their origin is doubtful in the extreme, but it is probable that they were a Turanian race, and Roesler has found them an aboriginal home in Ugria, a country situated eastward of the Ural mountains and the river Obi. Their savage nature, which long survived their advent into Europe, has been graphically described by several writers. Roesler, who has carefully studied their early history, says that they were mare-milking nomads living in tents, that they ate the half-raw meat of game or fish without knives. Mare's milk appears to have been what we may call their temperance beverage; whilst stronger drinks were the blood of wild animals or of their enemies on the field of battle; and the hearts of the latter were considered a sovereign remedy for diseases. Our own Hallam, in describing their appearance and ravages in Europe, calls them a 'Tartarian tribe' who moved forward in great numbers as a vast wave. Their ferocity, he says, was untamed; they fought with cavalry and light armour, trusting to their showers of arrows, against which the swords and lances of the European armies could not avail. 'The memory of Attila,' he adds, 'was renewed in the devastation of these savages, who, if they were not his compatriots, resembled them both in countenance and customs.'

But the nation who suffered the most severely from their irruptions, and whose history reflects their ferocity the most faithfully, were the Germans. Fortresses were erected to check their inroads, but 'exultingly and with scorn these wild horsemen brushed past them, and as though they were in pursuit of game they picked off the peasant at the plough, or the soldier mounting guard upon the walls. Men, women, and children were captured wherever they were found; were coupled by the hair of their heads and driven in herds, like cattle, into Hungary. If a regular army moved out against them, they dispersed like the winds of heaven, and the joyful cry went up, "God be praised, they are gone;" but soon they reappeared to harass the retreating soldiery. The horrors of desolation and rapine were the condition most congenial to them; in these they revelled and rejoiced; and most happy were they when they could anoint their beards with German blood, or, casting their firebrands into the houses of God, could witness the devouring flames as they rose up into the skies.'

Although in after times the Hungarians claimed the suzerainty over part or the whole of Wallachia (and we shall have occasion hereafter to refer to their relations with that country), their domination during the ninth and tenth centuries was of a very partial and transient character. They probably moved westward from the Ukraine at the beginning of the ninth century, and between the years 839 and 860 they were actively aggressive in Eastern Wallachia. They are said to have attacked Constantine, the Christian missionary, on his way through the district they occupied, but his venerable mien prevented them from doing him any injury. He is said not even to have allowed their cries to disturb him during prayer, in which he was engaged when they made their appearance. Towards the close of the century, as we have already said, they sustained a defeat at the hands of the Bulgarians, when, under their chief Arpad, they had formed an alliance with the Emperor Leo, who is said to have made peace with the enemy and left them in the lurch. After this they were driven into the Carpathians, A.D. 894, and, having first overrun the greater part of Transylvania, they commenced those aggression into Germany, France, and Italy, which for a considerable period rendered them the terror of all Europe. At the end of the tenth century, having met with severe reverses and been compelled to withdraw into Hungary, they at length settled down under an established government. The first king was undoubtedly Stephen (997 or 1008 A.D.), and they annexed Transylvania, which up to that time had been a debatable territory, either about 1002 according to some writers, or, as others affirm, not until the time of Ladislaus the Holy (1078-1095 A.D.).

VI.

In studying the historical records of this time, the reader will frequently encounter the names of two tribes which will cause him considerable perplexity, namely, the *Patzinakitai*, as they were called by the Greeks, and the *Wallachs*, who were variously called 'Vlaci,' 'Blaci,' 'Valachi,' 'Olachi,' &c. Of the former little can and need be said. They are sometimes called Romans; were dominant in certain parts of the country in the tenth, and probably also the eleventh, century; assisted the Bulgari to drive the Hungarians over the Carpathians, and were even strong enough to make war upon the Eastern Empire about the end of the eleventh century. About that time ineffectual attempts were made to christianise them, and the last we hear of them is at the close of the thirteenth century, when they were associated with the Wallachs in the Carpathians, and probably gave their name to a district in which they were settled. They are believed, later on, to have migrated into Hungary, and cease to be named as a distinct people.

Concerning the Wallachs, however, who have played a most important part in Romanian history, a good deal is known, but much is still obscure and the subject of heated controversy. First as to their origin. Some writers believe them to have been a branch of the Slaves; others think they were the Daco-Roman colonists of Mœsia, who, joining the Slaves, crossed the Danube with them, and that subsequently the fused races were known as Wallachs, who gradually spread themselves northward to the Carpathians. Other historians are silent about them until the foundation of the 'Wallacho-Bulgarian Empire,' and then they simply mention that the two races joined for the purpose of gaining their independence. There are, however, certain historians of the middle agea who accord to them a direct Roman origin and say they were the descendants of the Roman colonists who managed to retain their language and their hold upon the soil throughout the dark ages, and in spite of the irruptions and passage of the barbarian tribes of the north and east. This is now the view generally accepted.

As we have freely quoted the opinions of modern writers, many of whom, along with the authorities on which their views are based, are entirely unknown to the bulk of our readers, it is only fair that they should be made acquainted with the views of well-known historians who flourished nearer the time of which we are writing.

Anna Comnena says (between 1081 and 1118 A.D.): 'The Emperor Alexius commanded Cæsar Nicephorus to enlist as many soldiers as possible by conscription; but not veterans; new men who had not yet been in campaigns. He instructed him as to the tribes from which he was to select his recruits, namely, from the Bulgarians and from among those youths who had become hardened by a pastoral life; who possess no settled habitations, but wander about from place to place; those who, in the vulgar tongue, are called "Wallachs" ("Blachos").'

Bonfinius enters into details of their history. He tells how Trajan conquered the Dacians; how the province was evacuated; but that the colonists had multiplied to such an extent that the repeated incursions of barbarians failed to exterminate them; and he adds that they adhere so tenaciously to their language that one would imagine they had fought for that rather than for their lives. 'Who would not be astonished,' he says. 'when he considers the deluges of Sarmatians and Goths, the irruptions of Huns, Vandals, and Gepidæ, the incursions of Germans and Lombards, to find that traces of the Latin tongue should be met with among the Dacians and Getæ, whom we now call Wallachs, because they are such good marksmen? The Romanians are descended from the legions and colonists who were led into Dacia by Trajan and other emperors: they were called Wallachs from Pius of Flaccus (after a German pronunciation), but by us, because they are such good marksmen.'

Æneas Sylvius (Pope Pius II., 1458) is still more explicit. In a few pithy sentences he gives the geography of Wallachia and Transylvania; the history of Dacia from the time of the Persian and Greek wars to the Roman conquest; the fall of the colony; the derivation of the name from Flaccus; and then he adds: 'The people even now speak the Roman language, but so mutilated that an Italian can hardly understand them.'

And not only did learned writers recognise the descent of the Wallachs from the old Roman colonists, but crowned heads referred to it in their communications with the Bulgarian chiefs and with one another, as we shall see presently. Lauriani, from whose work we have made these extracts, says that the Hungarian writers were nearly always silent on the subject, or spoke of it with the utmost bitterness. He, however, quotes two who, in treating of the various nationalities, admit that Moldavia and Wallachia contain the descendants of the Roman colonists who speak a perverted Latin. One of them gives an extract from a poem by Martin Opitz (1621), who describes the national dance of Wallachia, the Hora, or 'Chora' as he calls it. After speaking of the vicissitudes through which the people have passed, he says of their language that the Roman tongue is still in vogue; and of the people who are dancing he says: 'The men, who are almost made (? clothed) upon the Roman model, are bad, but witty, think much and say little.'

We have already made a brief reference to the influence of the barbarian rule upon the language and habits of the modern Romanians, and it is very interesting to find that in the seventeenth century, when Opitz lived, this fact had already been noticed. Although it concerns chiefly the national sentiment of the Romanians of to-day and is no doubt very fascinating for them, the inquiry still presents some interesting problems for readers of every nationality.

VII.

As the reader is already aware, the first domination of the Bulgarians in the Danubian provinces was followed by that of the Eastern Empire after the victories of Basilius at the commencement of the eleventh century, and as a change of rulers in those days usually meant a change of oppressors, it is not surprising to find, about a century and a half later, that all the populations were ready for revolt. Among these, the most numerous and influential were still the conquered Bulgarians and the Wallachs. The Wallachs are first distinctly mentioned in the time of Basilius, in whose armies they fought as allies or mercenaries. Towards the end of the eleventh century they had spread widely; for mention is made of them as having settled all over the Balkan peninsula as far as Macedonia in the south, in Wallachia in the north, and in Moldavia, and perhaps even Bessarabia, in the north-east. That is to say, they had either spread into those countries, or their ancestors had been there from the Daco-Roman period, and, having become amalgamated with successive tribes of barbarians, were now once more the dominant race. They must always have been great warriors, for we find them at one time making irruptions on their own account into the neighboring territories, at others in alliance with the Eastern emperors against the Bulgari or the Hungarians; or, associated with neighboring tribes, warring against the last-named ruthless invaders.

And when, from about 1180 to 1200, the Greek power was approaching its dissolution, the people of the Danubian provinces were ripe for insurrection, and there were not wanting brave leaders to assist them in striking the blow for their independence. From the conflicting accounts of historians, neither the names nor number of those leaders, nor yet the precise events which led to the establishment of the new empire, are ascertainable with exactitude. Either there were two Wallachian brothers, Peter and Asan, to whom a near relative of the Greek emperor Isaac Angelos (1185-1195) treacherously allied himself, or three brothers, Peter, Asan, and John. The origin of the revolt is undoubted; it arose from the levying of what the people deemed an unjust tax upon them, and probably the refusal of the emperor to admit them into his army as paid mercenaries, as in the case of other tribes. In order to obtain redress for these grievances, an embassy, comprising the two brothers Peter and Asan, went to Constantinople. They were admitted to the emperor's presence, but their requests were refused, and one of the brothers, having displayed too much warmth on the occasion, received a box on the ear, which may be said to have laid the foundation of the Wallacho-Bulgarian Empire, and expedited the fall of the Greek dynasty.

At first the revolt was unsuccessful, and the Wallachs and Bulgarians in alliance were obliged to retreat across the Danube (1187); but soon returning with a powerful army, in which a new tribe, the Kumani, were also represented, they succeeded in inflicting a defeat upon the Emperor Isaac (about 1193), who narrowly escaped with his life. Pressing on to Adrianople, the allies threatened to overwhelm the Eastern Empire, and the Emperor Alexius Comnenus was only too glad to conclude a peace with them (about 1199) and to recognise their independence.

VIII.

The *Wallacho-Bulgarian* Empire lasted, according to different authors, from sixty to one hundred years, and contemporaneously with it the *Kumani* were also dominant in part of ancient Dacia; indeed, according to some writers,

Trajan's Dacia was called the land of the Kumani. The information concerning the latter is very scanty. One writer says that as the 'Uzi' they were found on the banks of the Danube at the end of the eleventh century; others say they entered Moldo-Wallachia about 1046. About 1089 they are spoken of as in Transylvania, and the period of their domination is variously stated as between these dates and 1220-1246. They were probably converted to Christianity about 1220-1223. About that time the tribe was broken up, and part of them wandered into Hungary, where they are said to have been guilty of great cruelties, and to have subsisted down to the fifteenth century.

During the same period also (1200) the order of *Teutonic Knights* had lands allotted to them in Transylvania by Andreas II. of Hungary, as well as in part of Wallachia, over which he claimed the sovereignty; but they sought to free themselves from his control, and the gift was soon withdrawn, and in 1224 they were compelled to leave the territory over which they had exercised jurisdiction. About 1247—1250 the *Knights of St. John* also enjoyed a brief authority in some parts of Transylvania and Wallachia.

The most interesting incident, of which the account has been handed down to us, in the Wallacho-Bulgarian *régime* was the negotiation between King Joannitz, one of the first rulers (to whom reference has already been made), and Pope Innocent III. (1198-1216).

Lauriani published the whole correspondence, which is so interesting that a brief epitome of it will not be out of place here. It not only throws light upon the historical events of the period, but also gives us a glimpse of the proceedings connected with the schism in the Catholic Church. It is only necessary to premise that in the separation between the Roman and Greek Catholics which took place in the latter half of the ninth century, the Danubian provinces followed the eastern section, that the union was complete under Basilius, but that, when the brothers Asan shook off the Byzantine yoke, there was a national feeling of antagonism in religion arising out of the political rupture. Of this Innocent took advantage, and in sending a nuncio to Joannitz he wrote him that God had seen the humility with which he had deported himself towards the Roman Church, and in the turmoil and dangers of warfare He had not alone mightily protected him, but also in his mercy had greatly enlarged him (*dilatavit*). 'We, however,' he said, 'when we heard that thy forefathers sprang from the noble city of Rome, and that thou didst not only inherit the nobility of their race, but also true humility towards the Apostolic chair, had contemplated ere this to address thee in writing as well as by word of mouth through our nuncios, but the cares of the Church have prevented us hitherto from carrying out our design.' He then goes on to tell him that he has sent him 'our beloved son Dominicus,' a Greek archpriest of Brundus, and he commends his nuncio to Joannitz, requiring that he should receive him with humility, treat him kindly, and through him communicate his further submission more explicitly. Should he (the Pope) be satisfied concerning his intentions and submission, he proposes to send him higher nuncios, or rather legates, to assure him and his (subjects) in the true faith.'

Joannitz evidently did not at first receive or treat the holy emissary quite so deferentially as he might have done; but at length he answers, beginning his epistle as follows:—'To the venerable and most holy Father, highest priest, I, Johannes, Emperor of the Wallachs and Bulgarians, send thee joy and health.' He acknowledges the letter, which he says is dearer to him than gold or any jewels, and thanks God for having remembered him, his race, and the Fatherland from which they originated.

Then he recites what the Holy Father said about his benevolent intentions, and adds that he, too, had attempted once, twice, and indeed three times to communicate with him, but was debarred from doing so by the number of his enemies; but now, knowing what are the Holy Father's feelings towards him, he sends, along with the nuncio whom the Pope had commissioned, also 'our pious and trusty priest Blasius,' to convey his thanks, friendship, and service to him, as his Holy Father and highest priest. Then, with an eye to business (which, by the way, pervades the whole correspondence), he adds that as by his sacred writing his Holiness had asked him to explain what he desired from the Holy Roman Church (which, however, was not the case), his Imperial Majesty desires of the Apostolic chair that he and his subjects should be fortified as children in the bosom of the Mother Church, and particularly he asks from the Roman Church, his mother, the crown and honor which his forefathers the old emperors received. 'One was Peter, another Samuel, and others, who preceded us in the government.' If his Holiness will do this, his every desire in regard to the demeanor of his Empire towards the Church shall be fulfilled.

'But,' he adds, rather significantly, 'you must not be surprised that your nuncio did not come back sooner, for we suspected him. Many persons have come and tried to mislead us, but we were proof against their machinations.' (False prophets he means.) 'But in this case, however, the prætext' (white robe) 'was convincing proof, and we were satisfied.' (But he was *not* satisfied.) 'But, most Holy Father, if it please thee, please send us the higher nuncios, and send this one with them, and then we shall be convinced that both the first and the second mission were from thee. May the Lord grant thee a long life!'

Then follows another letter from the Pope, which might have been drawn up by a modern conveyance. It recites the whole of the previous correspondence, and, referring to Joannitz's request for a crown, his Holiness says he has had the registers carefully searched, and finds that it is true many kings were crowned, and, moreover, that in the time of his predecessor, Pope Nicolas, the King of the Bulgarians, who had often sought his advice, had been baptized with his whole nation. Afterwards, he says, at the request of Michael of Bulgaria, Pope Adrian sent a subdeacon and some priests, but, in consequence of the bribes and promises of the Greeks, the Bulgarians cast them out and took Greek priests in their stead. In consequence of this 'light behavior,' therefore, he could not see his way clear to send any of his brothers the cardinals. Still he had decided to send his chaplain Johannes as a nuncio of the Apostolic chair, and, commending him to his good offices (in the usual terms), he wished him to understand that he was fully empowered to improve everything of a spiritual character in the realm. He also sent by him a robe (*pallium*) for the archbishop of his country, and a bull announcing the form and nature of the investiture. In fact this nuncio was authorized to ordain bishops and priests, and generally to substitute the Roman Catholic for the Greek faith. As to the crown there seems still to have been a hitch. The nuncio was to look up the older books and documents and learn all about the ancient manner of proceeding, so that 'we [the Pope] may with greater celerity make the needful arrangements.' And he bids him warn his 'nobles' also to treat the nuncio with proper deference.

Joannitz did his utmost to comply with the Papal behest. An archbishopric and two bishoprics were founded, and the 'Golden Bull' was promulgated, in which it was announced that Joannitz intended to receive his crown and investiture at the hands of the Universal Priest, Innocent III., and that certain ecclesiastical functionaries (naming them) had been established by the Church of Rome, and thereby received his (Joannitz's) sanction, which had previously been accorded to them by his ancestors. He also sent presents to the Pope as a token of submission; and all these matters having been duly weighed and considered by his Holiness, he at length nominated Joannitz King of the Wallachs and Bulgarians, and sent him the much-coveted crown and scepter by the hands of Leo, a cardinal of the Order of the Holy Cross, &c., who was commissioned on his behalf to perform the ceremony of coronation. Lauriani concludes the correspondence and narrative by saying that 'this Empire of the Romanians flourished from the year of our Lord 1186, in which it was restored by the brothers Peter and Asan, under the best and bravest kings of the family of Asanidæ, until the year 1285, when it was disturbed, but not destroyed, by the inroads of the Tartars. After the Turks had begun to make irruptions into the European provinces, in the fourteenth century, it was brought under the yoke by the Sultan Bajazet towards the close of that century, and wholly annihilated in the year 1392.'

Down to this period (the middle of the fourteenth century) we have been necessarily compelled to speak loosely of the territories which were overrun and held by the various barbarian races, for there is no clear information concerning the limits of their occupation; but henceforward our record will deal chiefly with Romania as at present constituted. The Wallacho-Bulgarian monarchy, whatever may have been its limits, was annihilated by a horde of Tartars about A.D. 1250. The same race committed great havoc in Hungary, conquered the Kumani, overran Moldavia, Transylvania, &c., and held their ground there until about the middle of the fourteenth century, when they were driven northward by the Hungarian, Saxon, and other settlers in Transylvania; and with their exit we have done with the barbarians.

CHAPTER XI.

FROM THE FOUNDATION OF THE PRINCIPALITIES, BETWEEN THE MIDDLE OF THE THIRTEENTH AND OF THE FOURTEENTH CENTURIES TO THE ACCESSION OF MICHAEL THE BRAVE, A.D. 1593.

State of the country at, the close of the barbarian era—Foundation of the Principalities of Wallachia and Moldavia—Traditions of Radu Negru and Bogdan Dragosch—Historical evidence—Description of the various rulerships in Wallachia in the thirteenth century—The clans Liteanu and Bassarab—Mircea the Old—His history—The First Capitulation (1393)—Character of Mircea— Verses in his memory by Bolentineanu (1826-1872)—John Corvin von Hunniad, Prince of Transylvania—His history, character, and exploits—Vlad 'the Impaler'—His cruelties—Capitulates to the Turks (1460 A.D.)—Moldavia—Its founders—Obscurity of records—Stephen the Great—His history—His flight to Niamtz—Verses by Bolentineanu—Recommends his son to capitulate to the Turks—His character—Neagu Bassarab, founder of the Cathedral of Curtea d'Ardges—His peaceful reign and works—- Radul d'Affumati completes the cathedral—His death—Turkish encroachments—Michael the Brave.

I.

When the title of barbarian immigration was ebbing in the Danubian Principalities, it is natural to suppose that there must have remained a very mixed population; and that, owing to the necessity for defense against such ruthless invaders as we have described in our last chapter, the inhabitants would congregate in various places under their ablest leaders, and would fortify themselves in the best manner possible. This was indeed the case, but until recently the historians of Romania have had little to guide them concerning the events of the period beyond traditions which, though very interesting, are now gradually giving place to recorded and authenticated facts.

Almost any history of the country which it is possible to find to-day, narrates the rise of the Principalities after the following fashion: The Daco-Roman colonists, historians say, fled into the Carpathian mountains before the Goths and Huns, and for nearly a thousand years they retained their nationality, from time to time making descents into the plains from one or other colony which they had established, always, however, to find new hordes of barbarians in possession. At length, when the great wave of barbarism had subsided, one Radu Negru, whose name is translated Rudolph the Black, the chief of the Daco-Roman colony of Fogaras in the Carpathians, descended into the plains with his followers, according to some writers in 1240 A.D., whilst others say in 1290, and, first fixing his capital at Campu-Lung, and then moving it to Curtea d'Ardges, where he built a beautiful cathedral, drove out the barbarians who remained in Wallachia, and became the first Voivode of that province. This is the tradition of the foundation of Wallachia.

About the same time, we are told, there dwelt in another part of the mountains, to the west of Fogaras, a colony of Daco-Roman descendants, namely, that of Marmaros or Maramurish, ruled over by one Bogdan, or Dragosch. This chief, as the story runs, was once out hunting the aurochs with a large following, accompanied by his dog Molda, and being arrived in a beautiful country through which flowed a pretty stream, he determined to settle there, called the river the Moldava, built a city which he named Roman, reduced the inhabitants and their chiefs to submission, and became the first Voivode of Moldavia.

Of late years these traditions have been subjected to the searching light of criticism, sharpened in some cases by national or political tendencies, and whilst the story of Radu Negru has fallen into discredit, that of Bogdan has undergone considerable modification. The very names of the heroes have been canvassed, and Radu, instead of Rudolph, has been shown to mean 'joy' (as Bogdan Dragosch was the God-given'), so that, instead of Radu Negru, we now sometimes meet with the name of Negru Voda, or 'the Black Prince,' who, according to the traditions of some parts of the country, is still believed to have descended from the Carpathians, and to have freed the land from the Tartar hordes.

II.

Thus far tradition. Romania possesses no historical records of the period, but the discovery of manuscripts in Hungary, Poland, and elsewhere, has established certain facts that are beginning to serve as a solid foundation upon which the early history of the country is being based.

First, it is admitted that the plains and the slopes of the Carpathians were inhabited by communities ruled over by chieftains of varying power and influence. Some were banates, as that of Craiova, which long remained a semi-independent State; then there were petty voivodes or princes, as the Princes of Zevrin or Severin, Farcas, Seneslas, &c.; and besides these there were khanates, called in French *kinezats*, and in German *knesenschaften* (from the Slav. *kniaz*, a prince), some of which were petty principalities, whilst others were merely the governorship of villages or groups of them. These are only a few of the small rulerships, which are every day multiplied as the State records of the neighboring countries are being more and more carefully investigated.

The names of prominent chieftains, too, are becoming clearer in the obscurity of the period. In or about 1285 a Prince Liteanu conquered and united three Wallachian principalities, and declared himself independent of the crown of Hungary, which claimed suzerainty over the western part of Wallachia. He was attacked by the Magyars under George Sowar, and slain in battle, while his brother was taken prisoner and executed. Some of the successors of this prince were more fortunate, and one of them, Tugomir, succeeded for a time in securing his independence. The clan *Bassarab* was mentioned at even an earlier period, a ban of that name having resisted the Tartars. Much confusion exists as to the origin of this clan, and whilst some writers call Tugomir (just referred to) by that name, others confound him with the Negru Voda of tradition. Whatever may be the obscurity, however, in which their rise is buried, it is certain that the Bassarab family gave many princes and rulers to Wallachia, and, after intermarrying with other members of the ruling classes, only became extinct about the year 1685.

In the mountains the state of affairs was somewhat different. There, no doubt from their greater proximity to the center of Magyar rule, the tie between the petty princes and the Hungarian crown seems to have been closer, and whilst some writers affirm that the Wallachs (or Romanians, as their countrymen like to call them) enjoyed privileges amounting to a quasi-independence, the Austrian chroniclers maintain that they were mere vassal retainers of the Court of Hungary. So, for example, they say that Bogdan, ruler of Marmaros, broke his allegiance to the King Louis of Hungary, and about 1359 descended, with a largo body of Wallachian followers, among whom were his sons, into the lower lands of what was already called Moldavia, and took possession of the country.

Shaking ourselves free as far as possible from controversial questions, we may state with safety, in regard to Wallachia, that for more than a century after the wave of barbarian immigration had ceased to flow over it, it resembled the condition of Independent Tartary of to-day; that the number of its petty princes gradually diminished, one of them, Vladislav Bassarab, having at length secured a great portion of the country under his rule, and almost, if not completely, shaken off the Hungarian yoke (1350-1376), until, under the reign of Mircea the Old (1386-1418), a new enemy, the Turks, so far obtained the ascendency over the country as to acquire permanent rights of suzerainty.

III.

Mircea, one of the heroes of Romanian history, not only secured the independent sovereignty, and called himself Voivode of Wallachia 'by the grace of God,' but in 1389 he formed an alliance with Poland, and assumed other titles by the right of conquest. This alliance was offensive and defensive with Vladislav Jagello, the reigning king, and had for its objects the extension of his dominions, as well as protection against Hungary on the one hand, and the Ottoman power on the other; for the Turks, who during the fourteenth century had been waging war with varying success against the Eastern Empire, were now rapidly approaching Wallachian territory. Although Constantinople did not come into their possession until the following century, Adrianople had already fallen, the Turkish armies had overrun Bulgaria, and about the year 1391 they first made their appearance north of the Danube.

At first the bravery of Mircea was successful in stemming the tide of invasion. The reigning Sultan was Amaruth II., who sent an army against him under the command of Sisman, Prince of Bulgaria, a renegade who had married the daughter of the Sultan, and had taken the offensive against the Christians; but he was signally defeated, and for a brief period Wallachia continued to enjoy her independence. A year or two afterwards Bajazet II., the successor of Amaruth, resumed the offensive, and this time, finding himself between two powerful enemies, the King of Hungary and the Sultan, Mircea elected to form an alliance with the latter, and concluded a treaty with him at Nicopolis (1393), known as the 'First Capitulation,' by which Wallachia retained its autonomy, but agreed to pay an annual tribute and to acknowledge the suzerainty of the Sultan. This treaty is dated 1392; but according to several historians Mircea did not adhere to it long, for he is said to have been in command of a contingent in the army of the crusaders, and to have been present at the battle of Nicopolis (1396), in which the flower of the French nobility fell, and, when he found their cause to be hopeless, once more to have deserted them and joined the victorious arms of Bajazet.

Of the continued wars and dissensions in Wallachia, during the reign of Mircea it is unnecessary to speak. He ruled with varying fortunes until 1418 A.D., and there is no doubt that the State was much better organised for defence, although his wars entailed great misery upon the peasantry. It is clear, not only from the Treaty of Nicopolis, but from other records, that the general condition of the country somewhat resembled that of England in the Saxon period. The prince was elected by the boyards, or barons spiritual and temporal, and by the nation (probably through representatives), and there was a general Council of State. There were probably freemen and serfs, although some writers maintain that there was perfect equality until after Mircea's wars commenced; then it is universally admitted that absolute slavery existed.

It has been said that Mircea kept a standing army of about 18,000 foot and 17,000 cavalry; but whether that was so or not, he certainly maintained a force sufficiently well organised to cope with his powerful adversaries the

Turks and the Hungarians. That these latter were still a fierce and untamed race is very probable, as were, no doubt, the followers of Mircea, and they committed ravages by their inroads, which have caused modern writers to class them with the barbarians whose rule had ceased. Whatever may have been his faults and vices (and his desertion of the Christians at Nicopolis, and the number of illegitimate children left by him, prove that he had both), his patriotism and courage endeared him to posterity, and his deeds are commemorated in the national poems of the present century. Here is a graphic picture of

>MIRCEA IN BATTLE.
>By D. BOLENTINEANU (1826-1872).
>
>Countless hosts of Magyars desolate the lands,
>E'en the sun in terror sees their roving bands;
>
>But the aged Mircea, firm and undismayed,
>With his braves, a handful, meets the furious raid.
>
>Knows, full well, to save the homestead's all but vain,
>Calmly still determines duty to maintain.
>
>Ah! the days of heroes surely now are fled,
>When, at duty's summons, Roumains nobly bled!
>
>Speaks the hoary chieftain: 'Hearken, brothers all,
>'Tis the will of God, as Roumain I should fall.'
>
>Dedicate thy life-blood, saviour of a nation;
>'Tis a puny flamelet in a conflagration.
>
>What is one poor lifetime in th' eternal day?
>'Tis a single blossom in a gorgeous May.
>
>Ere the noble falcon to the Jäger yields,
>Casts he nest and offspring down into the fields.
>
>Ere our arms or ankles should be locked in chains,

Lot us fall as heroes, die as free Roumains.

Ah! the days of heroes surely now are fled,
When, at duty's summons, Roumains nobly bled.

IV.

Before referring to the events which were passing in Moldavia during the period, it may not be out of place to say a few words here concerning another hero, who, although he ruled in Transylvania, was a Wallachian by birth, led the Wallachian armies against the Turks, and for a time succeeded in checking their advance in Europe. This was John Corvinus, as he is known to English readers, or, more correctly, Johann Corvin von Hunniad, Prince of Siebenbürgen, who was born about the year 1368 in the village of Corvin, in the Wallachian Carpathians. His father was a Wallachian, some say of ancient family, and his mother a Greek, to whom also a high ancestry is attributed. As his history was written by flatterers in order to gain the favour of his son and successor, these statements as to his high ancestry must be taken *cum grano salis*. Johann was at first the captain of a small party of adventurers, having served, as was the custom in those days, with a troop of twelve horse, first under Demetrius, Bishop of Agram, and then for two years in Italy under Philip, Duke of Milan. There he met Sigismund, King of Hungary, who induced him to join his standard, and, as a reward for his services, conferred upon him the estate of Hunnyades, from which he took his name. Subsequently he rose from post to post, until he was appointed Viceroy of Siebenbürgen (Transylvania), and eventually Regent of Hungary. In the former capacity he formed an alliance against the Turks (about 1443) with Vladislaus, King of Poland and Hungary, and Vlad, Voivode of Wallachia, and under his leadership the Christian armies frequently encountered the Ottomans, notably on three occasions—at Varna under Amaruth II. (1444) and Cossova (1448), in both of which encounters the allies were defeated, and finally at Belgrade (1456), where the Turks were completely routed. Various and conflicting accounts have been given of these battles, and of Hunniades's conduct during the encounters. At Varna, where Vladislaus was killed, the Poles charged Hunniades with cowardice; but the facts are probably that he defeated the right wing of the Turks, but that the temerity of Vladislaus caused the defeat of the army and his own death. The same charge was brought against him by the Poles in regard to the defeat at Cossova, but from his known bravery it was no doubt equally groundless. At Belgrade the city was completely invested by the Turks; but at the head of an undisciplined army Hunniades forced his way into the city, and by a subsequent sally, in which the Sultan Mohammed was wounded, he compelled the Turks to raise the siege and withdraw in confusion. John Hunniades died in the same year, and his son Matthias was elected to the crown of Hungary, over which country he ruled for more than thirty years.

The character of John Hunniades is well worth a brief consideration. As we have said, he was charged with cowardice by his Polish allies, but by the Turks he was so dreaded that they gave him the name of the Devil, and used it to frighten their children when they misbehaved themselves. Many anecdotes, of which the following is one, are related of his personal courage. After the battle of Cossova, whilst fleeing alone through the Carpathians, he was captured by two brigands, who deprived him of his arms. The cupidity of these men was aroused by a splendid gold chain which he wore, and one of them snatched it from his neck. Presently, however, forgetting the maxim that there is honour even among thieves, the two bandits began wrangling for the possession of the booty, and whilst they were so occupied Hunniades managed to recover his sword, and, engaging them in fight, he ran one through the body, whereupon the other fled.

If his biographers are to be believed, he must have been a remarkable man. 'As fishes are used to the water,' says one, 'as the deer to the forest glade, so was he adapted for the bearing of arms, a born leader of warriors, and the field of battle was his life-element.' The nobility of his bearing, another says, and his winning manner enabled him to secure the affection of his soldiers, whilst his readiness to serve, his piety and benevolence, and his shrewd policy, gained for him the confidence of his superiors, the leadership of armies, and the highest offices of the State. At his death he was universally mourned. Pope Nicholas ordered the cardinals to perform a magnificent *requiem* in his memory, as the pious and successful defender of the Christian religion. Even the Sultan Mohammed, whom he had just defeated—when George, Despot of Servia, brought him what he thought would be the gratifying news of the prince's death—lowered his head, and, after a long silence, exclaimed, 'There never was, under any ruler, such a man since the beginning of the world.'

As we have said, the Turks were so much afraid of Hunniades that they are said to have given him the name of 'the Devil;' but the same designation, as well as that of the Impaler, has also been bestowed upon Vlad, a voivode of Wallachia, who was probably the ally of Hunniades, and who, if one-tenth of what has been related of him be true, has a much better claim to the title. He is represented to have been one of the most atrocious and cruel tyrants who ever disgraced even those dark ages. One day he massacred 500 boyards who were dissatisfied with his rule. The torture of men, women, and children, seems to have been his delight. Certain Turkish envoys, when admitted into his presence, refused to remove their turbans, whereupon he had them nailed to their heads. He burned 400 missionaries and impaled 500 gypsies to secure their property. In order to strike terror into Mohammed II. he crossed over into Bulgaria, defeated the Turks, and brought back with him 25,000 prisoners, men, women, and children, whom he is said to have impaled upon a large plain called Praelatu. Notwithstanding his successes, however, Vlad was at length compelled to submit to the Turkish rule, and he concluded the 'Second Capitulation' at Adrianople (1460), in which the tribute to the Porte was increased, but no other important change was made in the terms of suzerainty.

V.

For a century after the foundation of *Moldavia*, or, as it was at first called, 'Bogdania,' by Bogdan Dragosch, the history of the country is shrouded in darkness. Kings or princes are named, one or more of whom were Lithuanians; two or three Bogdans, Theodor Laseu, Jurgo Kuriotovich, Peter, Stephen, Roman, Alexander, &c., and some of them are said to have been dethroned and to have reigned twice and even three times, until at length a prince more powerful than the rest ascended the throne, and by the prowess of his arms succeeded in establishing his name and fame in history. This was Stephen, sometimes called the 'Great' or 'Good,' but whether he deserved the latter title the reader will be best able to judge for himself.

He came to the throne about 1456 or 1458, and reigned until 1504, and his whole life was spent in wars against Transylvania, Wallachia (which he at one time overran and annexed to Moldavia), the Turks, and Tartars. Considered in conjunction with the acts of Hunniades and Vlad the Impaler, those of Stephen present a tolerably faithful picture of the condition of Romania in the fifteenth century. We shall therefore ask the reader to bear with us whilst we hurry through the leading events of his life. Five years after he came to the throne, Stephen overran Transylvania. In 1465 he married Eudoxia, a Byzantine princess, and two years afterwards we find him at war with Matthias of Hungary (the son of John Corvinus), by whom he was defeated at Baja. Between that time and 1473 he once, if not twice, defeated Radu (the brother of Vlad the Impaler), King of Wallachia, and in 1475 he was at war with the Turks, whom he defeated on the river Birlad, between Barnaba, and Racoviça. This battle he is said to have won by stratagem. He concealed a number of men in a neighboring wood, and when the battle was at its height they were ordered to commence playing various instruments as though another force were approaching, and this created such a panic among the Ottomans that they gave way and fled precipitately, followed by Stephen, who put many to the sword. In that year also Stephen again defeated Radu and completely overran Wallachia. Having reduced it to submission, he placed a native boyard on the throne as his viceroy, who showed his gratitude to Stephen by rebelling and liberating the country from his rule; but he was in his turn murdered by his Wallachian subjects. In 1476 Stephen sustained a terrible defeat at the hands of the Ottomans at Valea Alba (the White Valley), but eight years afterwards, allied with the Poles, he again encountered this terrible enemy. His army was at first forced to give way, and he is said to have fled for refuge to Niamtz, where he had a castle, but his mother refused him admission and bade him return to his army. Here is the story, with its sequel, as it is told by the poet who has already once been quoted (Bolentineanu):—

> 'Blows are heard resounding at the outer gate.
> 'Tis the hour of midnight; whose the voice so late?
> "Hasten, dearest mother"—ha! that well-known sound—
> "From the host I'm driven, bleed at every wound!
> Fearful was our fortune, terrible the fray,
> Scattered all my army, fled they in dismay.

Mother, open quickly; infidels pursue,
Icy is the night wind, purple blood their cue."
"Ha! what say'st thou, stranger? Stephen's far away,
Dealing death, strong-handed, where he stands at bay.
Of him the mother I; such my son is he.
Be thou who thou may'st, my son thou canst not be.
(Yet can Heaven have fated, dealt this fearful blow?
Can his soul be craven, quail before the foe?)
If in truth thou'rt Stephen, faint returning home,
Not within these portals shalt thou ever come.
Hasten to thy brave ones; for thy country fall;
Then maternal love with wreaths shall deck thy pall!"
Once more Stephen rallies; lusty sounds his horn;
Heroes flock around him on the battle morn.
Fierce and dire the slaughter; on that glorious day
Falls the Moslem chivalry like the new-mown hay.'

Notwithstanding the great victory which he obtained, the Moslem power was too strong for him, and he is found, before the century's close, allied with them against Poland, to whose sovereign he had but a few years previously sworn fealty, and into which he now made a raid. In 1504 he died a natural death, and it is said that before his decease, either from fear of the Turks, or distrusting the power of his son Bogdan, he advised the latter to make a permanent treaty with the Porte, which he did shortly after his death. The most favorable traits in Stephen's character seem to have been his courage and patriotism, notwithstanding the story which is told of his flight to Niamtz. Like Mircea, he organized an army which is estimated at about the same strength, with the addition of irregular troops. That he was pious after a fashion is most likely, but that he also practiced the tyrannic cruelties of his age is undoubted. Shortly after his advent to the throne, the Tartars entered his dominions, carrying fire and sword everywhere, but they were eventually repulsed and driven out by Stephen. In the course of this campaign he took a son of the Tartar chief prisoner, and when envoys came to treat for his liberation he ordered the prince to be decapitated in their presence, a deed which may have been justified as a lesson to the ruthless tribe who had invaded his country. Not content with this, however, he impaled all the envoys but one, whose nose and ears he cut off, and sent him back to his master in that dreadful condition. 'But,' adds the chronicler, 'Stephen, who was a man of his period, only regarded this act as a manifestation of zeal in the faith. Shortly afterwards he built the monastery of Putna, dedicated it to Jesus and the Virgin, and caused to be transported thither the wooden chapel which Dragosch had constructed at Volovitz.' 'These were the ordinary practices of the age,' remarks another commentator; 'and if such treatment was reserved for the high and noble, one may guess what was the fate of the humble.'

VI.

What that fate was may easily be imagined by anyone who follows the narrative of the wars which devastated the land. But, before treating of the condition of the country and the customs of the period, we must refer to one or two voivodes whose rule was pacific, and whose energies were directed to the promotion of civilizing influences. Concerning these, too, we have the trustworthy records already cited in our description of the cathedral of Curtea d'Ardges. One of them was Neagu Bassarab, the other John Radul, known as Radul d'Affumati, and both were voivodes of Wallachia.

The first-named, Neagu, came to the throne either in 1511 or 1513, and died a natural death in 1520, a rare event in those days. He was conspicuously a man of peace in a country and age of war and bloodshed, and was eminently pious and benevolent. He repaired several churches, restored the cathedral of Tirgovistea, roofed other churches with lead, both in and out of Wallachia, and built the beautiful cathedral of Curtea d'Ardges, the erection of which, as we have heard, was attributed by tradition to Radu Negru, the reputed founder of Wallachia. The tablet in his memory has already been referred to elsewhere. In war he never took any personal part, and, as we have already remarked, he died peacefully in his bed.

He was followed on the throne by 'Radu the Monk,' who met with the usual fate, having been slain by the Turks; and this prince was succeeded by the Radu d'Affumati above named, a nephew of Nyagu (1522), who occupied the throne for seven years.

War, war was still the cry; he had numerous vicissitudes during his short reign; participated in the defeat of the Hungarians and Poles in the battle of

Mohacs, 'which witnessed the slaughter of a king, seven bishops, five hundred nobles, and twenty thousand soldiers; not only laid open the whole country to the inroads of the Turks and established them for nearly a century and a half in its capital, but changed the reigning dynasty of Hungary and introduced for the first time a German sovereign to the Hungarian throne.' Radu was dethroned, and in his attempt to leave the country he was seized by two of his nobles and decapitated. During part of his reign, however, Wallachia enjoyed some tranquility, and Radu continued the works begun by his uncle; among others, as we know, he completed the cathedral of Ardges.

After the battle of Mohacs the Turks began to encroach more openly upon Romanian (Moldo-Wallachian) territory. They occupied and fortified Braila, Giurgevo, and Galatz; interfered in the election of the princes, in one or two instances securing the appointment for men whose sole claim to the crown was their willingness to pay a heavy bribe. One of those was a Saxon Lutheran of Transylvania, who was, however, a favorable example of the princely race. He was elected Voivode of Moldavia about 1580, and built a church for the Lutherans. In addition to the intrigues for the voivodeship, internecine wars broke out between the two Principalities, and the boyards made lawless raids upon one another. In these civil broils the Turks intervened, adding to their own influence, and rendering the princes more and more subservient to their will. This state of things lasted until the end of the sixteenth century, when another hero, Michael the Brave of Wallachia, restored tranquility and independence to the Principalities, and raised them for a season in the esteem of surrounding nations. As his victories were solid, and the heroic age in the early history of Romania may be said to have closed with his death, we feel justified in making more than a passing reference to his exploits and career, more especially as in so doing we shall also be able to present a trustworthy account of the condition of society in his day.

CHAPTER XII.

THE TIMES AND CAREER OF MICHAEL THE BRAVE.

The state of society—Greater and lesser boyards—Taxation and oppression of the peasantry—Immorality of the boyards—The priesthood—Officers of State—Classes of peasantry—Rise of the towns—The soldiery—Aggressions of Turks and Tartars—Michael the Brave—His rise to power—Accession to the throne (1594)—Remonstrances with the Porte—Alliance with Hungary and Poland—Massacre of the Turks—Anecdote—Conspiracy against Michael quelled—The Turks attacked and routed on the Danube—Invasion of Wallachia by Achmed Pasha—His defeat—Michael swears fealty to Sigismund of Transylvania—Second Turkish invasion by Sinan Pasha—Determined stand of Michael at Giurgevo—Retreat of Michael and battle of Kalugereni—Defeat of Sinan—Retreat of Michael—Occupation of Wallachia by Sinan—Michael and his allies take the offensive—Flight of Sinan and slaughter of the Turks at Giurgevo—The Turks expelled—Peace in Wallachia—Intrigues of Michael—Accession of Andreas Bathori—Invasion and conquest of Transylvania by Michael—His triumph—Michael, Prince of Transylvania—Further intrigues—Invasion and conquest of Moldavia—Michael in the zenith of his power—Feud with the nobles—Michael encounters them at Miriszlo—Their Austrian ally, General Basta—Defeat and flight of Michael—Anecdote—Continued misfortunes of Michael—Petitions the Emperor—Is permitted to visit him—Recall of Sigismund Bathori—Michael reinstated by the Emperor—Invades Transylvania in alliance with Basta—Defeat of the nobles at Gorozlo—Quarrels of the victorious generals—Basta determines to remove Michael—Employs a Walloon officer to assassinate him—Michael murdered in his tent (1601)—Flight of his boyards—The German Court refuses to reward Basta's treachery.

I.

As the state of the northern Danubian territories before the foundation of the Principalities has been compared by us to the present condition of what is called Independent Tartary, and at a subsequent period to that of the early Saxons, so in the reign of Michael the Brave (1593-1601 A.D.) the state of society resembled that of England under the Norman kings; indeed, there is a remarkably interesting agreement in some of its phases. As in England there were greater and lessor barons, so in Moldo-Wallachia there were greater and lesser boyards. These seem to have possessed all the rapacity of our robber barons, with but little of their *reputed* chivalry. They oppressed the peasantry, who since the time of Vlad the Impaler were to a large extent serfs, with unbearable taxes, and endeavored on all occasions to shift the burdens of the State upon those whose shoulders were the least able to bear them. One of these imposts was the poll-tax, similar to that which gave rise to Wat. Tyler's riots in the time of Richard II., but which, strange to say, still survives in Romania, to the dissatisfaction of all her right-minded citizens.

Besides the poll-tax, there was the 'Standard gift' (Poklon), which was levied at the installation of the Voivode; the Easter present; the extra tax (*ajutoriţă*), which was raised when the other taxes ran short. Moreover, there were taxes in kind on malt, salt, fish, cattle, and horses, payable to the prince. The landlord (boyard) was entitled to land and pasturage tax, the tenth of the earth's productions, feudal service, bee, pig, and sheep taxes, and in addition to these a rate was levied upon bees, pigs, tobacco, wine, and sheep, for the benefit of the prince. Whilst these imposts and the extraordinary levies and ravages of war often reduced the whole of the peasantry to the most abject poverty, bordering on starvation, the boyards lived in comparative ease, and led a life of immorality and self-indulgence. Concubinage widely prevailed, and many boyards had, besides their legitimate wife, ten or a dozen mistresses. They appear to have been gradually growing in influence, and the greater boyards filled all the chief offices of State as well as the leading military posts in the districts. Personal distinctions existed also, the leading boyards being allowed to wear long beards, a practice which was forbidden to the lesser boyards.

Besides the boyards and their serfs there was hardly any native population worth speaking of, and no middle class whatever; all trade being in the hands of Greeks, Jews, and Armenians. There was, however, a priesthood, who were as ignorant as the peasantry; indeed many of them followed both occupations, the only exceptions being the metropolitan and the higher clerics, who possessed considerable influence there as elsewhere in the middle ages. The power of the prince had no definite limits, and, with the exception of the counteracting influence of the boyards, it was practically absolute. There was a council of twelve boyards, whose signatures along with that of the prince were visually appended to all important State documents.

In the time of Stephen (some writers say, at an earlier period), the various offices of State were established, which were maintained down to a recent date, both in Wallachia and Moldavia; and as it is impossible for the reader to interest himself in any question bearing upon the past history of the country without finding some mention made of one or other of them, it may be useful here to enumerate a few of their titles.

1. The Ban of Craiova was Viceroy of Little Wallachia, and his authority reached back, in all probability, to the foundation of the principality. 2. The Vel-Vornic, or Minister of the Interior, was Governor of the Carpathians and of the neighbouring districts. 3. The Great Vornic was governor of the lowlands. 4. The Logothet, or Chancellor, was Minister of Justice. 5. The Great Spathar was Minister of War. 6. The Great Vestiar, Treasurer and Master of the Robes. 7. The Great Postelnik, Master of the Post. 8. The Paharnic, chief butler and cup-bearer (this was a title of Hungarian origin). 9. The Great Stolnik, chief cook. 10. The Great Comis, Master of the Horse. 11. The Aga, Chief of Police. 12. Great Pitar, Inspector of Commissariat. 13. Serdar, general of infantry of three districts (3,000 men). In Moldavia the Spathar was called the Hettman; in both principalities there were minor offices, and in Stephen's time the first six only formed the Council of Ministers.

Although, as we have said, the peasantry were chiefly serfs, there were differences in their condition. The chief body were called Scutelnici, and the peasantry generally were divided into two classes, those who possessed land of their own, and those who worked on the estates of the prince, the boyards, or the monasteries. Part of the latter were free to move about in search of employment, and the rest were absolutely serfs attached to the soil; the term of service in every case was fixed at forty-eight days in the year. The towns were growing in importance, the capital being Tirgovistea, but Bucharest(to which place Constantine Brancovano transferred his capital about a century later) was already an important place, owing chiefly to its situation. Another town or large village was Curtea d'Ardges. But the Wallachian Voivodes shifted their 'capital' as it suited their pleasure, and the removal in those days was probably not a very onerous undertaking. It appears that Vlad Dracul (the Devil) preferred Tirgovistea, whilst another Voivode, Michna, favored Ardges. Other towns of note Craiova, Ploiesti, Buzeu, and two or three ports on the Danube. In Moldavia, Iasi, Suceava, and Roman were the chief towns. The government of the towns was carried on by a burgomaster, or mayor, a prefect, and a council of twelve citizens.

The army was very heterogeneous both as regarded its nationalities and its armament. It was then, or perhaps at a somewhat later period, divided into three sections, the regular army, the militia, and the landsturm, the last-named being without pay and only called out in times of great danger, and it consisted mainly of the servants and slaves of the boyards. The arms of the regular soldiers were originally, as in this country, bows and arrows and lances, but in Michael's time there were already musketeers and primitive artillery. Besides the native soldiery there were mercenaries, namely, Hungarians, Szeklers, Poles, Cossacks, Servians, Bulgarians, Albanians, cavalry as well as infantry. The whole country was at that time divided into military districts answering to the present Judeztu or departments, each district being under the control of a captain who united military, administrative, and judicial power in his own person. The names of most of the districts remain unchanged to the present day.

To this account of the state of Moldo-Wallachia it is only necessary to add that in time of war, and that was the normal condition, the people were subjected to terrible privations. When an army advanced, the peasantry were laid under contributions for the troops; when it fled before the enemy, everything was burned or destroyed in its retreat, so that the pursuing force might be checked for want of supplies.

Schools for the people there were none, and all the knowledge that existed was confined within the walls of the monasteries, which were, however, numerous and well endowed. At no period of its history was Wallachia in such a deplorable condition as when Michael ascended the throne. Besides possessing the suzerainty of the principality the Turks completely occupied the whole southern bank of the Danube, along with some posts and what is known as Temesvar, on the northern side. The Transylvanian slopes of the Carpathians and the country beyond were a fief of the German, or, as it was called, the Roman Empire, over which at that time Rudolph II. reigned, whilst the territory north of Moldavia formed part of Poland. But although Wallachia was nominally autonomous, and was allowed to choose its own rulers, it was in reality an oppressed province of Turkey. The treaties had been completely set at defiance. Mosques had been erected and houses built by Turkish residents, contrary to the stipulations of the Treaty of Nicopolis, with the connivance of the voivodes, who, as we have said, were raised up and deposed as it suited the greed or policy of the Porte. Their fortresses and garrisons on the Danube served as centers from which the Ottomans made raids into Wallachian territory, spreading desolation far and wide, and in addition to this scourge the suffering inhabitants had from time to time hostile visits from the Tartars. Hordes of these savages were in alliance with the Turks against Hungary, and it was not unusual for them to deviate from their route, fall into the plains of Wallachia, and renew the scenes of rapine and outrage which had characterized the passage of the Eastern barbarians.

Michael, who was probably the posthumous son of a former voivode of Wallachia called Petraschko, was born about the year 1558, and in 1583 he married the widow of a boyard, by whom he had at least one, if not two sons, and a daughter. He occupied several honorable positions in the State, and was Ban of Craiova before he ascended the throne of Wallachia. This step he accomplished through intrigues at Constantinople with the aid of his father-in-law, whereby he succeeded in deposing his predecessor Alexander. Some marvelous tales are told concerning the hairbreadth escapes of Michael in his struggles for the ascendancy, one being that, when he was captured by Alexander and ordered for execution, the headsman was so terrified at the majesty of his countenance that he dropped the axe and fled, and no one else was to be found willing to undertake the odious duty. Be that as it may, he succeeded eventually in removing his rival, and mounted the throne of Wallachia in 1593. For some time after his accession Michael addressed remonstrances to his suzerain at Constantinople concerning the lawless proceedings of the Turkish and Tartar soldiery, but, finding these to be of no avail, he sought the alliance of Sigismund, Prince of Siebenbürgen (Transylvania), and Aaron, Voivode of Moldavia, and determined to rid his country of the oppressors. Aaron of Moldavia, it should be added, was a feeble prince, who would not have joined Michael but for the circumstance that, having been attacked and defeated by the Poles, he was compelled to seek refuge at Michael's court. After the alliance between the three princes was completed the first blow was struck for independence, and on November 12 or 13, 1594, all Turks who were found in Bucharest or Jassy were slaughtered without mercy. Michael is said to have invited a large number of true believers, who were pressing for the settlement of unlawful claims, to meet him in a khan in Bucarest, and when they were assembled he had them all put to the sword, and this was the signal for a massacre throughout the Principalities. A few Turks escaped through the humanity or friendship of private individuals, and one instance of this is specially recorded. The Cadi of Giurgevo, who happened to be at Bucarest, was walking out on the morning of November 13, when he was stopped by a Wallachian friend who said, 'Ali-Gian-Hogea, how many years have I eaten of thy bread and salt?' 'About twenty years,' answered the Turk. 'Well, then,' said his friend, 'out of gratitude I will give thee a word of counsel.' 'Speak,' said Ali. 'Do not stay in this city until three or four o'clock; neither remain in Giurgevo, but hasten thee as speedily as possible to Rustchuk' (on the opposite bank of the Danube). 'But wherefore?' enquired the Turk. The Wallachian walked away, but, turning round and seeing his friend still undecided, he called out: 'Forget not what I have told thee!' Wandering on in the city, the Turk could not help noticing greater activity than usual in the streets; suspecting mischief, but without saying a word to any person, he ordered his horses to be harnessed and fled to Giurgevo. The interior of Wallachia having been thus cleared of the Turks, Michael proceeded to attack their positions on the Danube. First he stormed Giurgevo and compelled the Turks to leave it, some crossing over the Danube, and others taking refuge in the fortress which was situated on an island in the river; but this latter he was unable to capture, as troops, ammunition, and provisions were sent into it from the Bulgarian side. Content, therefore, with his victory, he retired to Bucharest.

II.

Shortly afterwards a conspiracy against Michael was set on foot by adherents of the Turks, and under the pretence of desiring simply to march through the country, a Turkish Emir, with two thousand men, entered Bucharest. Michael, who know of the conspiracy, made a pretence of acquiescence in this movement, but shortly afterwards withdrew quietly to the camp of the allies, and returning with a sufficient force surrounded the house of the chief conspirator, in which the Emir and his escort were quartered, and put them to the sword. The fury of his troops was unbridled, and no quarter was given, the last of the enemy being put to death. But Michael did not stop here. In order to protect Wallachia from Turkish inroads, he determined to clear both banks of the Danube of their garrisons. With this view he sent the noted and successful Transylvanian general, Albert Kiraly, with a sufficient force, who took, plundered, and burned the Turkish town at the mouth of the Jalomitza, where it falls into the Danube. The fortress, however, he was obliged to leave in the hands of the Turks. Michael, following with the remainder of the army, crossed the river itself and besieged Oroschik (now Hirschova). This place was strongly reinforced by the Turks, but after an obstinate battle, which was fought partly on the frozen waters of the Danube, the allies were victorious, and retired across the river with an immense booty.

Shortly afterwards he moved up the river to Silistria, where he a second time encountered the Turks, gained a victory, and reduced the place to ashes. These victories of Michael struck terror into the rulers at Constantinople, and an Ottoman army, under Achmed Pasha, was sent to Rustchuk, whilst the Khan of the Crimea, an ally of the Turks, was ordered to enter Wallachia from the east, the Porte hoping by these vigorous measures to reduce its rebellious vassal to submission. The Turks did not, however, know of what material Michael was made. Dividing his army into two parts, he succeeded, by the rapidity of his movements, not only in keeping the allies asunder, but in completely routing both. The Tartars were twice defeated, and their fugitives spread terror among the Ottoman forces. Michael next gave the Turks battle at Rustchuk with his whole force, defeated and dispersed them, and slew their general. After these exploits he returned in triumph and with great booty to Bucharest.

Without, however, resting long under his laurels, he once more divided his army into several detachments, which, under different generals, marched once more to the Danube, the result being that the allied princes of Wallachia and Moldavia were soon able to report to Prince Sigismund that both banks of the Danube eastward to the Black Sea had been swept clear of the Ottoman forces.

III.

But Michael's troubles were far from terminated by these victories. Before securing the co-operation of the Prince of Siebenbürgen, he had, with a duplicity which characterized his whole career, agreed to acknowledge Sigismund as his suzerain, his object being to free himself from Turkish rule and then assume independent power. But the Transylvanians were not to be so easily disposed of, and after the victories over the Turks they in their turn demanded homage from the two Voivodes, and backed their claim by an irresistible force. The Voivode of Moldavia was seized and imprisoned, and Michael, deeming prudence the better part of valor, submitted to the terms which were dictated to him. These were in appearance worse even than the Turkish 'capitulations,' but, as they were never kept, it is unnecessary to mention them. Sigismund assumed the title 'By the grace of God, Prince of Siebenbürgen, of Moldavia and Wallachia, and of the Holy Roman Empire, &c.' (he in his turn being the vassal of the German Emperor), whilst Michael was denied the claim to divine right, was restricted in his princely powers, and was addressed as 'Dominus Michael Voivoda regni nostri Transalpinensis.' He was not permitted to employ the national seal, but was allowed the use of red wax.

Perhaps it was well for Michael that he submitted to these humiliating conditions at the hands of his ally, or his reign might have been even shorter than it was, for the Turk was again at his gates with an overwhelming army. The Sultan Murad III. was dead, January 1595, and was succeeded by Mahommed III.; nineteen brothers, we are told, having been slaughtered to obviate dissensions, a custom which is still followed, as the reader is doubtless aware, in certain oriental realms. Shortly after his accession, the Porte again proceeded to assume the sovereignty of the Principalities, and an army variously estimated from 100,000 to 180,000 men, under Sinan

Pasha, was concentrated at Rustchuk to take possession of the provinces. Michael was at the time able to collect only 8,000 men, for the Transylvanian troops had been withdrawn, but his encounter with the overwhelming Turkish force arrayed against him on this occasion undoubtedly presents the most brilliant phase of his remarkable career. Marching rapidly to Giurgevo with his handful of men, he managed to detain the Turkish army for weeks on the south side of the Danube, destroying their bridges and preventing them from crossing the river. Turned at length by a Turkish detachment, which had succeeded in crossing at a point above Giurgevo, he was compelled to withdraw to a village about halfway towards Bucharest. His little army had been strengthened by an accession of Transylvanian and Moldavian troops, the former under brave Albert Kiraly, but even then it barely numbered 16,000, whilst the army of Sinan Pasha must have been at least six times as strong. Kalugereni, the village at which this stand was made, is still to be found on the maps, on the line of railway from Giurgevo to Bucharest; and it only differed from Thermopylæ in the fact that the enemy was not alone checked in his career, but for the time the little army of Romanians and their allies were completely victorious.

Nothing could have exceeded the astonishment of Sinan Pasha when he found Michael ready to give him battle with his handful of patriots; but as he proceeded to make his dispositions for the onslaught, he found that his adversary possessed in his favorable position much to compensate him for his inferior numbers. The nature of the ground was such that Sinan could not employ the whole, nor even the major part, of his forces, and Michael and his allies were protected by a morass and river, which rendered it necessary for the Turks to concentrate their whole attack upon a single road and bridge crossing the latter. At this bridge the battle was practically fought. Michael and his forces for a long time sustained the attack of the Ottomans, who had posted their guns so as to commit havoc in the ranks of the allies, until these, fighting hand to hand, were obliged to retreat. The Turks followed and had made sure of their victory, when Albert Kiraly succeeded in bringing two guns into a favorable position, and by a flank fire threw the enemy into confusion. Of this circumstance Michael availed himself once more to renew the attack, this time with the most happy results. The enemy retreated in disorder over the bridge, and by the furious onslaught of the allies his hosts were driven helter-skelter into the morass. On the one hand Michael is said to have performed prodigies of valor, whilst on the other Sinan Pasha, who fought with equal bravery, was unhorsed and thrown into the bog, from which he only escaped with his life through the fidelity of one of his followers, who was afterwards known as the 'Marsher.' Michael recovered his own guns, which had been captured early in the fight, as well as many of the enemy's, along with a great booty comprising many Turkish standards, and including the sacred standard of Mohammed, which was believed to be invincible. Thus ended a struggle of which to this day Romanians are proud, and which they associate with the memory of their greatest hero. This battle was fought and won at some indefinite date between August 13 and 26, 1595. The rest of the campaign may be dismissed in a few sentences.

That Michael with his small force could draw no advantage from his victory may be readily imagined; and, a council of war being held during the night, a retreat was decided upon. Passing rapidly through Bucarest, which was sacked by the Transylvanian troops in order that the Turks might not profit by its treasures, the allies retired to Tirgovistea, followed by the inhabitants on their route; and after a few days' rest they proceeded to a village at the foot of the Carpathians to await succor from Siebenbürgen. The Turkish commander, meanwhile, instead of following them promptly, entered Bucharest at leisure, where he divided his army into numerous detachments, to take possession of various parts of the country and garrison fortresses, and spent his time in turning churches into mosques and substituting the crescent for the cross. Then he marched on, took possession of Tirgovistea, and sent a large force to occupy Braila.

Meanwhile Sigismund had collected a powerful and well-disciplined army, consisting of imperial troops and Transylvanians, and numbering 20,000 horse and 30,000 foot with 53 guns. With these he crossed the Carpathians, and, joining Michael and Albert Kiraly, he resumed the offensive against the Turks, driving them before him wherever he encountered them. Sinan took fright, and retired to Bucharest. Tirgovistea was recovered by the allies after three days' fighting, and many guns were captured. Sinan continued to retire before the advancing foe. Having set fire to the city and burned many churches, he hastily withdrew to Giurgevo; and, thinking that the allies would enter Bucharest, he is said to have left it mined ready for explosion. In this, however, he was mistaken. Sigismund and Michael passed by Bucharest and pursued him in all haste, arriving at Giurgevo whilst the Turkish army was still crossing the river. Sinan had managed to reach the Bulgarian side with a portion of his troops, but the rearguard was still at Giurgevo, and a fight ensued in which the greater part of the Turkish force was cut to pieces either on land or in their attempt to traverse the stream. The Danube was reddened with the blood; 5,000 Turks are said to have fallen, and 4,000 to 5,000 Christians to have been liberated from their chains. The whole campaign is said to have cost the Turks 30,000 men and 150 large and small guns.

IV.

Having, with the aid of his allies, effectually freed his country from external enemies, Michael had now a brief space of time for improving its internal condition, for it is hardly necessary to say that these desolating wars had reduced it to the very lowest stage of misery. Fields were tilled, cattle imported from Transylvania, seed corn distributed among the peasantry, and soon the face of the land assumed a smiling aspect, and new towns and villages sprang from the ruins of the old. Minor wars he had with the Tartars, and conspiracies were formed against him and quelled. He was even accused of treachery against his suzerain, whom, however, he managed to satisfy during a visit to Weissenburg; and well would it have been for Michael and his country if his ambition had not prompted him to over-estimate his powers, and if he had been content to reign in peace over his own principality. But this was not his policy. His victories had given him a high rank among the powers of the Orient; and the changes which were taking place brought him into communication with one and another, and favored a scheme of aggrandizement which, though it was for a time successful, eventuated in his downfall and death.

Sigismund Bathori, weary of government, had abdicated in favor of his brother, the Cardinal Andreas, with whom Michael had nothing in common, and then it was (if not previously) that the latter began to nurse the design of becoming the independent ruler over what had been ancient Dacia, namely, Wallachia, Moldavia, and Siebenbürgen. With this view he commenced negotiations with the Porte, which were eagerly welcomed; and he also approached the German emperor, from whom he needed money to pay his mercenary troops. Indeed, for the purpose of accomplishing his ends, he at one and the same time did homage and acknowledged himself the vassal of both powers. For a long time he temporized and contented himself with strengthening and drilling his forces. At length taking advantage of unfriendly relations which subsisted between Andreas Bathori and the emperor, from whom he had succeeded in obtaining a subsidy on the plea that he required it for his operations against the Turks, who constantly threatened the Empire, Michael hastily assembled his forces, and, against the warnings and wishes of his wife and some of his more discreet counselors, he crossed the Boza Pass in the Carpathians in 1599, and proceeded to overrun Siebenbürgen, as he professed, in the name and interests of his suzerain, the German emperor.

After striking terror into the inhabitants of Transylvania by the excesses of his troops, Michael's first step of any consequence on entering the country was to appear before Kronstadt with his army and demand its surrender. This was granted, and Michael deemed it politic not to enter the city, but to march forward and get possession of other towns, which yielded to him one after the other in rapid succession.

Andreas Bathori was staggered and perplexed by this sudden inroad into his dominions, but when he became fully alive to the danger the whole country was roused by the carrying round of the 'bloody sword.' He also sent emissaries to induce Michael to return to his own country, but the latter kept these in confinement until the conclusion of the campaign. What made the matter more serious for Andreas was that a vast number of discontented inhabitants and freebooters, lusting after plunder, had joined the army of Michael, and had swelled it to the number of 25,000 men. A council of war was hastily called by Andreas, and after considerable delay the Transylvanian army was collected at Hermanstadt. Michael, not expecting serious opposition so soon, had recourse to stratagem in order to gain time and deceive his enemy. To his shame be it said that he sent emissaries to Andreas who were instructed to represent the whole proceeding as an unfortunate mistake, and to express Michael's regret at the excesses of his troops. All he wished, he said, was a free passage through Siebenbürgen into Hungary, where he desired to join his forces with those of the Empire against the Turks. And when the cardinal sent him word that he must return to Wallachia with his forces before he could consider their old friendship restored, Michael carried his duplicity so far as to conclude a truce with the emissaries and make a proposal to exchange hostages. The negotiations were, however, in all probability insincere on both sides; and, after further delay, the emissaries returned to their respective camps, and the opposing armies met in hostile array upon a plain between Hermanstadt and Schellenberg. Here each prince addressed his troops previous to the encounter. Cardinal Andreas, divested of his clerical robes and fully equipped and mounted, denounced Michael in the bitterest terms. His brethren, he said, still herded sheep and pigs in Wallachia. He had associated himself with robbers and with a miscellaneous rabble collected from all parts to ruin the country. 'Be not afraid,' he added, 'of this nation of Sclaves, who, from time immemorial, have been conquered subjects of the Hungarians, and who should be punished rather with rods and blows than with the sword.' Thus, and much more in the same strain, spake Andreas. Michael, on the other hand, spoke of his enemy with contemptuous jocularity, as a mounted and perjured priest who had allied himself with the Turks, the enemies of Christendom, whilst he himself claimed to represent fidelity to Christianity and the Empire. Moreover, he held out to his troops tho prospect of great booty if they were victorious.

We shall not attempt to describe the engagement which followed. At the very outset it declared itself to some extent in Michael's favor through the desertion of one of the most influential leaders in Andreas's army. It was chiefly a series of encounters between isolated detachments of troops, and in many cases not only were men of the same nation arrayed against each other, but the opposing forces were under the leadership of near relatives. The first to yield, after a fierce and protracted contest, was Andreas, who fled from the field believing the battle to be lost. His brave generals, however, rallied his men, and to a great extent retrieved the fortunes of the day. In fact they fought so successfully that a portion of the Wallachian army, where Michael himself was in command, took to flight, and for a time dragged its leader along with it. The cowardice of Andreas prevented the Transylvanian leaders from taking advantage of this turn in their favor; and Michael, seeing that all was not lost, made strenuous efforts to rally his troops. By threats, blows, and angry exclamations, he at length succeeded in arresting the stampede, but it was not until he had with his own sword run two fugitive captains through the body that he was once more successful in leading his followers into the field, and this time in effectually routing the enemy. This end was facilitated by an event similar to the one which commenced the fight. The Poles in Transylvanian service, seeing their leader flee, and regarding his cause as lost, deserted in a body in order that they might not lose their share of the booty.

This battle, which is called by some the battle of Schellenberg, and by others of Hermanstadt, laid Transylvania at the feet of Michael. Hermanstadt would have opened its gates to him, but instead of entering it he marched onward, and on November 1, 1599, he entered the capital, Weissenburg, in triumph. On that occasion the magnificence of his apparel and surroundings scarcely seems to have been consistent with his reputation as a hardy warrior. We read of a white silk mantle embroidered with gold lace; of buttons of precious stones; of a girdle, in which was carried a scimitar rich in gold and rubies; and of his wife and children being in similar state. One other feature is worthy of mention. With booming of cannon, tolling of bells, sound of fife and drum, and tramp of richly-caparisoned steeds was associated the Wallachian national music performed by gypsies (Laoutari), an incident which enables one who has even to-day heard their wild music to picture to himself a vivid representation of the scene.

V.

Michael now assumed the direction of affairs in Transylvania, notwithstanding that the German general, Basta, who had hoped to acquire the government for himself, was present with an army to control his action. Soon he heard of the capture and murder of Andreas Bathori, on whose head he had set a price, by the peasantry of the mountains; and, calling an assembly of the notables, he succeeded in securing their adhesion to his viceroyalty. After long-protracted negotiations the emperor, seeing that Michael was firmly installed in his government with the consent of the Assembly of States, and finding him willing to submit as a vassal of the German crown, accepted the situation, and permitted him to do homage. This was done with great reluctance and in spite of Papal remonstrances, as the murder of Cardinal Bathori had caused great bitterness against Michael at Rome. As soon as the latter felt or deemed his position in Siebenbürgen secure, he turned his arms against Moldavia, with a view to depose Jeremiah Mogila, the reigning voivode, and complete his incorporation of that country with the two over which he already ruled. The manœuvres of Michael were questionable previous to his contest with Andreas; but now he excelled himself. In order to obtain his ends, he threatened the emperor with an alliance with the Turks, unless he gave him further supplies of money. The Porte he pacified by receiving its envoys and doing homage. To the Pope he turned for support against the infidel, but his only response was that Michael should first adopt the true faith—he being, of course, a member of the schismatic Greek Church; and just before entering Moldavia with his army he had the effrontery, in order to throw Mogila off his guard, to propose a marriage between his daughter and Mogila's son. Finally, in order to secure the obedience of his subjects in Siebenbürgen during his absence in Moldavia, he sent a large number of Transylvanian nobles to his son in Wallachia, to be detained there as hostages until he had accomplished his ends.

The King of Poland, who was in alliance with Moldavia, was aware of Michael's schemes, and appealed to the emperor to check them; but Michael, little heeding, collected a heterogeneous army, and in May, A.D. 1600, he commenced his march into Moldavia, announcing it as his intention to avenge the death of the late Voivode Stephen, who had been murdered by Jeremiah Mogila. His passage across the Carpathians was beset with difficulties, his army being often almost bare of supplies; but, once in Moldavia, all yielded before his arms. Jeremiah was at a wedding in fancied security, and had barely time to collect a small army when Michael was upon him. A battle was fought near the capital Suczava, which decided the fate of the principality. A great part of Jeremiah's army deserted to Michael, who defeated his enemy without difficulty, and obtained possession of Suczava. After remaining for a short time in Moldavia, Jeremiah escaped to Poland, and succeeded in raising the Poles in his support. These, however, were so terrified at the successes of Michael's arms that they contented themselves with sending an army to the frontier, and there standing on the defensive. Michael won over the Moldavians by exempting them from taxation, and, having placed the government in the hands of a military commission, he turned his face towards Transylvania, and re-entered Weissenburg in triumph, within two months of the day on which he had departed on his mission of conquest.

VI.

The authority of Michael was readily recognized by the Transylvanian States General, and with great misgiving by the Emperor Rudolph. He was now at the pinnacle of his fame, styling himself, modestly enough, Viceroy, but acting with the authority of a despotic ruler. Gold and silver medals were struck in his honor, some of which are extant; emissaries waited upon him from the German and other courts, and were received in royal state.

From his effigy upon these medals, and from a portrait of him which was painted subsequently, he appears to have been a man of striking presence and somewhat stern aspect. His face was characterized by an aquiline nose, a beard and mustache, and it is said to have been full of expression.

Would that we could leave him at this triumphant stage of his career; but that is impossible, for rapid and remarkable as was his ascent, his fall and ruin were still more precipitate. Scarcely was he installed in his threefold authority when his troubles commenced. He had never been heartily accepted by his nobles, many of whom were ambitious and self-seeking, and considered him in the light of a usurper. The nation itself was composed of antagonistic races, Szeklers, Saxons, Hungarians, &c., and where he pleased one race he displeased the other. The Poles, too, were only watching their opportunity to disturb his government in Moldavia. A rising at home, which Michael endeavored to quell by the execution of some of the leaders, soon became very formidable, and the nobles assembled a considerable army of retainers and encamped at Thorda. Michael endeavored by various stratagems to get them into his power, but failed to do so. General Basta, who was eager to be revenged upon him for having kept him out of the viceroyalty of Siebenbürgen, joined the Transylvanian army; and Michael, finding all his efforts at pacification unavailing, at length encountered General Basta and the nobles at Miriszlo, a village which the reader will still find marked on the railway, between Karlsburg and Klausenburg. The position of Michael was a very strong one, and, had he awaited the attack of his enemies, the probability is that he would again have been victorious. But in Basta he had a wily adversary. Finding it impossible to attack Michael where he was encamped, he feigned a retreat, whereupon Michael, asking contemptuously of his generals 'whither the Italian hound was fleeing,' allowed his army to follow in disorderly pursuit. They were, however, soon checked, and Michael was then obliged to give battle under far less favorable conditions. His army was more numerous than that of his enemy; but not only was the latter composed of seasoned troops, but it was far better officered. The encounter was a fierce one, and it was decided against Michael by a clever manœuvre of Basta. One of his generals noticed that Michael's artillery, which was so posted as to harass the army of the allies, might be seized by a flank movement. He sent three hundred musketeers, who succeeded in capturing the guns and turning them upon Michael's forces. All was soon lost, and after vain attempts to rally his men he at length yielded to the solicitations of his officers and prepared to fly. His conduct on this occasion is characteristic of the man. 'So he ordered the national flag to be brought, which was made of white silk, and bore a device consisting of a raven with a red cross in its beak upon a green field. This was torn from the staff, and Michael hid it in his bosom. The officers followed his example with the remaining ensigns. Then he gave spurs to his horse, and with loosened rein, accompanied by his officers and some Polish and other cavalry, took to flight. Had he waited a few minutes longer, he would surely have been made prisoner.' With the enemy at his heels Michael reached the banks of the Naros river, and instead of allowing himself to be ferried across he sprang into the waves on horseback, and his faithful horse, which was of Turkish breed, landed him safely on the other side. Here, filled with gratitude and affection for the animal, and knowing that it was unable to carry him further, he patted it on the neck, stroked its mane, kissed it, and let it run free into the fields. To follow Michael's adventures after this terrible defeat would be impossible. At first he took refuge in the Carpathians, in the Fogaras mountains as they are called; he then returned, and, joined by his son, succeeded for a short time in maintaining a foothold in Transylvania. But threatened by Rudolph and by the Poles, he was glad to escape into Wallachia.

Here he was again followed by the Poles, and, to complete his perplexities, the Turks commenced making raids into his country. Once more he was defeated by the former on the Telega river, near Ploiesti. A brother of Jeremiah Mogila having been put upon the throne of Wallachia, Michael found it necessary to take refuge in the Banate of Craiova, his first seat of government. Then it was that he appealed for protection to the German emperor, expressing his desire to present himself before him to plead his own cause. Rudolph granted him a safe-conduct for himself and a moderate following through Siebenbürgen, and Michael proceeded to the German Court. Notwithstanding the safe-conduct, however, his journey was fraught with peril. He was fired upon from castles, was followed by hostile bands, and was at last only allowed to cross the river Theiss at Tokay with a hundred men. He reached Vienna in safety on January 12, 1601, and was there prevented from proceeding to Prague, where the Emperor was, by orders from the imperial court.

Shortly after this, however, the Transylvanian nobles, as faithless to Rudolph, to whom they had sworn fealty, as they had been to Michael, recalled Sigismund Bathori, and, without the sanction of the Emperor, placed him on the throne of Siebenbürgen. Then it was that Rudolph found it convenient to allow Michael to approach his person. The latter, on his arrival, presented a petition embodying his defense which might have been drawn by a special pleader, and which was accepted by the Emperor as a justification of his proceedings. A complete reconciliation took place between them, and Michael was formally re-appointed vicegerent of Transylvania. A sufficiently well-appointed army and a large sum of money were placed at his disposal, and he was requested to join with his old enemy, General Basta, in dethroning Sigismund. An apparent reconciliation took place between the two chiefs, Michael and Basta, and they marched as allies into Siebenbürgen. Sigismund, finding that his case with the Emperor was hopeless, and after, it is said, vainly endeavoring by foul means to prevent the junction of Michael and Basta, sought and obtained the aid of the Turks and Moldavians. That is to say, the former would have sent him a contingent of troops had not Michael, by means of forged letters, purporting to be signed by Sigismund, kept them at a distance. The opposing forces met at Goroszlo near Klausenburg, and after a hotly contested battle the Transylvanians were defeated with terrible slaughter. Hardly, however, was the victory won when jealousies and recriminations between the two generals followed.

Michael considered himself, as viceroy of Siebenbürgen, called upon to manage the affairs of the country. Basta, smarting under the disappointment of having failed to secure the viceroyalty, continued to assume the position of commander-in-chief of the forces, and not only interfered with the orders and wishes of Michael, but charged him with various offenses, the chief one being that he was again usurping the supreme power. Believing that he would be safe in using this charge as a justification for his acts, and that his removal would pave the way for his own accession to the viceroyalty, Basta then determined to have Michael assassinated. Knowing that it was his intention to proceed to the Carpathians and liberate his family which had been kept there in confinement, Basta sent a captain with three hundred Walloons to effect his purpose. This man applied at Michael's tent for permission to accompany him on his journey, and asked him to obtain the necessary permission from Basta. Michael assented, whereupon the officer entered the tent hastily, and, approaching the prince who was reposing, addressed him as his prisoner. Michael exclaimed that he would not yield himself alive, but before he could obtain possession of his sword to defend himself, the officer had ran him through the body with his halberd. This foul deed was perpetrated between August 17 and September 1, 1601, and it is said that the assassins struck off his head and sword-hand with Michael's own sword. Afterwards they tortured and assassinated his minister, a veteran of eighty years of age, and spread such terror among the troops who had remained faithful to their murdered prince, that his boyards and their followers took to flight and sought refuge in Wallachia.

Thus fell Michael the Brave, rash, courageous, false, ambitious, patriotic, the central figure in the past history of Romania. Basta sought to justify his act of treachery in a letter to the Emperor; but whilst on the one hand the German court dared not quarrel with him in the then condition of Transylvania, on the other hand they refused to reward him for a deed of blood which has sent down his name with execration to posterity.

CHAPTER XIII.

FROM THE DEATH OF MICHAEL THE BRAVE (A.D. 1601) TO THE DEPOSITION OF PRINCE COUZA (A.D. 1866).

Turkish exactions after Michael's fall—Transition from native to Greek Voivodes—Matthew Bassarab (Wallachia) and Basilius Lupus (Moldavia)—Their severe criminal codes—Serban II. (Cantacuzene)—His good deeds—Betrays the Turks before Vienna—Growing power of Russia—Treaty of Carlowitz—Brancovano (Wallachia) and Cantemir (Moldavia) negotiate with Peter the Great—First Russian invasion of the Principalities—Repelled by the Turks—Flight of Cantemir—(Note: Anecdote of Russian cupidity)—Arrest and execution of Brancovano and his family—His great treasures—The Phanariotes—Their origin and rise—Massacred in Wallachia—Second appearance—Extortions and expulsion—Panaiotaki, Dragoman of the Porte—The Mavrocordatos—Nicholas, first Phanariote Hospodar—Suppresses the boyards' retainers—Constantine modifies slavery—Mode of appointing hospodars—The Caimakam—Homage and servility of boyards—Conduct of Phanariote rulers at home—Court customs—Reputed effeminacy—Rapacity and exactions—Extortions of officials—Extravagance of princesses—Treatment of peasantry—Princes encourage brigandage—Usually deposed and executed—Corruption of clergy—Other baneful effects of Phanariote rule—(Note: Divorces in Romania to-day)—Another view of Phanariote princes—Their good works—Ypsilanti, Gregory Ghika—Nicholas Mavrojeni and his cowardly boyards—Ennobles his horses—Russo-Turkish wars—Treaty of Belgrade—Russian successes and Austrian interference—Treaty of Kainardji—Russian protectorate—Cession of Bucovine to Austria—Treaty of Jassy—Amelioration of state of the Principalities, 1802—French and English consuls appointed—Russo-Turkish war and occupation—Treaty of Bucharest—Hetairia or Greek rising—Rebellion in the Principalities—Career and fate of the patriots Vladimiresco and Ypsilanti—End of Phanariote rule—Russian intervention and occupation—Treaty of Adrianople and restoration of native rulers—Patriotic efforts of Heliade and others—Rise of Romanian learning and art—The year of revolutions, 1848—Partial success of the rising in Romania—Suppression by Russia and Turkey—Escape of the patriots—Review of the benefits of Russian interference in the Principalities—Renewed Russian aggression—Brief history of the war of 1854-1856 between Russia and the Western Powers and Turkey—Treaty of Paris—Return of the patriots—Union of the Principalities under Prince Couza—Incidents of his reign—His deposition—How planned and effected—The provisional government—Evil influence of Couza's conduct.

I.

The history of Moldo-Wallachia during the seventeenth century—that is to say, from the fall of Michael to the dispossession of the native voivodes at the beginning of the eighteenth century—possesses little interest for English readers. Some of the more important incidents will be referred to in connection with the subsequent *régime* of the Greek, or, as they are called, the Phanariote rulers appointed by the Porte, and it will only be necessary to make a few brief comments upon the condition of the country, and the character of two or three of the Voivodes who reigned during the century.

It may well be imagined that the humiliating defeats inflicted by Michael upon the Turkish armies would not tend to mollify the severity of their subsequent rule, and that the chief aim of the Porte would be to extort as large a revenue as possible from the conquered provinces, without regard to the sufferings of any class, This was effected by taking advantage of the jealousies and intrigues of the boyards who aspired to the rulership to obtain an increase of the tribute, and bribes; and a reference to the records of the time shows that whilst in Wallachia the rule of only three voivodes, and in Moldavia that of two only, exceeded five years, there were often two new princes appointed in the same year. A noteworthy circumstance in connection with these voivodes is their gradual transition from native to Greek families. Here and there we have an Italian appellative, such as

Quatiani or Rosetti, but in the main there is a change from the Bassarabs, the Bogdans, and the Radus, to the Ghikas, Cantacuzenes, Brancovanos, and eventually to the Mavrocordatos. The explanation of this change will be given presently, but amongthe native rulers we may select two or three for brief comment. Between 1627 or 1633 and 1654 Matthew Baasarab ruled over Wallachia to the advantage of the nation. He drove out the Tartars who had overrun the country, and afterwards devoted himself to the welfare of his subjects. Bucharest was not yet the acknowledged capital, but he established a printing-press there, and also reformed the administration of justice. At the same time Basilius (known as Basil the Wolf), Prince of Moldavia, between whom and Matthew there had been great jealousy, followed his example in his own country, and a criminal code was introduced into both principalities, which, among its other provisions, legalized slavery in some of its most iniquitous forms. A few extracts from this code may be of interest, as showing the condition of the people at that time.

Anyone guilty of arson was burned alive.

Anyone harboring a fugitive serf was liable to a fine of twelve silver lions into court and twenty-four to the seigneur.

If the gypsy of a boyard or his children stole some such trifle as a chicken or an egg twice or three times, he was to be pardoned, but if he stole anything more considerable he should be punished as a thief. If he committed a theft to ward off starvation, he was pardoned, and also if he stole from the enemy.

A treasure discovered by means of sorcery became the property of the prince.

Besides the very severe punishments directed against other forms of murder, poisoning, which must therefore have been frequent, has two clauses provided for it. One is that, in addition to the punishment of a murderer, his children shall be declared infamous.

If a man gave another a box on the ear, and was stabbed in return, no punishment was inflicted, even if death ensued; and the whole code of honor is of a like savage nature.

Doctors are to be believed in matters of hygiene before barbers or sorcerers.

Bigamy was punished by the culprit being whipped through the town, riding naked on a donkey.

If a person to whom the training of young girls was confided corrupted and betrayed them to licentious men, hot lead was to be poured down his (or her) throat until it reached his heart (*sic*), 'for it was from thence that the seductive counsels had proceeded.'

A slave or paid serf who committed rape was not put to death as were others, but he was burned alive.

Torture was evidently quite common, for judges are forbidden to torture innocent persons even by order of the prince.

Nobility clearly gave immunity to crime—at least it mitigated the punishment; for 'neither nobles nor boyards nor their sons could be condemned to the galleys nor to the mines, but they might be banished for a longer or shorter period; they might not be hung, nor impaled, nor dragged through the streets like ordinary malefactors, but they should be decapitated.'

A wise and good Prince of Wallachia was Serban II. (Cantacuzene), 1679-1688, who built and improved churches and monasteries, and erected factories and workshops for the people. He also encouraged education and literature, founded the first Romanian seminary, translated the Bible into Romanian, and, so far as it was possible in the unfortunate condition of the country, he diminished the taxes of the poor. He was compelled to join the Turks in their wars against Germany, but, summoning courage at a critical moment, he turned his arms against—or perhaps it would be more honest to say he betrayed—those of whom he was the unwilling ally. This happened during the siege of Vienna in 1683, where Serban was at the head of a contingent of four thousand Wallachians in the army of Cara Mustapha, and the duty was entrusted to him of constructing bridges and works. He took advantage of his position to communicate with the Germans, facilitated the destruction of the works which he himself had raised, and it is said that he loaded his guns with straw. He is said also to have erected a high cross opposite his tent, on which an inscription was graven capable of bearing a double interpretation, and which gave courage to the besieged. After the defeat of the Turks before Vienna through its relief by Sobieski, King of Poland, Serban fostered the idea of asserting his independence of Turkish rule; but before he was able to carry his plans into execution, he died (1688), it is said, poisoned by his brother and nephew.

II.

But another great Power was drawing nearer and nearer to Romania, which was eventually to exercise a grave influence upon her destiny. Already the Muscovites had taken part with the Christian Powers in their struggles with the Ottoman Empire, and in 1699 the Treaty of Karlowitz was concluded, which gave Transylvania to Austria and Azov to the Russian Empire. The position of the Principalities as vassal states of Turkey remained unaffected, but the indirect influence of the growing power of Russia soon became manifest. In the beginning of the eighteenth century there ruled two voivodes, Constantine Brancovano in Wallachia, and Demetrius Cantemir in Moldavia, both of whom had been appointed in the usual manner under the suzerainty of the Porte; but these princes, independently of each other, had entered into negotiations with Peter the Great after the defeat of Charles XII. at Pultawa (1709) to assist them against the Sultan, their suzerain, stipulating for their own independence under the protection of the Czar. Encouraged by these advances Peter approached the Pruth with his army; but the Moldavian boyards were generally opposed to the alliance, and Cantemir found himself supported only by three or four of his ministers. Notwithstanding this, the Russian army crossed the Pruth, and pitched their camp near Jassy. A general massacre of the Turks throughout Moldavia followed, but no advantage accrued to the Russian arms, as the Moldavian prince was unable to furnish the Czar with the promised supplies for his army. It is even said that one of the boyards, who enjoyed the confidence of Cantemir, appropriated certain funds which he had received for the supply of the army to his own use, and placed himself in communication with the Grand Vizier. The Porte, aided by its allies, raised a powerful army, which crossed the Danube; and although one of Peter's generals is said to have obtained some temporary advantage, the Czar soon found himself so hard pressed by the superior forces of the Ottomans that he was glad to conclude a treaty with the Porte and make the best of his way home, harassed on his return by fierce Tartar hordes.

At Stephanesti the Czar was met by Cantemir, who sought and obtained his protection, and returned with him into Russia, where it is said that his representations inflamed the desire of Peter to possess the Principalities, if not Constantinople, and led to those subsequent wars of which Romania afterwards became the seat and the victim.

Brancovano, Prince of Wallachia, who had not taken any active part in the war, met with the fate which his neighbour had escaped. His secret correspondence and alliance with Peter the Great were betrayed to the Porte by a member of his own family, and after the conclusion of peace steps were taken to depose him. With this view the Kapidgi Mustapha was sent with a small escort to arrest and bring him to Constantinople with his whole family. The story of his deposition is narrated with great dramatic effect: how the Kapidgi with twelve janissaries entered the throne-room where Brancovano awaited him unconscious of his impending fate; and how the former, refusing to take a seat by his side, drew a long crape shawl from his breast and, throwing it over the shoulders of the prince, pronounced the terrible word 'deposed.' He then called the boyards together, read the decree of the Sultan, and threatened them with an invasion if they resisted. The cowardly boyards allowed their prince and his family to be carried off to Constantinople without an effort to save them. On his arrival at Constantinople, Brancovano was declared a traitor, and, having refused to embrace Islamism, he and four of his sons and his son-in-law were decapitated (A.D. 1714) in the Sultan's presence. Satiated with their blood, it is said that the Sultan Achmet III. spared the last member of his family, a young grandchild, and that this one, with the widow, were permitted to retire into Wallachia.

One of the temptations to put an end to the life as well as the reign of Constantine Brancovano was undoubtedly his great wealth. Along with his person his papers were seized, and his property was confiscated, an inventory having been made of the latter, in which the following are said to have been included:—A service of gold plate; the ancient crown of the voivodes, valued at 37,000*l.*; a gold belt and a rich collar set with jewels; the effigy of the hospodar in gold pieces of ten ducats; harnesses embroidered with gold and precious stones; a vast sum of money in coinages of different countries; and deposit-receipts for sums lodged in his name in Vienna, Venice, &c. Also landed property in various places, making an estimated total of three and a half millions sterling. The immense value of his treasures, and the sums of money which he possessed in various coinages and countries, led to the charge against him of having betrayed the interests of the Porte for bribes, received from Austria, Poland, and Venice, and, what was more unfortunate for him, to the suspicion that still larger treasures were secreted. Previous to his execution he and his eldest son are said to have been tortured for five days, to compel them to make discovery of further possessions, but without result. After the deposition of Brancovano, Stephen Cantacuzene, the son of one of his accusers, was made Voivode of Wallachia, but like his predecessors he only enjoyed the honor for a brief term, and two years afterwards he was deposed, ordered to Constantinople, imprisoned, and decapitated; and with him terminated the rule of the native princes, who were followed, both in Wallachia and Moldavia, by the so-called Phanariote governors or farmers-general of the Porte.

III.

But who and what were the Phanariotes? the reader may inquire; and in order fully to answer the question we must revert to the beginning of the seventeenth century, and hastily review a series of events which, during that century, laid the foundation of their subsequent rule. About the commencement of the century many Greeks, coming chiefly from the islands of the Archipelago and from Asia Minor, sought refuge in Constantinople, where in the course of time they founded a colony in a parish or district known as the 'Phanar:' hence their name of Phanariotes. Being more learned, or at least better instructed, than the people among whom they resided, and moreover well acquainted with trade, they assumed similar functions to those performed by the Jews of the west of Europe, and like the latter they at once became the objects of cordial dislike, and indispensable factors in society. Not content with settling in Constantinople, they spread themselves into the Turkish pashaliks and dependencies, among others into the Danubian Principalities, where, too, owing to their extortionate practices, they became thoroughly detested; and it is said that Michael the Brave issued an edict excluding them from all public offices of trust. About the year 1617 they had so greatly increased in numbers, and excited such hatred, that the native population could no longer be restrained; a second edition of the Sicilian Vespers was enacted, and they were massacred, men, women, and children, a deed for which their successors took ample vengeance. For a time we hear nothing more about them, but about half a century afterwards (1665) they returned in great numbers in the suite of two Voivodes, who had purchased the thrones of the Principalities, and once more sought to establish themselves. Two of these seem to have played the part for the reigning prince that Empson and Dudley filled for our Henry VII., namely, that of extortioners, but with far greater tyranny and cruelty. They were at length cut in pieces by the populace, and the Greeks were once more expelled from the country. Meanwhile, however, they had grown in favor in Constantinople, where, through their learning and intelligence, they began to fill confidential offices under the Porte. To their ordinary avocations some added the practice of medicine, in which they were adepts; and one of them, Panaiotaki Nicosias, a medical attendant of the Grand Vizier, managed to ingratiate himself with his patron, and then, having exerted his influence in favor of his fellow-countrymen, he succeeded in obtaining minor offices for some, and toleration for all. He was appointed Dragoman or interpreter to the Porte, and, proving an able and faithful servant, he was permitted to nominate as his successor Alexander Mavrocordato, who is said by some to have been a common laborer and to have married a butcher's daughter, whilst others call him a silk-dealer of Constantinople or of Chio. Be that as it may, he made himself so useful to his employers, especially during the negotiation of the Treaty of Carlowitz, that after the execution of Brancovano he managed to secure the succession to the throne of Wallachia (1716) for his son Nicholas Mavrocordato, and became the ancestor of a long line of rulers in both principalities.

IV.

The selection of Greek princes, or, as they are often called, 'farmers-general,' by the Porte, was probably the result of the distrust which the native voivodes and boyards had engendered, as much as the respect entertained for its faithful dragomans; and if Nicholas Mavrocordato did not receive explicit instructions on the subject, he knew that the most welcome change he could make in the interests of his patrons would be to introduce an entirely new *régime* into his dominions. The most important step taken by him was to suppress the guards of the native boyards, which made them as dangerous to the ruler as the retainers of our barons had been to the Crown until they were suppressed by the Act of Henry VII. He established new tribunals and disbanded the militia. His successor, Constantine (about 1731), was superior in his views and aspirations to almost any of the princes who had ruled over Wallachia. He abolished the old form of slavery, but unfortunately political considerations still caused the retention of the peasantry in servitude; for, in order to weaken the native boyards, a large number of serfs, it is said 60,000 in all, were transferred as labourers from their old masters to the Crown, and to the newly created Greek boyards. Whilst their bodies were nominally freed, these poor creatures were required to render such an amount of feudal service to their new masters, that their wretched condition was rather aggravated than improved. The Greek or Phanariote boyards who were created, found it politic to intermarry with the native boyard families in order to improve their position in the land of their adoption, and the servile Wallachian nobles deemed it to their interest to encourage such alliances; indeed it was necessary to save themselves from extinction. New officers of State were appointed in the supposed interests of the Porte, but, as we shall see presently, the ruling prince, or, as the reader will find him called, voivode or hospodar, managed to turn these changes to account and make them serve for his own aggrandizement.

The new hospodar was always appointed by the Porte with great ceremony. 'The kukka or military crest,' says Wilkinson, 'is put on their heads by the Muzhur Aga; the robe of honour is put on them by the Vizir himself. They are honored with standards and military music, and take the oath of allegiance in the presence of the Sultan, to whom they are introduced with the ceremonies usual at a public audience.' They were appointed by 'Beratt,' an imperial diploma, of which Wilkinson gives a formula, and wherein the Sultan commands the Wallachian and Moldavian peoples to acknowledge and obey the bearers of it, as the sole depositories of the sovereign authority. As soon as the prince was appointed, he at once sent an *avant-courrier*, a Kaimakam, to make preparations for his arrival; and this one, who was practically the chief of the State for a period of two months, generally managed, whilst he was carrying out his mission, to do a little profitable business on his own account. The prince followed in great state, accompanied by a number of dependents and hangers-on who had succeeded, by means of presents or otherwise, in ingratiating themselves in his favor. The bribes, flatteries, and meanness of which these sycophants were guilty, either before the departure of the prince from Constantinople or after his arrival in Bucharest(which had been the capital of Wallachia since the close of the seventeenth century) or Jassy, have been described in vivid colors by modern historians, some of whom have drawn pretty freely upon their imagination for the purpose. It is a fact, however, that the boyards sent presents to the prince before his departure, and even lodged sums of money in Constantinople for the purpose—money which had been wrung from the unfortunate peasantry. The new hospodar, who had paid pretty dearly for his post, submitted to all this homage, accepted everything, and then acted as it seemed most politic, often punishing and exiling those who had stooped the lowest or bribed the highest. Arrived at the principality he generally made a complete change in the *personnel* of the court and government, giving the most lucrative offices to his own relatives, honorary appointments to some, and pecuniary ones to a few of his best supporters. To Mahommedans he took care to assign posts of little or no influence, so that it might not be in their power to expedite his downfall, which took place, at farthest, at the end of three years, and was usually effected by intrigues at Constantinople. His dispositions thus gave him almost absolute power, which he took care to use in such a manner as to enrich himself and his family during the brief term of his dearly-bought hospodarship.

After their arrival at the capital, the princes delivered an address to the assembled boyards, promising happiness and prosperity to the people; but as soon as the first ceremonies were concluded, the greater number gave themselves up to self-indulgence, exacted servile attentions from all about them, and practiced every kind of unlawful extortion upon all those who were able to furnish supplies to the treasury.

'It was the custom that the prince never asked for anything at table. All is prepared for him; even his bread is cut into small pieces. He refuses food which does not please him. Wine is served to him in carafes of crystal. The cup-bearer (Paharnik), who is always a near relative, stands up before him holding a glass half filled.' When he has finished his dinner, coffee is handed to him, and when, subsequently, he withdraws to sleep, silence is enforced, not only in the palace, but throughout the city, so that his rest (which he does not, however, always take) shall not be disturbed. At a fixed hour, when he is supposed to have risen, the bells of the city are tolled, and all is again activity. All kinds of stories, more or less authentic, are narrated concerning the effeminacy of the Phanariote rulers, such as that they were lifted about by attendants, who supported them under the armpits, so that there might be no need for them to place their feet on the ground; but although such statements may be correct in regard to some of them, there were undoubtedly princes with whose character and actions such practices were quite inconsistent.

V.

It may, however, be readily believed, that various devices were resorted to by the princes to enrich themselves as speedily as possible. Their regular income was augmented by the granting of monopolies, the depreciation of the currency, and frauds in collecting the revenue and in providing supplies for the Porte. A poll or capitation tax was levied upon the nomadic and stationary gypsies, and money was even exacted under all kinds of pretenses from the heads of the religious orders. The annual income of the princes is said to have exceeded 40,000*l.* in addition to the tribute payable to the Porte. Nor must it be supposed that this was the whole amount that was extorted from the unfortunate inhabitants. It was 'like master like man,' and every official and underling followed the prince's example, each being aware that a change of rulers meant dismissal for himself. The princess, too, had special sources of income, which were usually squandered in rivalry with the boyardesses, in jewellery, dress, and other luxuries. It is said that one of the princesses, being offended with a lady of rank for excelling her in the ostentatious richness of her dress and personal adornments, caused her to be exiled; and that when she had secured a sufficiently large sum to purchase a more magnificent apparel than her rival, she allowed her to return to court, in order that she might enjoy her humiliation. The complaints of the oppressed peasantry were at best unheeded, and when these were driven to desperation and ventured to appeal in person to the prince, a number of them were seized and cast into prison, 'pour encourage les autres.' The result was that many turned brigands, and united to form bands; but even these, it is said, ministered to the rapacity of some of the Phanariote rulers. The prince secretly encouraged or winked at their misdeeds, until he thought they had amassed a considerable treasure by free-booting. Then, making a raid upon them with a strong military force, he deprived them of their plunder and decapitated or imprisoned them. The greater number were sent to work in the salt-mines, where (as already stated elsewhere) they usually died after the expiration of about four years.

This system of extortion and tyranny usually continued until the Porte could no longer refuse to listen to the call for redress, and in such cases intriguers for the succession were only too ready to take up the cry, and even to exaggerate the crimes of the reigning prince. The result was that one by one they were deposed, and often recalled to Constantinople, only to be disgraced, exiled, or executed. According to the historical records, there were eleven distinct hospodars in each principality between 1716 and 1768; in Wallachia the government was changed twenty-one, and in Moldavia seventeen times. In one year (1731) Constantine Mavrocordato ruled twice, and Michael Racoviça once; the former is noted as having reigned six times; the latter was re-elected in 1741, and was eventually exiled to Mitylene. Charles Ghika (1758) was exiled to Cyprus; Stephen Racoviça (1765) was strangled by order of the Porte; and so on.

But although the rulers were changed so frequently, the system not only continued, but became more and more demoralizing to the whole nation. For a time the clergy were content to bleed without drawing blood in their turn, but at length they, too, began to extort money from rich and poor alike, in order to meet the demands upon them, and prostituted the sacred offices of religion to gain their ends. Another terrible result of the Phanariote rule was the seizure by the officials of the Porte of Romanian men and women, the former to replace those who had fallen in the wars between the Turks and Russians; and the best blood of the country was sacrificed in a cause in which it had no interest. The moral degradation of the boyards also became deeper and deeper. Many turned renegades, and adopted the Mussulman faith, partly from servility, often to save themselves from being condemned to death. Others pursued that course that they might not be harassed by the Turkish officials, and others again because the oriental dress pleased them, and they desired to indulge in the practice of polygamy. Fathers educated their sons in every kind of deceit and hypocrisy to minister to their advancement in life, teaching them how to approach the dominant seigneurs and ingratiate themselves in their favor, whilst, in the eyes of the common people, the boyards had sunk so low that they had earned for themselves the name of 'sleeping dogs.' The women were even worse than the men. The height of their ambition was to form advantageous alliances without reference to their happiness in after life; the marriage tie was treated with the utmost indifference, and the clergy were often compelled, much against their will, to grant divorces in order to retain their offices and influence.

So much for the dark side of the Phanariote rule; and it is much to be regretted that all modern historians have contented themselves with looking at its unfavorable aspect, and have sought to shift all the sins and errors of the period upon the shoulders of the Greek princes. It is not our intention to follow their example, for we believe that the government of the Greek hospodars was by no means an unmixed evil. The modern descendants of those men still occupy honorable positions in Romania, but these have little to say in their defense; indeed we have heard Greeks express the opinion that it would be more creditable to them if they were to lay bare the exaggerations of evil, and bring into prominence the better traits in the character of their ancestry. That they were not all tyrants and extortioners is certain, although many, especially the earlier ones, were only too faithful servants of the Porte who may have played their part *con amore* in remembrance of the massacre of their ancestors, and in conformity with the customs of the period. But among them were brave, religious, charitable, and learned men, who contributed to raise the Romanians from a condition of barbarism to one of comparative civilization. Of this we have evidence in the law reforms, imperfect as they were, introduced by Constantine Mavrocordato; in the buildings and charitable foundations of Ypsilanti and Gregory Ghika in both Principalities (between 1768-1778); in the courage of the latter, who paid with his life the penalty of serving his adopted country; and of Nicholas Mavrojeni (1786-1790), whose boyards were too cowardly to follow him in the defense of their country against a Russian invasion.

The last-named is rather a notorious incident in Romanian history, and some writers have devoted pages to the narrative. It appears that Nicholas had received instructions from the Porte to raise a force and set himself in motion against the combined Russians and Austrians who menaced Wallachia. He thereupon assembled the boyards and called upon them to take up arms. Too cowardly, in the opinion of certain writers, or distrusting the prince, according to others, each excused himself on some flimsy pretext, whereupon Nicholas, indignant and furious, called upon one of his attendants to bring forth thirty horses, which were soon standing caparisoned in the court-yard. The prince invited his boyards to descend, and when they were arrived below, 'Now,' he cried, 'to horse!' They maintained a sullen silence, however, and no one moved. Casting a look of contempt upon them, he turned round to the horses, and, addressing one after the other, he cried, 'I make you Ban; you, Grand Vornic; you, Grand Logothet;' and so on, until he had exhausted all the offices of the State. Then, turning again to his cowardly boyards, he reminded them of the deeds of their ancestors, of Mircea, Vlad, and Michael, and denounced them as women, puppets, worse than eunuchs. Several he ordered into exile; while others, stung with shame by his taunts, mounted and followed him to victory.

This is the story of how Nicholas Mavrojeni is said to have ennobled his horses; but, if the reader wishes to hear how, after disputing every yard of ground with the invaders, he was rewarded by the Porte with an ignominious death, we must refer him to the pages of the historian.

VI.

Nothing can be more dreary and wearisome than to wade through an account of the wars between Russia and the Sublime Porte from the accession of the Phanariote rulers down to the Crimean campaign of 1853-6, and yet, for any but Romanian readers, the history of the country contains little else of interest during that period. There are two aspects of these struggles, however, which devastated the unfortunate Principalities almost as much as the incursions of the barbarians, that are well worthy of our consideration. The first is the tenacity and perseverance with which the Czars, one after the other, sought to tighten their grasp upon the Principalities, with ultimate aims upon Constantinople; the second, the occasional efforts which were made by a few patriots, backed up not so much by the boyards as by the common people, to relieve the country from foreign domination, whether Mussulman, Russian, or Austrian—for the last-named nation also sought to gain a foothold in the land.

Let us briefly review the leading events of the period referred to, and consider their bearing upon Romania of to-day. After the unsuccessful campaign of Peter the Great in which the voivodes, Cantemir and Brancovano, were enlisted on the side of the Russians, the latter made no serious attempt to interfere with the government of the Principalities until about the year 1735, when, under the Empress Anne, and in alliance with the German Emperor Charles VI., they endeavored to expel the Turks, and partially succeeded in doing so. After two campaigns, however, the allies were ingloriously defeated at Belgrade; and by the treaty of that name (1739 A.D.) they were not only compelled to restore all their conquests, but even to relinquish some of the territory of which the Porte had been deprived in the seventeenth century. The hospodars who ruled at that time in Wallachia and Moldavia were Constantine Mavrocordato and Gregory Ghika.

About twenty-five years later the Russians returned to the charge under Catherine IV., and this time with better success. Their operations extended over about six years, and the war commenced in 1768 by an act of hostility on the part of the Sultan, provoked by a Russian propaganda. In 1769-70 the Muscovites overran Moldavia and Wallachia; the former, it is said by some, with the connivance of the reigning prince, Constantine Mavrocordato III.; and, having defeated the Turks in several pitched battles, and even penetrated into Bulgaria, they actually ruled in the country until 1774 A.D., and introduced many useful reforms. Then, however, owing to the interference of Maria Theresa, Empress of Germany, who, as Queen of Hungary, herself claimed rights of suzerainty over Wallachia, and largely also in consequence of the passive resistance of the Porte, the Czarina agreed to the Treaty of Kainardji, by which, under conditions favorable to the Principalities, they were once more restored to the Porte. Among the conditions were a complete amnesty; the restitution of lands and goods to their rightful owners; freedom of worship for Christians, and liberty to build or restore places of worship; the privilege of sending two *chargés d'affaires* (one from each principality) to Constantinople; and the right on the part of the Court of St. Petersburg to speak in favor of the Principalities in cases of complaint, with the further provision that such remonstrances should be treated with the respect due from one friendly power to another.

In 1777 the Porte ceded Bucovine to Austria. The signature of the ruling Hospodar of Moldavia, Gregory Ghika, was necessary to validate the cession, but that patriotic 'Phanariote' refused to append it, whereupon he was deposed and cruelly murdered by the creatures of the Porte. We have already referred to his patriotism and its results.

In 1781-2, by an arrangement with the Porte, Catherine II. secured the right to send consuls to Bucharest and Jassy, who were maintained and served in great state at the cost and provision of the Principalities, and were authorized to exercise a certain control over their public income and expenditure for the protection of the inhabitants. This new influence was secured by Russia through the complaints of the Romanians in regard to the rapacity of the Turkish rulers; through her growing influence; and, last but not least, her threatening attitude on the Turkish frontiers. In 1788 an alliance was again formed between Russia and Austria, having for its object the dispossession of the Porte in the Principalities. This was the occasion on which Nicholas Mavrojeni is said to have ennobled his horses. He was afterwards defeated at Calafat, and after several reverses the Porte was glad to conclude treaties of peace, first with the Austrians and then (1792) with Russia at Jassy. By this treaty the Russians gained territory and secured the promise from the Porte of a more merciful government in Moldo-Wallachia, the condition of which at that time is represented to have been desperate, owing to the Phanariote exactions and the frequent change of hospodars.

Consequent upon the bitter complaints of the inhabitants the Russians again interfered in 1802, forcing the Porte to extend the duration of the rulership to seven years and to repress other abuses. About this time the first English Consul was appointed. Vaillant refers to him as 'Sir Francis,' and charges the English Government with having sent him to co-operate with Russia against Turkey. A French diplomatist also appeared at Bucharest, and, whatever part these representatives may have played in the matter, it is certain that in 1806 another Russo-Turkish war broke out. The Russians under General Michaelson overran the Principalities, held possession of the country until 1812, and then only restored it after the peace of Bucharest, by which the Russians gained the whole of Bessarabia (the river Pruth being fixed as the boundary), with the ports of Ismail, Khilia, and other places at the embouchure of the Danube.

VII.

Shortly after this time, the Hellenic regeneration, or the Hetärie as it was called, commenced in the south-east of Europe. This movement, which liberated Greece from the Ottoman yoke, brought much misery but ultimate gain to Romania. In 1821 there reigned in Wallachia Alexander Soutzo III., and in Moldavia Michael Soutzo III., two Phanariotes who, true to their traditions, had pressed upon the people with their exactions until they were ripe for a revolt. This took place in Wallachia under Theodor (or, as he is sometimes called, Tudor) Vladimiresco, an ex-officer in the Russian army (indeed, Russia is said to have fomented the Greek revolt everywhere); whilst in Moldavia a Greek called Alexander Ypsilanti joined with the reigning hospodar to drive the Turks out of that principality. Vladimiresco soon succeeded in establishing himself in Bucharest, where he ruled supreme for a short time, and whence he sent representations to the Porte complaining of the conduct of the Phanariotes, requiring their recall and the reinstatement of the native hospodars, as well as a restitution of the rights of the people under the old 'capitulations.' The reply to this was the entrance into Wallachia of a considerable army under the Pasha of Silistria, whereupon Vladimiresco withdrew towards the mountains and stationed himself at Pitești. Ypsilanti, meanwhile, had also approached Bucharest with his forces, but was unable to come to an understanding with his companion in revolt. When he heard of the withdrawal of Vladimiresco and the march of the Turkish Pasha, he believed, or professed to believe, that the former was about to betray him, and the scene of Basta and Michael was acted over again. Ypsilanti sent one of his lieutenants with a strong escort who decoyed Vladimiresco out of his tent by vain promises, carried him off by force, and then murdered him with great barbarity.

After the assassination of his rival, Ypsilanti, who claimed to represent the movement for Greek regeneration, found himself face to face with a well-organized Turkish army, whilst his own, consisting of enthusiastic Greeks and volunteers from various countries, was inferior in numbers and comparatively undisciplined. Holding discretion to be the better part of valor, he retired before the enemy, who, however, brought him to bay and offered him battle at Dragosani on the river Oltu. Here enthusiasm and devotion to their cause inspired the 'sacred battalion,' as the Greeks called themselves, with unwonted courage, and at first the Turks were unable to resist their impetuous charge with the bayonet. Ypsilanti was, however, no general, and, failing to profit by the bravery of his troops, the advantage was lost; the Turks rallied, a rout ensued, and Ypsilanti fled, leaving his lieutenants to resist for a time and then to die gloriously in defense of their liberties. He escaped across the Carpathians into Austria, was seized by order of the Government, imprisoned in the fortress of Munkács, and some writers say he was afterwards executed.

VIII.

Two important results for Romania resulted from the Greek rising. The first was the termination of the Phanariote rule and the restoration of the native princes, Gregory Ghika being appointed Prince of Wallachia, and John Stourdza of Moldavia. The reason of this change was that the Greek hospodars had made common cause with the insurgents; and we cannot do better than close this eventful period in the history of the country than by summarizing the Phanariote rule in the words of Consul Wilkinson, who says: 'From the period at which this system was introduced to the beginning of the present century, being a space of ninety years, Wallachia alone has passed through the hands of forty different princes independently of the time when it was occupied by the Russians from 1770 to 1774, by the Austrians and Russians from 1789 to 1792, and by the Russians again from 1806 to 1812.' 'Few of them died of natural death, and the Turkish scimetar was perhaps frequently employed with justice among them. In a political point of view, the short reigns of most of these princes offer nothing of importance or interest to deserve a place in history.' From this brief judgment of one who lived at the time of their extinction, our readers will see that we have not dealt uncharitably with the *régime* of the Phanariotes.

Another of the results of the Greek insurrection was the inevitable Russo-Turkish war. Then followed the occupation of the country by the Russians; what Carlyle might have called the hand-shaking of incompatible tyrannies; and eventually the Peace of Adrianople, to which city the Russian arms had penetrated (1829). The stipulations of that treaty may be summed up in a few words. A large indemnity to Russia, with continued occupation until it should be liquidated, and a Muscovite protectorate of the Principalities; the suzerainty and an annual tribute for the Porte, and complete autonomy with the appointment of life-long hospodars for the Principalities. By a subsequent ukase known as the 'Reglement Organique,' the Court of St. Petersburg further expressed its wishes in regard to the internal government of the Principalities; and this document having been confirmed by the Porte after great procrastination, the Russian forces were withdrawn from the Principalities in 1834, and two princes of the houses of Stourdza and Ghika were again appointed hospodars.

IX.

We have said that two phases in the history of this period are interesting to the historian—the gradual encroachments of Russia on the one hand, and on the other the patriotic efforts of the nationalists to secure independence. With the Greek rising of 1821-2, and the prospect of complete liberty, a new spirit was awakened, which took the form first of a national intellectual regeneration, and then of what proved to be an unsuccessful struggle for independence. With both these movements the name of John Heliad Radulesco (known in history as Heliade or Eliad) is inseparably connected as *littérateur* and patriot. His name first appears conspicuously about the year 1826, when, in conjunction with Constantine Golesco, a returned exile and friend of the unfortunate Vladimiresco, and with the concurrence and support of the reigning hospodar, Gregory Ghika, he endeavored to revive the national language, which had been displaced by Greek in consequence of the long-continued Phanariote rule. He was himself a poet of no mean order, and by his national songs he stirred the hearts of the people. But poetry did not absorb his whole attention. An able man of science, for that day, he himself imparted instruction in geography, logic, and mathematics, in the colleges of which he promoted the establishment. Of these one was founded on the remains of an ancient convent at St. Sava, the other at

Craiova, and concurrently with this effort, to promote collegiate education primary and normal schools were also established. But the march of enlightenment did not end here; national journals and a national theater were included in the scheme of the patriots. The hospodars, too, performed their share of the general advancement. They founded hospitals, promoted agriculture, welcomed back those who had emigrated before the scourge of war, and sought by every means in their power to give security to the national industry.

But the unfortunate geographical position of the Principalities, which made them the battle-field of the two contending powers of the Orient, still militated against the complete liberation of Romania, and her efforts at regeneration were watched with jealousy by both her powerful semi-barbarous neighbors. The period soon arrived, however, when, for a time at least, the intrigues of emperors, sultans, and courts were unavailing, and when crowns were at a decided discount—the great European convulsion of 1848. Then, when the French monarchy fell and the rulers of other European States fled from their dominions into a more or less abiding exile, the awakening of nationalities extended to Moldo-Wallachia, and caused a patriotic rising far more hopeful and for a time more successful than the revolt of 1821; and the Principalities would no doubt have been permanently freed from foreign domination had not disunion among the national leaders once more prevented such a desirable issue. In the year of revolution, Nicholas I. being the Czar, and Abdul Medjid (the 'Sick Man') Sultan, simultaneous risings took place in the Principalities. The one in Moldavia was headed by a number of leading boyards, who at first contented themselves with petitioning for the restoration of their liberties. They were seized by order of the hospodar, Michael Stourdza, and sent into confinement, but most of them escaped and returned to reorganize the revolt. In the same year, however, as we shall hear presently, the Russians invaded the principality, entered Jassy, and quelled the revolution.

In Wallachia the rising assumed more serious proportions. It was led by Heliad and the brothers Golesco, George Maghiero, a Greek by descent, Tell, Chapka, a priest, and by three young men, two of whom will hereafter be spoken of in connection with the Romania, of to-day—Demetrius and John Bratiano and C. Rosetti. Although all these men were united in the desire to liberate their fatherland from the heavy burdens with which it was oppressed, they disagreed as to the best mode of proceeding. Long experience had taught them that between the two fires of St. Petersburg and Constantinople there was little hope of escape, and some leaned to the former, others to the latter power, whilst the younger men, the Bratianos and Rosetti, looked anxiously to Western Europe and its advanced civilization for succour. The hospodar Bibesco soon yielded before the storm, and fled to Kronstadt in Transylvania. A provisional government was formed, dissolved, and formed again. Great assemblages of the people took place at Bucharest; proclamations were issued and oaths administered and taken; but the whole thing eventually resolved itself into a 'Princely Lieutenancy,' under the suzerainty of the Porte. This was at first recognized by the Turkish general, Suleiman Pasha, who along with Omar Pasha had entered Wallachia with Turkish armies; for it suited the policy of the Porte to look favourably upon a rising which was chiefly directed against Russian influence in the Principalities. But the Muscovite Cabinet was not easily outwitted. Nicholas witnessed the rising with equal satisfaction, for it justified a new intervention in the affairs of Moldo-Wallachia. He issued a proclamation, calling the revolution the work of a turbulent minority whose ideas of government were plagiarized from the socialistic and democratic propaganda of Europe. This proclamation was followed by a march of the Russians into the disturbed provinces as 'liberators.' The nationalist leaders were glad to escape to France, Omar Pasha having occupied and plundered Bucharest on the Russian approach, and a convention—that of Balta-Liman—was entered into between Russia and Turkey, which deprived the Principalities of all their electoral rights, substituted a divan, or council of ministers, and reserved to the two contracting powers the nomination of hospodars. Russia, however, managed to get the lion's share even in this negotiation, for, contrary to the understanding, she succeeded in appointing both hospodars, Stirbei in Wallachia, and Alexander Ghika in Moldavia, thus largely increasing her influence in both Principalities.

X.

Much has been said here, and a great deal more in the works of those French writers who were unfriendly towards Russia, concerning her intrigues and encroachments in the Principalities, but it is only fair to admit that her interference invariably resulted in the ameliorating of their condition. This the French writers sometimes grudgingly admit, and the facts of history clearly prove. In nearly every instance Russian interference meant relief to the peasantry and enforced moderation in the rulers. In 1710, when Cantemir III. of Moldavia sought the aid of Peter the Great, it was 'to put an end to the spoliations of the Porte.' In 1769 Constantine Mavrocordato entered into secret relations with Catherine II., and after the Russian invasion the Porte was compelled by the Treaty of Kainardji to grant autonomy to the Principalities, and to diminish its exactions; in 1802, through Russian remonstrances, abuses were suppressed and the evil-doers punished. In 1812 the chicanery of the rulers and the exactions of the Porte had brought the people to the brink of starvation; the Russians interfered, and put a limit to the demands of the Porte; but after their departure, we are told, the current value of agricultural produce again fell so low that it was impossible for the cultivator to live, and this circumstance, along with the renewed exactions of the rulers and officials, once more brought ruin upon the peasantry. In 1820 Wilkinson, who, it must be remembered, was Consul at Bucharest, and who was far from being enamored of Russia, says: 'During my residence in the Principalities several instances have occurred within my observation of very active exertion on the part of Russia to keep the accustomed system of extortion in restraint, and to relieve the inhabitants from oppression, and such exertion has certainly on many occasions prevented the condition of the inhabitants from becoming worse.'

But that the ultimate design of Russia was to secure and incorporate the Principalities as part of her general scheme of aggression, there can be no doubt in the mind of anyone who has followed her operations previous to the Crimean campaign. That and subsequent events may be said to belong to contemporary history; but we must briefly refer to such incidents of the war as affected the Danubian Principalities and laid the foundation of Romanian freedom. The Emperor Nicholas had picked a wolf-and-lamb quarrel with the Porte, of which the ostensible ground was the protection of subjects professing the Greek Catholic faith in the 'holy places;' and little expecting, perhaps little caring, that he would arouse the jealousy of France and England, he had sent an ultimatum to the Porte, demanding the right of intervention in conformity with the Treaty of Kainardji, threatening the invasion and occupation of the Danubian Principalities in default of immediate acquiescence. Not having received the satisfaction he required, he ordered General Gortschakoff to cross the Pruth and to take possession of and hold the Principalities. This was done in the month of July 1853. In September the Turkish Commander-in-Chief on the Danube demanded an immediate evacuation of those territories, and, failing compliance, war was declared. For some time the Russians, fearing the enmity of Austria, which had massed troops on the Wallachian frontier, remained on the defensive, but in October Omar Pasha assumed the aggressive, sending a small force across the Danube at Vidin, and it was thought that the straggle between the contending forces would take place in 'Lesser Wallachia.' Omar Pasha, however, either intended this as a feint, or changed his plan, for he soon afterwards occupied strong positions on the Danube at Turtukai and Oltenitza, between Silistria and Rustchuk, and was there attacked by a Russian force, which he succeeded in repulsing. No results followed this encounter; the Russians retreated towards Bucarest, and the Turks fell back across the Danube into Bulgaria.

In February 1854 the French and English Governments sent an ultimatum to Russia, requiring her to evacuate the Principalities, and in March they declared war against her. In June Austria followed suit, so far as demanding the evacuation of Moldo-Wallachia, and received permission from the Porte to drive the Russians out of the Principalities, and occupy them with her troops. She, however, contented herself during the continuance of the war with accumulating forces on her frontiers, and no doubt it was this threatening attitude which at length compelled Russia to evacuate them. Meanwhile active hostilities were proceeding between Omar Pasha and Gortschakoff. In the early part of 1854, the Russians having met with a reverse at Cetate, near Calafat, the Russian army was ordered to invade Turkey, and, having succeeded in crossing into the Dobrudscha at Galatz, Braila, and Ismail, it was deemed necessary to capture Silistria as a strategic post, in order to ensure the safety of the advancing army. In May 1854 the Russians attacked that fortress unsuccessfully, and after they had attempted to storm it four times, the Turks (in June) assumed the offensive, and made a sally, during which one of the Russian generals was slain. In the same month Nicholas, finding himself threatened by the Western allies in the Black Sea, and fearing to make an open enemy of Austria, whose forces were constantly increasing on her frontier, gave orders for raising the siege of Silistria, and subsequently for the entire withdrawal of his troops from the Principalities. This was not, however, effected until July, nor before the Russians had sustained another defeat from the Turks at Giurgevo.

Then it was that the army was completely withdrawn, the Turkish vanguard entered Bucharest, and, says one of the historians of the war, 'the Wallachian nobles celebrated a Te Deum in the metropolitan church to commemorate the restoration of Turkish supremacy—the same boyards who, in 1829, kissed the hands of the Russians who had freed them from the Turkish yoke.'

As for the hospodars. Stirbei of Wallachia, and Alexander Ghika of Moldavia, they had retired for safety to Vienna shortly after the outbreak of hostilities, and remained there until September, when the Austrians occupied the country with the approval of the Porte. They then returned for a short period, but Stirbei again abdicated permanently a month afterwards. The Romanians wore compelled by the Russians to serve in their armies as long as they occupied the country, but a Turkish amnesty relieved them from the consequences of this procedure.

The military operations of the contending Powers external to the Principalities have an interest for us only in their results. After the termination of the Crimean campaign, when Russia was compelled to sue for peace, the Treaty of Paris was concluded, and it contained stipulations of vital consequence to Moldo-Wallachia.

These stipulations may be summarized as follows:—The neutralisation of the navigation of the Danube, which was placed under the control of a European Commission; the cession by Russia to Turkey (and thus to Moldavia) of a portion of Bessarabia at the embouchure of the Danube; and the re-organisation, on an entirely autonomic basis, but still under the suzerainty of the Porte, of the Danubian Principalities. In the year 1857, before the deliberations of the European Powers had given permanent effect to the stipulations of the Treaty of Paris, a movement was actively proceeding in both Principalities, the object of which was to effect their union under one governing head.

The exiles of 1848, who had fled to Paris, and there endeavored by their published works to keep alive the spirit of independence in Romania, now returned to their native country and renewed an active agitation at home. Among those who then and thereafter strove for the liberties of their country were John Bratiano, C.A. Rosetti, two members of the family of Ghika, Demetrius Stourdza, John Cantacuzene, and other laymen, and Golesco and others of the military profession. These so far attained their end that, after a great deal of idle intervention on the part of Turkey and the other European Powers, most of whom were intriguing for their own hands rather than for the welfare of the Principalities, they succeeded in obtaining from a conference of the Powers at Paris, in 1858, a kind of agreement, which, whilst it insisted upon the retention in each Principality of a separate prince or hospodar, gave to each an elective parliament, and admitted of a partial fusion, under a kind of central commission, for the 'united Principalities.' This was a species of compromise which was no doubt satisfactory to the guaranteeing Powers, with their conflicting interests, but was not at all to the taste of the young nation struggling for union and independence. By a clever and perfectly justifiable manœuvre the people of Moldavia and Wallachia proceeded to supplement the deliberations and decisions of the Powers, by each choosing the same ruler, Captain John Couza, and, in spite of protestations from the Porte, which refused to recognize this as a lawful proceeding, Couza, under the title of Alexander John I., mounted the united throne as *Prince of Romania*. In 1861, chiefly in consequence of the recommendation of the guaranteeing Powers, the Porte assented to the union.

XI.

Prince Couza was born at Galatz in 1820. He was of an old boyard family, and was educated at Jassy, Athens, and Paris. In 1845 he married Helena, the daughter of another boyard, Rosetti, and subsequently held high offices in the State. His princess was a patriotic lady who founded and supported many charitable institutions, among others the orphan asylum known as the Asyle Hélène, of which we have already spoken; and had her husband recognized her virtues, and remembered his own obligations to her; he would probably have still sat upon the throne of Romania. For there is no doubt that during the earlier part of his reign, which lasted from 1859 to 1866, he enjoyed the cordial support of all parties in the State; but he soon endeavored to render himself absolute, and in 1864 he effected a *coup d'état*, very similar to the one which has recently been perpetrated by the Prince of Bulgaria, in all probability under the same tutelage. In his case, however, the nation refused to submit to such an arbitrary proceeding, and although it succeeded for a time, that, coupled with his avarice, gross immorality, and general misgovernment, led to his ultimate downfall. In 1864 the monasteries were secularized, that is to say, they were claimed as State property, a proceeding which was sanctioned by the guaranteeing Powers against payment of an indemnity. In 1865 a complete reform took place in the relations between the landed proprietors and the peasantry, who were freed from feudal obligations and became part owners of the soil. Of this reform we have already spoken at length. As we have said, however, the personal actions of the Prince, who enriched himself at the expense of a still suffering country, sought by every means in his power to obtain absolute rule, and led an openly immoral life, against which his advisers protested and warned him in vain, led to what some have called a conspiracy, but which was an uprising of all the leading representatives of the people, lay and military, who united to drive him from the throne.

The so-called abdication, but really the deposition, of Prince Couza, as it was narrated at the time, was effected as follows. The conspiracy being ripe, on February 11 [23], 1866, a sufficiently strong body of military, acting under the orders of General Golesco and others, surrounded the palace in which the Prince was lodged, and a number of officers then forced their way inside. On entering the palace they proceeded to the room of the Prince, arresting on their way thither M. L—— and two officers of the body-guard. Before they forced the door the Prince, it seems, had a presentiment of some danger, and cried from within, 'Don't enter, for I shall fire.' Before the sentence was finished, however, the door was burst open, and he saw before him the conspirators with revolvers in their hands. He was cowardly enough (says the narrative) not to fire once. It is possible that if he had known that they had an order not to fire, whatever might happen, he would have killed one or other of them. Or, perhaps, the presence of Madame —— prevented him from offering resistance, for she was there undressed.

'What do you want?' he asked, trembling.

'We have brought your Highness's abdication,' said Captain C——. 'Will you sign it?'

'I have neither pen nor ink,' he answered.

'We thought of that,' said one of the conspirators.

'I have no table.'

'For this once, I offer myself as such,' said Captain P——.

Having no alternative, the Prince then signed the following act of abdication, as it lay on the shoulders of the stooping officer who had condescended to serve as a desk for the occasion.

'We, Alexander, according to the will of the whole nation, and the oath we took on ascending the throne, this day, February 11, 1866, lay down the reins of government and relegate the same to a princely *locum-tenens* and to the ministry chosen by the people.

(Signed) 'ALEXANDER JOHN.'

'This has been my wish for a long time,' said the Prince after having signed; 'but circumstances not dependent upon myself have caused me to postpone. Spite of all this, I was willing to do it in May.'

After he had signed the act of abdication the conspirators made him dress, and led him to a carriage where Ch——, in the dress of a coachman, received him and drove him to the house of M. Ciocarlanu. Madame ——, on the other hand, was taken home to her own house after she had habited herself. Immediately after Couza's arrest the bells rang out a merry peal, a band of music struck up before the theatre, and masses of people collected before the palace where the Provisional Government had installed itself, and shortly afterwards issued the following proclamation:—

'Romanians,

During seven years you have shown Europe what can be effected by patriotism and civic virtue. Unhappily you were mistaken in your selection of the prince whom you called to lead the nation. Anarchy and corruption, violation of the laws, squandering of the national finances, degradation of the country at home and abroad, these have characterised the conduct of this culpable Government. Romanians, the princely *locum-tenens* will maintain the constitutional government in its integrity. It will uphold public order, and remove personal ambition from the altar of the Fatherland.

'Romanians, by the election of a foreigner as Prince of Romania, the votes of the Divan will become an accomplished fact.'

Let us add a few words concerning this proceeding. We have heard blame attributed to the revolutionists, who, as already stated, comprised the leading statesmen of the country, for using force in order to ensure Couza's abdication, and so far as the mere legality of the document is concerned, his signature, thus obtained, was of course valueless. But in order to be able to form a correct opinion on the crisis and the acts of the revolutionists, it would be necessary to understand not only the character of the prince (which would alone have justified extreme measures, if one half be true that has been written concerning him), but also to estimate the effect of any delay that might have arisen from a more pacific and deliberate course of action. The popular leaders had not forgotten the lessons of 1848, and it was not likely they would be so insensate as to give time for Russian or Turkish intrigues once more to break down the barriers of their hardly-won liberties. That the nation was satisfied is proved by the sequel. No one troubled himself about Couza, who was allowed to withdraw from Romania laden with the spoils of his reign; and when afterwards the name of the present ruler was placed before the people it was accepted with joy and acclamation.

But we have had another reason for dwelling at greater length than has been customary with historians upon this incident in Romanian annals. It was to show the kind of example in morality, or rather immorality and faithlessness, which was set by one of the princes of the country so recently as fifteen or sixteen years since. Such conduct may be treated with contempt in countries having a well-established and settled constitution, but in a new-born nationality it could not fail to work great mischief, which has not yet been fully remedied despite the example of an unblemished Court.

CHAPTER XIV.

FROM THE DEPOSITION OF PRINCE COUZA (1866) TO THE CORONATION OF KING CHARLES (1881).

Accession of Prince Charles of Hohenzollern—Signs the Constitution—Former differences between the Prince and the Parliament—(Note: State of parties with leaders in 1881)—Action of Russia prior to the war of 1877—Turkish incapacity and obstinacy—Perplexing position of Romania—Reluctance of the nation to interfere—First attitude of neutrality—The Porte declares the Prince an enemy—The Prince and army organization—Value of Romanian co-operation to Russia—The Russian army of operations—Crosses the Danube and occupies Sistova and the Shipka Pass—Repeated defeats at Plevna and elsewhere—Gloomy outlook for the Russians—The Romanians cross the Danube—First estimates of them—Contemptuous criticisms and anecdotes—Changing views regarding them—Prince Charles appointed Commander-in-Chief of the allies before Plevna—Defenses of Plevna—The Grivitza redoubt—Strength and composition of the armies—Commencement of the attack (August 31, 1877)—Capture of Loftcha by Skobeleff—Russian operations against Plevna—Great assault of September 11—Defeat of the Russians—Ineffectual bravery of Skobeleff—His appearance after the repulse—The Romanians—The 'indomitable' Grivitza redoubt—Romanian approaches (September 7 to 10)—Assaults and final capture and retention of the redoubt by the Romanians (11th)—Carnage in the redoubt—Unsuccessful attempt to capture a second redoubt—Flattering criticisms upon their bravery—Further Romanian victories and services in the war—Failure of Osman Pasha to break the lines of the allies—His submission—Interview between Osman, the Grand Duke, and Prince Charles—Russian ingratitude to Romania—'Exchange' of Bessarabia for the Dobrudscha—Treaty of San Stephano and Berlin Conference—Romania independent—Coronation of the King and Queen—Conclusion of historical review.

I.

After the fall of Couza the two Chambers elected the Count of Flanders, a younger brother of the King of Belgium, as his successor, but, owing probably to the threatening attitude of the Porte, that Prince declined the honor. Their choice then fell upon the reigning sovereign, Prince Charles of Hohenzollern (son of Prince Charles Anton, of Hohenzollern-Siegmaringen), who accepted the nomination, and was proclaimed Prince of Romania on the anniversary of his birthday, April 20, 1866, and was received with great joy on his arrival at the capital. The Sublime Porte protested as usual, but this time the Romanians threatened—at least, they determined to uphold their choice, and collected a strong force with that object. After vainly endeavoring to enlist the Powers on his side, the Sultan gave his assent to the nomination, and the Prince was invested with the sovereignty for himself and his heirs.

Meanwhile the national leaders had prepared the draft of the constitution under which Romania is now governed, of which the leading stipulations, along with the names of its framers, will be found in the Appendix (III.), and on June 30 [July 12] it was approved and signed by the Prince, who at the same time took the qualifying oath, first at Bucharest, and shortly afterwards at Jassy, where he was received with equal enthusiasm by the Moldavians.

Few rulers have had the obstacles to contend with that greeted Prince Charles on his accession to the throne of Romania, and few indeed have managed so completely to overcome their difficulties and to win the affections of their subjects—a task which has, however, been materially lightened in his case by the co-operation of his talented consort, whom, as Princess Elizabeth of Wied, he espoused in November 1869. The liberties of Romania had not been of slow growth, and the people who for sixteen centuries had been the downtrodden vassals, first of this and then of that dominant race of barbarians, were naturally, a little awkward when they were called upon to assume the responsibilities, as well as to enjoy the privileges, of emancipation. We will not dwell upon the party dissensions which for a series of years militated against the smooth working of the new Constitution, nor upon the known fact that the Prince well-nigh relinquished the reins of power in consequence of the repeated changes of ministry and the unworthy jealousies of those who, having first selected him as a foreigner, subsequently charged this against him as a disqualification. Nor must we examine too narrowly all the causes of this restlessness in the people. They had been so often betrayed by their rulers, and were so jealous of their newly-won liberties, that, it may be, the acts of a prince of the house of Hohenzollern were not always in accord with the tastes of a semi-republican legislature. This friction, through the devotion of the ruler and the good sense and patriotism of his advisers, has ceased to exist; and, far from there being now a bitter strife of parties, one of the Romanian leaders deplores that there is not a more active and powerful opposition to the ministry, which was last elected in 1875, and has for more than six years guided the destinies of the nation.

II.

Let us now consider the circumstances which lately enabled Romania to throw off the last traces of her vassalage, and to take her place in the comity of European nations; and with a brief narrative of those events we must bring this imperfect outline of her past history to a close. The story of the last Russo-Turkish war must be within the memory of all our readers who take the slightest interest in Oriental politics. How Russia, chafing under the restrictions which had been put upon her by the Treaty of Paris, had succeeded in obtaining a modification of that treaty, which gave her once more the right of entrance into the Black Sea; how, resuming her favorite *rôle* of protectress of the Christian inhabitants of Turkey, she intervened in the affairs of those nations who stood between her and Constantinople; how the Servians and Montenegrins, incited by her, rose in revolt, and the Bulgarians followed suit; how the European Powers, sympathizing with Turkey on the one hand, in consequence of the renewed machinations and transparent designs of her powerful northern enemy, and on the other despairing of her on account of the barbarities with which she endeavored to quell the rising in her vassal provinces, the inherent weakness of her rule, and the bankrupt condition of her finances, they were compelled at length to leave her at the mercy of her foe. To repeat the narrative of these would be telling an oft-told tale. But when, after the final break-up of the Conference of Constantinople in January 1877, the Cross and the Crescent were once more opposed to each other, and when the Russian forces were massed on the eastern bank of the Pruth, then came the moment at which it behooved the newly-liberated nation, which had so often been the victim of the 'holy' strife, to decide on which side it would array itself. Indeed, Romania had little choice in the matter; the critics who have censured her policy, and have charged her with breach of faith towards her suzerain the Porte (and we know there are many such in this country), cannot have carefully considered her past history; nor have reflected upon the position in which she was placed. As a matter of preference, the young nation which was about being dragged into this ruthless strife could have none, and might with justice have exclaimed, 'A plague on both your houses!' What cared they, on the one hand (and this was the popular sentiment), for the hypocritical crusade undertaken for purposes of aggrandizement; or, on the other, what sympathy could they have with the moribund State which had ever been to them as the daughters of the horseleech, and whose atrocities were identical with those that were perpetrated in the days when Huns and Vandals devastated their own fair plains? If Romania in her then condition (now it would be different) had opposed the passage of the Russian forces, they would have entered her territory as enemies, the war would have been carried on once more within her borders, and, beggared and prostrate, she might at best have reckoned upon retaining her political independence through the intervention of the European Powers; though, looking at the fact that these had recognized Russia as their executioner in Turkey, it is very questionable whether they would have interfered for the protection of Romania, and whether she would not have fallen to Russia along with Bessarabia. On the other hand, if she had actively sided with either Power, her national independence and the happiness of her people would have been staked upon the result. She chose the wise, and indeed the only course, namely, that of allowing her powerful neighbor to pass through her dominions, stipulating that, so far as Russia could help it, she should be spared the desolation and horrors of war within her frontiers. But what course did the Porte adopt? Not recognizing the *force majeure* which had driven Romania to this decision, she was suicidal enough to declare her an enemy, and to threaten to depose the Prince, thus giving to her bitterest foe an ally who, at a critical period, in self-defense, turned the scale against her, and caused her to lose some of her fairest provinces. For the Romanians well knew, after the declared enmity of the Porte, that the defeat of the Russians and their withdrawal into their own territories would at once have been followed by all the incidents of Turkish rule, of which for centuries they had had such a bitter experience.

Among the valuable services which Prince Charles had rendered to his adopted country before the outbreak of the Russo-Turkish war was the organization of a national army on the German model. Under Prince Couza the whole standing army of the two Principalities was at first 8,400 men, but he raised it to 25,000 strong, and officered it on the French system. When Prince Charles received the investiture at the hands of the Sultan in 1867, the army was limited to 30,000 men of all ranks; but he substituted German for French officers, and sent young Romanians to Germany to study military tactics. In 1874 the standing army numbered 18,542 men of all arms, and the territorial forces 43,744, making a total of 62,286 men and 14,353 horses; these were armed with 52 steel Krupp guns, besides about 200 of an inferior description; 25,000 Peabody rifles, and 20,000 Prussian needle-guns, raised in 1875 to 100,000 rifles of the best description.

The sanitary services and the military hospitals had been organized by General Dr. Davila, a French physician, of whom we have frequently spoken elsewhere, and who still occupies the post of Director of Hospitals, &c., and of the Medical School at Bucharest.

III.

With an army thus constituted and disciplined, Prince Charles went into the Russo-Turkish war as an ally of the Russians, although, at first, not as an active one; and as the success of that terrible war relieved Romania from the last vestiges of her dependence upon Turkey, we will endeavor to collect within as narrow limits as possible a few of the leading events wherein she participated, and which affected her claim to European attention.

That the Romanians rendered valuable services to the Russians before they co-operated actively in arms is well known, and also that the latter had pressing need for such assistance. In May 1877 every facility was given for the passage of troops over the Romanian railways, hospital equipment taking the precedence, and the Romanian civil and military hospitals opened their doors to receive the Russian sick; in fact, disastrous as were the Russian reverses throughout the war, they would have entailed far greater misery upon their wounded soldiers if it had not been for the systematic aid which they received from the Romanians. Then, in preparing for the defense of their own bank of the Danube, the latter were diverting the attention of the Turks, whose gunboats amused themselves in making harmless excursions up and down the river, pretty much as our fleet did between Besika Bay and the Dardanelles, and they were making a line of defense for the Russians in case they should have been obliged to recross tho Danube. Here it is that we first make the acquaintance of Prince Charles, who traveled from post to post on the river inspecting the defenses. 'Born a Hohenzollern, and reared an officer in the Prussian army,' says a writer who accompanied him on this tour, 'it is little wonder that Prince Charles of Romania is above all things a soldier. Since his election to the headship of the Principalities he has sedulously devoted a large share of his energies to the improvement, or rather, in the first instance, to the creation of a Romanian army, and that his labor has not been lost is apparent to any man having any conversation with military matters, who has spent the last few weeks in the territory over which Prince Charles holds sway.' The prince had at his disposal two army corps, each numbering 28,000 men, fully equipped, whilst the militia, whose strength was about 100,000, was ready for mobilization at the shortest notice. As to the fighting qualities of these troops writers differ, and we shall refer presently to the changes that took place in the estimation in which they were held as the war progressed; but even at the commencement there were those who lauded their coolness, and said that they did not exhibit any of that tremor under fire which is not wholly unnatural in young soldiers.

Before these men were called into action, however, their powerful allies had suffered terrible defeats at the hands of the enemy. Dealing only with that division of the Russian army which was engaged in Bulgaria, we have to note the following events. On June 27, 1877, the main body of Russians, or the 'army of operations,' as it was called, which was under the command of the Grand Duke Nicholas, crossed the Danube in floating ferries from Simnitza to Sistova, feints having been made to concentrate and pass over in other places at the same time, so as to mislead the Turks as to the intended point of crossing. Although some efforts were made by the latter to prevent the landing on the Bulgarian shore, which resulted in many being killed and wounded on either side, the Russians effected the passage in safety and occupied Sistova, where they found all the houses of the inhabitants sacked and plundered by the Turks, who had beaten a retreat. The Emperor and the Grand Duke Nicholas were either on the spot or in the immediate vicinity at the time of the crossing, the headquarters being then at Ploiesti, on the Bucharest and Orsova, railway, and from that time forward they sustained a series of terrible reverses.

As soon as a sufficient force was landed, they divided the army into three sections, one of which, under General Ghourko, pressed on to the famous Shipka Pass in the Balkans, where he encountered the brave enemy; he occupied the pass on July 19. Another section under the Grand Duke himself—part of the 9th Army Corps—marched onwards to the equally well-known position of Plevna, where Osman Pasha was in command of the Turkish forces, and where the Russians met with their first check. General Krüdener, who commanded the attacking force, was not only repulsed, but, being assailed in his turn by the Turks, he was badly beaten. Two days afterwards, having been reinforced, he, in conjunction with General Schahofskoy, commanding a force of 32,000 men, made a second assault on Plevna, but they were again defeated with terrible loss. On July 31 Ghourko met with a still more serious defeat. He had penetrated with a Russo-Bulgarian force as far as Eski-Zagra (or Zara), where he met the Turks under Suleiman Pasha, and, after a sanguinary encounter, he was not only repulsed, but compelled to withdraw to the Shipka Pass. Suleiman Pasha followed him and succeeded in occupying the village of Shipka, but his attempts to drive the Russians from the pass were unsuccessful, and on August 27 he discontinued his operations and telegraphed for reinforcements, the Russians having in the meantime also received theirs. Suleiman Pasha did not renew the attempt until September 17; and, although at one time he had so far discounted his success as to telegraph a victory to Constantinople, he was finally repulsed.

Added to these and other reverses in Europe, there came tale after tale of disaster in Asia. Kars, which had been besieged by the Russians, was successfully relieved by the Turks under Muktar Pasha, just as, a few months later, Erzeroum was twice attacked by the Russians, who were as many times repulsed. Then it was, when the skies were lowering on all sides, that the Russian emperor and his princes and generals began to look eagerly for aid from their ally north of the Danube; and then, for the safety of his own country, Prince Charles entered the field with his brave little army of Romanians, and, recalling the days of Stephen and of Michael, and emulating the prowess of the field of Kalugereni, he succeeded in turning the tide of victory, and in saving the honor of that ally, from whom lie subsequently received such poor acknowledgment.

IV.

Up to August 25 we hear little or nothing of the movements of the Romanians, and in every case the fighting was done by the Russians, either alone or in conjunction with their ruthless allies the Bulgarians, the operations being then spoken of as those of the 'Russo-Bulgarian' forces; but on the date named, or thereabouts, the main portion of the Romanian army crossed the Danube, and thenceforward the Bulgarians are seldom mentioned, and the contest is prosecuted by the 'allies,' or the 'Russo-Romanian' army. At first the Romanian soldiers receive scant regard at the hands of the chroniclers: indeed, on one or two occasions they are referred to with marked contempt. Writing from Giurgevo on June 5 (that was before the Russians had crossed the Danube at Simnitza), one of the correspondents says:—'Whilst eating and talking, I heard one or two curious incidents that occurred here when the Cossacks first came. In the course of reconnoitering the country, five Cossacks, with an under-officer, came upon a post of twenty Romanian soldiers, likewise under the command of an under-officer. The five Cossacks immediately arrested the twenty Romanians, brought them in to headquarters, and reported them to General Skobeleff as prisoners of some unknown army. The Cossacks were not quite sure, apparently, whether they were Turks or not, so they thought that they had better bring them in, an operation to which the Romanians, although vastly superior in numbers, consented with not a little murmuring.'

This anecdote, it must be understood, was told by a party of Russian officers, and is unworthy of critical examination, but it shows in what estimation they held the men who were afterwards to be their indispensable helpmates, and in a sense their leaders and preservers. Other writers represented the Romanian soldiers in a more favorable light from the beginning of the war. Their coolness under fire has already been mentioned, and the same correspondent, in describing the defensive operations at Kalafat, says: 'I was struck with the admirable conduct at this time of the Romanian gunners, who never flinched in the slightest degree under the trying ordeal.' After their defeats before Plevna and elsewhere, the Russians, too, began to estimate their allies at something nearer their real value.

'The Russian authorities,' writes the same correspondent in the month of August, 'are greatly pleased with the appearance and apparent efficiency of the Romanian artillery. Indeed, the Romanian troops are everywhere now spoken of with a consideration not previously evinced.'

No more talk now of five Russians running in twenty Romanians; and we shall hear quite a different story presently. And not alone had the soldiers risen in Muscovite esteem, but the Russians were beginning to understand that there might be some virtue in the commanders also; for about September 1, or a day or two previously, they so far admitted their superiority as to invite Prince Charles to take the command-in-chief of the whole Russo-Romanian army before Plevna, which he did, with the Russian general Zotoff as chief of his staff and second in command.

On this occasion he issued an address to the Romanian soldiers, reminding them that success for the Turks would mean pillage and desolation in their fatherland, assuring them that, although their numbers were few, he had confidence in their courage, and in their ability to retain for Romania the good opinion which she deserved and enjoyed among the nations of Europe. He concluded by announcing, in modest terms, his own appointment as Commander-in-chief of the allied armies.

V.

On August 31, Osman Pasha had made a sortie against the besiegers, in which he was eventually repulsed with heavy loss, and then it was that under the new command a fresh attack on Plevna was decided upon. In order, however, to understand the events which followed, and the part taken therein by the Romanians, it is necessary that we should briefly describe the position and constitution of the forces engaged, and refer to the operations which preceded the assault.

The scene of the long-continued struggle is an undulating country, and Plevna, the center of attack and defense, is in the hollow of a valley running in a northerly and southerly direction. The ground adjacent to this valley was described by one of the war correspondents as consisting of great solid waves with their faces set edge ways to the valley of Plevna. To describe it in detail here would be impossible, but the positions of the attacking and defending armies were very simple. The Turkish positions were, roughly speaking, 'a horseshoe, with its convexity pointing east, and the town of Plevna standing about the center of the base.' Another writer compares it to 'a reaping-hook, with the point opposite Bukova, the middle of the curve opposite Grivica, the junction of the handle close on to Plevna, and the end of the handle at Krishine.'

The Russians had been surrounding this horseshoe, leaving the base open, and the form of their attack on this occasion was in the line of their environment straight to their front. The main point of interest in the struggle, so far as we are concerned, is the Turkish redoubt of *Grivica* or *Grivitza*, the strongest of all the positions of defense: this was situated on the toe, if we may so call it, of the horseshoe, and directly opposite was the Russo-Romanian center.

The Russo-Romanian army numbered about 80,000 infantry, of whom 28,000 were Romanians, in two corps, under Colonels George and Alexander Angelescu, and 10,000 cavalry, whereof 4,000 were Romanians. The whole Romanian division was commanded by General Cernat; the Russians by Baron Krüdener, General Kriloff, Prince Meretinsky, and the brave but erratic General Skobeleff; and this army of 90,000 men was provided with 250 field and 20 siege guns. The number of the defenders under Osman Pasha is estimated at about 70,000 men.

Here is a concise account of the attack. After the unsuccessful sortie of Osman Pasha on August 31, in which the Russians recovered all the positions temporarily occupied by the enemy, there was a partial cessation of hostilities before Plevna until September 6. Meanwhile, on the 3rd, a force of 22,000 Russians under Meretinsky, including a brigade of Cossacks commanded by Skobeleff, succeeded, after a sanguinary conflict, in driving 7,000 Turks from the village of Loftcha and a defensive position west of it, which they permanently occupied. This operation had the effect of cutting off the supplies of Osman Pasha from the south. An artillery duel then followed between the whole of the attacking and defending armies, which lasted until the 11th, and, judging from the long and careful accounts of the correspondents, the firing seems to have had little effect on either side. In the interim the Romanians were posted opposite the Grivitza Redoubt, which, as we have already said, was the most formidable of all the Turkish defenses. Meretinsky and Skobeleff were in the vicinity of the Loftcha road; and Kriloff and Krüdener were moving about in co-operation, the former having posted himself on the Radisovo height with the forces under his command. Of the Grivitza and the Romanian operations we shall speak more fully hereafter. At the other points of attack nothing serious happened until the 11th, when, a general assault being ordered, the attack of Kriloff and Krüdener was directed against a position known as the 'Mamelon,' south of Plevna, whilst Skobeleff made a vigorous assault upon a double redoubt on the south-east, the object being to carry these positions which were believed to be the most vulnerable, whilst the Romanians were 'holding' the Turks at their strongest redoubt—the Grivitza. Supported by Romanian artillery, Kriloff attacked the 'Mamelon' three times during the day, each time with fresh forces; but he was as often repulsed with terrible loss, the third attack and defeat lasting only twenty minutes. In fact, Kriloff and Krüdener were repulsed all along the line. Skobeleff was somewhat more fortunate, having begun his attack after Kriloff's second reverse. With a loss of 2,000 men he succeeded in carrying the Turkish position; and at a further sacrifice of 3,000 he held it for a time only, for it was commanded by the Krishine redoubt (which was the ultimate object of his operations) on his left, and by Plevna on the north. The Turks attempted in vain five times to dislodge him. Skobeleff supplicated time after time for support, but it only arrived when, after the sixth Turkish attack—this time successful—he had been forced to withdraw, and was retreating to his old ground. The closing scene of his day's operations has been frequently described, but as his recent escapade gives fresh interest to anything concerning him, it will lose nothing by repetition: 'It was just after this that I met General Skobeleff the first time that day. He was in a fearful state of excitement and fury. His uniform was covered with mud and filth, his sword broken, his cross of St. George twisted round on his shoulder, his face black with powder and smoke, his eyes haggard and bloodshot, and his voice quite gone. He spoke in a, hoarse whisper. I never before saw such a picture of battle as he presented. I saw him again in his tent at night. He was quite calm and collected. He said, "I have done my best. I could do no more. My detachment is half destroyed; my regiments do not exist. I have no officers left. They sent me no reinforcements, and I have lost three guns." They were three of the four guns which he placed in the redoubt upon taking it, only one of which his retreating troops had been able to carry off. "Why did they refuse you reinforcements?" I asked. "Who was to blame?" "I blame nobody," he replied; "it is the will of God!"'

VI.

We have thus loosely described how the Turks had effectually disposed of the whole Russian attack excepting that of the Romanians, and now we must turn for a moment to inquire what was occurring at Grivitza. This redoubt is constantly referred to by the correspondents as the most formidable of all the Turkish positions. It is called 'the indomitable Grivica redoubt;' 'the dreaded redoubt;' 'they' (the Russians) 'may bombard it for a week, sacrifice a brigade of infantry, and not succeed in taking it.' 'The Turkish positions,' says one writer, 'opposite to the Romanian section, are the stronger both by nature and art. But there are but 28,000 Romanians to 50,000 Russians. It seems logically to follow that the function of the Romanians is intended to be chiefly of a demonstrative character.' How 'demonstrative' it was we shall see presently.

Already on the 7th and 8th, the Russian siege guns had been pushed forward in closer proximity to the Grivitza, and on the 9th the Romanians worked their batteries nearer to it; whilst on the 10th their infantry occupied a natural shelter-trench, from which they were picking off the Turkish gunners in the redoubt. On the same day a couple of companies of Russians, thinking the redoubt was evacuated, made an attempt to take it, but when a small party of advancing skirmishers arrived within a hundred yards of the foot of the glacis, they were confronted by a row of rifle muzzles and Turkish heads, and thought it more prudent to retire.

On the 11th, however, the Romanians, with whom were three battalions of Russians, made their 'demonstration' against the Grivitza simultaneously with the Russian attacks on the other redoubts. Little attention appears to have been paid to them in the slaughter of that terrible day, but on the following the correspondents narrated the result of their operations, and as those not only substantiated the title of the young army to *élan* and bravery, but really constituted the turning point in the war, we will endeavor to follow their brief descriptions of the events.

'It appears,' writes one of the chroniclers, 'that at half-past two p.m. the redoubt was attacked by two Romanian brigades each consisting of four battalions, and three battalions of Russians. The Romanians attacked from the east and south-east, the Russians from the south and south-west. The attack was made in the following manner:—First a lino of skirmishers with men carrying scaling ladders, gabions, and fascines among them. The latter had their rifles slung on their backs, and were ordered in no case to fire but merely to run forward, fill up the ditch, and place their ladders behind. Then followed the second line in company column formation for the attack, followed by the third line to support the assault. At half-past two p.m. the attack was made by the Romanians, and it is said that by some mistake the Russians arrived half an hour too late. Be that as it may, the assault was repulsed, and all retired except two companies of infantry, which rallied, and, keeping under cover, maintained a brisk fire against the work.

'At half-past five the attack was renewed by a battalion of the Romanian militia, followed by two Russian battalions of the 17th and 18th regiments. The redoubt was then carried, and the Turks withdrew to the other redoubt a little to the north of the captured work. But it was soon apparent that the redoubt could not be held without reinforcements, and three Romanian battalions with a battery of artillery were ordered forward. They lost their way, however, in the fog, and were thus precluded from rendering the required assistance; consequently, when the Turks returned to the attack, the allies were driven out.

'The third assault soon followed, and the work was finally captured at seven p.m. Four guns and a standard were the trophies of the feat of arms. More than once during the night did the Turks advance with shouts of "Allah," but no serious attack was made. Thus, to my surprise, when I reached the Plevna valley this morning, I beheld a flagstaff up defiantly exposing the Romanian flag in that hitherto dreaded Grivica Redoubt.'

How sanguinary had been the struggle which is here described in a few commonplace sentences is manifest from the subsequent appearance of the captured redoubt.

'The interior of this large work was piled up not only with dead but with wounded, forming one ghastly indistinguishable mass of dead and living bodies, the wounded being as little heeded as the dead. The fire had hindered the doctors from coming up to attend to the wounded, and the same cause had kept back the wounded-bearers. There were not even comrades to moisten the lips of their wretched fellow-soldiers, or give them a word of consolation. There they lie, writhing and groaning. I think some attempt might have been made, at whatever risk, to aid these poor fellows, for they were gallant men, who, twenty-four hours before, had so valiantly and successfully struggled for the conquest of that long-uncaptured redoubt; and it was sad now to see them dying without any attempt being made to attend to them. I could fill pages with a description of this harrowing scene and others near it, which I witnessed, but the task would be equally a strain on my own nerves and on those of your readers.'

But the Romanians were not contented with holding their position. Within 250 yards of the Grivitza was another Turkish redoubt whose fire commanded the former, and that they attempted in vain to take on the 11th. Nothing daunted, however, they held their ground day after day, and on the

18th they made another gallant but futile attempt to expel the enemy from his position. 'It is said they will renew it,' writes one of the spectators, 'and there is plenty of fight in Prince Charles's gallant young army, but, in my opinion, there is little chance of success unless they work up to the hostile redoubt by sap.' On September 24 they were progressing by trenches, and were only 80 yards from the second Grivitza redoubt. 'Their fighting spirit and cheerful endurance of hardships are admirable,' we hear. And again, on the 26th: 'The Romanians are pushing forward their works against the second redoubt with a perseverance and pluck worthy all praise, and which is the more remarkable as the Russians are doing absolutely nothing on their side.' This contrast comes from the pen of the chronicler who told the story of the twenty Romanians being taken prisoners by five Russians, and whose views of the relative merits of the combatants had evidently undergone considerable modification; for he now says of the Russians: 'They are waiting for reinforcements, which are arriving slowly, and which, when they are here, will hardly more than cover the losses by battle and by sickness during the last two months. I think history offers no such example of a splendid army in such an utterly helpless condition. The Romanian generals are showing far more pluck and energy.'

The Romanians were unable to capture the second redoubt, but they managed not only to hold their advanced position before Plevna, but to give material assistance elsewhere in turning the siege into an investment. On November 21 they captured Rahova, on the Danube, which greatly facilitated operations against the doomed fortress and aided to make the works of the allies impregnable. In the closing incidents of the investment of Plevna the Romanians took little or no part in consequence of the position which they occupied. On the morning of December 10, Osman Pasha made his brave but unsuccessful attempt to break through the Russian lines, a struggle in which both sides performed prodigies of valor. One whole Russian regiment was annihilated in the effort to check the enemy, whose general was himself wounded; and after having kept the Russo-

Romanian army at bay with an inferior force for more than four months, he was at length obliged to surrender with his whole army. Here is a glimpse of the final scene, as the wounded hero met his conquerors:—

> 'The Grand Duke rode up to the carriage, and for some seconds the two chiefs gazed into each other's faces without the utterance of a word. Then the Grand Duke stretched out his hand and shook the hand of Osman Pasha heartily and said: "I compliment you on your defense of Plevna; it is one of the most splendid military feats in history." Osman Pasha smiled sadly, rose painfully to his feet in spite of his wound, said something which I could not hear, and then reseated himself. The Russian officers all cried "Bravo! bravo!" repeatedly, and all saluted respectfully. There was not one among them who did not gaze on the hero of Plevna with the greatest admiration and sympathy. Prince Charles, who had arrived, rode up, and repeated unwittingly almost every word of the Grand Duke, and likewise shook hands. Osman Pasha again rose and bowed, this time in grim silence.'

VI.

How easy it is to be magnanimous to a fallen foe; how difficult, with some people, to be honorable in their dealings with an ally, especially if he has been successful where they failed! The first is a claim of superiority, and the higher the meed of praise awarded by us to the vanquished the greater appears our victory; but the less we admit to be due to our comrade in arms, the greater credit is left for ourselves. And yet what will be the judgment of posterity upon the conduct of Russia towards her brave ally who had saved her honor, if not the integrity of her empire? Whatever she may think, the joy-bells would have rung throughout a great portion of Europe, and certainly the party then dominant in England would have rejoiced exceedingly, if she had been driven back over the Pruth, and had been compelled to busy herself with much-needed reforms in her own country instead of meddling with the affairs of her neighbors and seeking to extend her already overgrown possessions.

The war was never popular with the masses in Romania, and although, at the opening of the Chambers in November 1877, the royal speech predicted that the fall of Plevna would mean a complete emancipation for Romania, much uneasiness prevailed concerning the designs of Russia—uneasiness which was justified by subsequent events. On December 17, a load having been lifted from the mind of the nation by the surrender of Osman Pasha, there was great rejoicing at Bucharest on the occasion of the Czar's visit. He was on his way to St. Petersburg to receive the congratulations of his subjects, having left Plevna behind him, 'full of horrors.' He is dead now, but his son and all princes who live by the sword would do well to peruse and reperuse the accounts of the tragical scenes that the victors left upon the battle-field when they departed to receive the ovations of the fickle populace. The Romanians fêted their victorious allies, to whom it must be admitted that we have here done ample justice in all their proceedings. But they were the same Russians who, under Peter the Great, were reported to have stolen the boots from the feet of their sleeping hosts; the same whose hands the Romanians had kissed when in 1829 they had released them from the Turkish yoke; who it 1853 overran the Principalities with a view to their permanent occupation, and who a few months after the events above recorded betrayed their allies, and, for the risk they had run of once more sacrificing their national existence, deprived them of Southern Bessarabia, a province inhabited almost entirely by Romanians.

Still the war brought its compensating advantages. The Dobrudscha which the Romanians received in exchange for Bessarabia, is proving a more valuable acquisition both for trade and for strategical purposes than was at first anticipated.

The Treaty of San Stephano, which was executed between Russia and Turkey on February 19 [March 3], 1878, and was practically confirmed by the Berlin Conference, contained among its other provisions this one (part of Article V.): 'The Sublime Porte recognizes the independence of Romania, which will establish its right to an indemnity to be discussed between the two countries;' and (part of Article XII.): 'All the Danubian strongholds shall be razed. There shall be no strongholds in future on the banks of this river, nor any men-of-war in the waters of the Principalities of Romania, Servia, and Bulgaria, except the usual *stationnaires* and the small vessels intended for river police and custom-house purposes.' And

Article XIX. gave to Russia that part of Turkey bordering on the Danube, known as the Dobrudscha, which Russia 'reserves the right of exchanging for the part of Bessarabia detached from her by the treaty of 1856,' and which, to the great indignation of the Romanians, she subsequently forced them to relinquish in 'exchange' for her newly acquired territory.

But *n'importe*. Romania was free; and this time she had fought for and won her complete independence.

VII.

There is something unsettled in the nature of an independent principality. The title fails to convey the idea of a free and sovereign people, and we are always disposed to regard it as the possible province of some annexing neighbor. So thought a writer on Romania four years ago, at the close of the war of liberation. 'Situated as it is, as an independent State, it must sooner or later fall to Russia or Austria, more probably to the former.' So, in all probability, thought the Russian diplomatists when they created a number of weak principalities south of the Danube to serve them as stepping-stones to Constantinople. And so, too, thought the Romanians themselves. They knew that a name is 'neither hand, nor foot, nor arm, nor face, nor any other part belonging to a man,' and so they 'doffed the name,' and on May 23, 1881, with the concurrence of the great Powers of Europe, they invested their prince and princess with the royal dignity, placing upon their sovereign's head a crown made from the very guns which he had captured whilst he was fighting for their liberties.

The poetic sentiment which attaches to this last act of the people of Romania brings vividly before our mind's eye the dramatic character of her whole national career. Twice have we found the course of her history lost in darkness—first in the clouds of antiquity by which the early life of every nation is obscured; then in the still impenetrable gloom of the so-called dark ages, which continued to hang over the Danubian plains long after it was lifted from every other part of Europe. Conquered first, and civilized by one who ranks among the greatest heroes of the Roman Empire, she has inherited a high antiquity of which she may be justly proud, remembering, however, that honorable ancestry alone is not the measure of a nation's greatness. But then, for ages we might almost say, the blast which swept across her plains with all the fury of a tempest, but, as it traveled westward, broke and moderated under the influence of the older civilization, caused a second blank in her existence; and when she once more rose from her prostration, she found herself whole centuries behind the western peoples. But hardly had she time to breathe again, and ere the wounds inflicted on her by the Goths, and Huns, and Avars were yet fully healed, another ruthless conqueror had laid hands upon her; and spite of all her efforts to regain her liberty he held her fast, and sent her taskmasters as cruel and exacting as the leaders of barbarian hordes had been before. And yet her spirit was indomitable; bowed but not broken she continued to live on, and ever strove for freedom. Mircea, Stephen, Michael, those are the names which vindicate her claim to courage, and which shield her from the charge of cowardly submission. And next she is the object of contention between two neighboring despots, the one endeavoring to hold, the other to annex her. It is a marvelt hat between them she was not dismembered limb from limb.

At length for her, as for all suffering peoples, the day of liberation was at hand; the iron bonds which Oriental despotism had forged were loosened by the agency of Western progress, and, lightened of her load, she this time struck a more effectual blow for liberty, and was among the first to unfurl the flag of freedom in the East. But a long succession of barbarian governors, the license of repeated military occupations, the proximity of Tartar savagery on the one side and of Oriental effeminacy on the other, these incidents of her long-continued vassalage have necessarily, and, it is to be hoped, but for a time, left their evil influence upon the nation, which it is now the earnest endeavor of her patriotic leaders to exterminate.

CHAPTER XV.

PRESENT ROMANIAN LEADERS AND THEIR POLICY.

The King—Customs of the Court—The Queen—Her attainments—Extract from her poetry—Madame Rosetti—Her patriotism and adventures—M. Constantin A. Rosetti—His career and public services—M. Bratiano—Other leaders of public opinion—The party of progress—Their past foreign and domestic policy—Geographical boundaries—Panslavism and Panroumanism—The future policy of Romania—Growth by pacific means—(Note: Comparative values of Russian, Turkish, and Romanian securities)—Romania and Great Britain—Conclusion.

I.

We have passed in hasty and imperfect review those features in the national life of Romania which we believed would be of interest to our readers, and will now endeavor to present to them sketches of a few of the persons of distinction who are forming public opinion, and are the leaders of progress in the country, premising, however, that there are many omissions, due partly to our own ignorance, and partly to the fact that the discussion of the merits and demerits of some of the public men would not have been fitting in this treatise.

By his rank and patriotism, and not least by his extensive knowledge, his Majesty King Charles is entitled to our first consideration. Of his political career we have spoken in our historical summary, and little more need be added. He was born on April 20, 1839, and is therefore about forty-three years of age. On November 15, 1869, he married Pauline Elisabeth, Princess of Wied, who was then about twenty-six years old; but, unfortunately, the sole offspring of their union, a little girl, lies interred in the grounds of the Asyle Hélène. The King is a handsome man, rather above the average height, and, so far as his regularly formed features are concerned, he might belong to any nationality of Western Europe. He usually wears a somewhat severe expression, but the moment he begins to converse this at once disappears. His manner is quiet and earnest, although he often warms into enthusiasm, and he has the happy faculty of placing all with whom he comes into contact at perfect ease. He possesses a wide range of information, and speaks with evident knowledge on all matters of interest to his subjects or to civilization. Of course he is well acquainted with his adopted country and its resources, takes a lively interest in its trade and capabilities; and so far as the geographical configuration of Romania is concerned, he not only knows all about the level country, but has either ridden or walked through every part of the Carpathians. His scientific knowledge is such as one might expect in an educated German, and is chiefly of a practical kind. He is deeply interested in arboriculture, about which he knows more than many who are entrusted with the care and fate of the vast woods that clothe the mountain districts, and he has often pointed out to such persons errors in their mode of felling timber. In private life the King is hospitable, genial, and very regular in his habits; he is a devout Catholic, but a constant attendant upon the services of the Greek Church.

But of course our interest in him is necessarily rather of a public than of a private character. Is he constitutional? or is Europe likely some day to be favored with a Romanian *coup d'état*? The answer to these questions is clear and emphatic. Although a Hohenzollern, he is a Constitutional Liberal, we should say of an advanced type. We spoke before of his misunderstandings with his ministers; but even those who were originally opposed to him, and who watched his every act with suspicion, state that he has managed with great tact to steer clear of unconstitutional courses; indeed, from their own admissions and the facts of history, it is clear that he must have served a very trying apprenticeship in the art of constitutional rule. His demeanor towards his subjects and that of his queen, of whom we shall speak presently, is everything that can be desired, and both are winning their affections more completely year by year.

When the court is at Bucharest a great portion of the king's time is devoted to giving audiences, not only to officials, but to all who desire to know their sovereign, and even to seek his counsel or that of his amiable consort. Two books are kept at the palace, one for callers only, and the other for persons who desire to see and speak with the king or queen, for they give audiences apart. Those who enter their names in the second book must give notice to the 'Hofmarschall,' and they are then sent for in turn, and punctuality above all things is insisted upon. The king gives audiences from 1 to 3 or 4 p.m.; The queen for a longer time, and young as she is, for she has not yet attained her fortieth year, she is regarded as the mother of her people, and many there are who come to her for advice or consolation. But we are digressing. If the king interests himself in the civil affairs of Romania, he is a soldier before everything else. The virtual as well as the nominal head of the army, he always wears uniform, and nothing is too unimportant for his consideration in the organization of his army. Those who have been in the field with him and much about his person extol his coolness, bravery, and endurance. He has often risked his life in battle, was always to the fore visiting outposts and bivouacs in the most inclement weather, and there can be no doubt that it is to his bravery as a general, and to his tact and patience as a statesman, that Romania is largely indebted for her independence and her promise in the future.

II.

The Queen of Romania is almost too well known in Europe, through her literary attainments, to need any description here; still a few particulars concerning her may be of interest to our readers. She is of the middle height, has an amiable face and still more affable manner. She, too, might pass for a lady of any western country, having very little to indicate her German nationality. Her voice is soft and melodious, and although she can speak well on literary and scientific subjects, there is not the slightest pedantry or affectation of learning in her discourse. She is said to speak six languages, and she certainly speaks Romanian, French, German, and English.

We do not know what the other two may be, but if she speaks the four languages here named as fluently and with as little foreign accent as she does our own, she may fairly claim to be an accomplished linguist. All educated Romanians speak French, and most of them German, besides their own tongue; indeed French is almost the universal language of the middle classes, whilst those who have been educated here, especially the younger men, naturally speak English well, and therefore the Queen is in this respect only somewhat ahead of her more accomplished subjects. But, as we have already stated, she is a poetess, and her verses are often marked by great depth of feeling. She possesses, too, considerable scientific knowledge and great taste in art, and one of her chief desires is to promote national industry. She sets the example by wearing the national costume (in which her portrait is usually taken) whilst in the country, and requires it to be worn on State occasions, her main object being, we were told, to encourage the peasant women who make these costumes in their own homes. But whilst in these matters, as in her devotion to public duty, the Queen identifies herself with the Romanian people and their interests, she would not be a German if she had forgotten the 'Fatherland.'

> 'Land of greenwood and of vine,
> Sparkling wavelets of the Rhine,
> Hushed thy song, afar thy gleam.
> All to me, now, but a dream.
>
> 'Oft when I these eyelids close,
> Purling sounds haunt my repose,
> Vessels in the sunlight's ray,
> 'Fore the wind, speed on their way.
>
> 'Lovely home on German plain
> Once my own, but ne'er again,
> Thou wilt be to mem'ry dear
> Till they place me on my bier.'

III.

But her Majesty, who is a Protestant, is not the only lady now living who has made her mark in Romanian history. There is another of whom we are sure our readers will be glad to hear something, for she is an accomplished Englishwoman, and it is very questionable whether, after all, the Romanians do not owe their independence as much to her energy and devotion as to any other cause; we mean Madame Rosetti, the wife of the Home Secretary. It was mentioned in our historical summary that the patriots of 1848 made their escape to France in that year, and that they returned after the Crimean war in 1856. That is a long story told in a couple of sentences, and but for Madame Rosetti it is probable they would never have escaped, but would have languished and died in a Turkish prison in Bosnia, whilst Romania might have been at this day a Turkish pashalik or a Russian province. The fact is that all the leaders of the revolution, fifteen in number, were arrested and conveyed on board a Turkish man-of-war lying in the Danube; and Madame Rosetti, whose heroic adventures have formed the theme of a work by Michelet, helped them to escape from their captors. As we have already said, she is an Englishwoman, whose maiden name was Grant, and she had only been married about a year when the revolution broke out. Her first child was born a day or two before her husband and his comrades were arrested, but she at once left her bed, and, taking her infant in her arms, prepared to follow them. First she managed to obtain an interview with the patriots on board the Turkish vessel to which they had been conveyed, and there plans were formed which she skilfully and courageously executed. Disguising herself as a peasant, and carrying her child, she followed them up the Danube to Orsova, communicating with her friends from time to time by signals. At Orsova the prisoners were landed, and whilst they were on shore she succeeded in making their guards intoxicated, and, with the connivance of the authorities, prepared suitable conveyances, in which the patriots made their escape. First they passed through Serbia, and reaching Vienna in safety they entered that city the day after the bombardment, and subsequently they made their way through Germany, accompanied by their deliverer, and found a hospitable asylum in Paris. Since her return Madame Rosetti has been as valuable a coadjutor to her husband in his prosperity as she was in his adversity, and she is also a useful and willing adviser to any of her countrymen who, visiting Romania, may stand in need of her assistance.

IV.

Her husband, his Excellency Constantin A. Rosetti, has also reaped the reward of his devotion to his country's welfare. He is of an old boyard family of Italian origin, and in his early youth he was not only a soldier in the national army, but his pen also gained for him a considerable reputation, for he composed and published many interesting Romanian poems. At the age of about thirty-two years he married the English lady to whom he owes so much, and of his adventures in 1848 we have already twice spoken. Before he permanently took up his residence in Paris after his escape, we believe he spent some time in Constantinople. In Paris he was the companion of Michelet, Quinet, and other leading writers, and with them and his countrymen the brothers Bratiano and Golesco he managed by his patriotic publications to keep the lamp of liberty burning in his own country. Here, too, he is said to have enjoyed the support of our own distinguished statesman, William Ewart Gladstone, who was subsequently made a Romanian citizen by an Act of the legislature about the year 1861, and whom the Romanians still regard with feelings of great respect and admiration. On the return of M. Rosetti to Romania after the Crimean war he founded the 'Romanal' a daily paper which still occupies a high position among the journals of the capital, and which remains his property. He took a conspicuous part in the union of the Principalities under Prince Couza, and supported that prince whilst his proceedings were constitutional, but he was one of the most active agents in his deposition, and the only serious objection that has been taken to his acts and those of his colleagues on that occasion is that he employed the army to bring about the prince's overthrow. To this matter, however, we have already referred in our historical summary. In 1866 he was one of the provisional government, and was at first by no means favorably disposed towards the present king, who was, we believe, recommended to the Romanians by the Emperor Napoleon III. In later times, however, he became one of his Majesty's most faithful advisers.

M. Rosetti is about sixty-seven years of age, full of life and energy. His career of hardship has somewhat bowed his physical frame, but it has in no way interfered with his cheerful and kindly disposition. In appearance he is an Italian, has very prominent but mild eyes, and a most thoughtful, somewhat careworn countenance. He is *vif*, hot and excitable, and not unfrequently lets his voice be heard if anything is going wrong in public affairs, and something is very often going wrong in Romania. He speaks Romanian, French, and German, and can write English (of which he is fond of interjecting an expressive word now and then when he is speaking in French) fairly well. Unfortunately for scandal-mongers, of whom there are a good many in the capital and elsewhere, M. Rosetti lives with great simplicity on the premises of the 'Romanul,' and upon, the profits of his paper and his salary; so they are unable to charge him with peculation, which they would certainly do if he gave them the slightest justification. He is a Radical, and an uncompromising enemy of *coups d'état*, and of despotism or unconstitutional proceedings in any form, a man of unflinching honesty and the leader of political thought in his country. In fact, he is a patriot, and his countrymen know and appreciate the fact.

They usually couple his name with that of M. Bratiano, who is President of the Council and Minister of Finance, and, so far as temperament is concerned, the very opposite of his colleague. M. Bratiano is a quiet, courteous gentleman, somewhat younger than M. Rosetti. His features are regular and handsome, his beard and hair iron-grey, and his voice even and melodious. He is full of pleasant humour, and has the bearing and manner of an English gentleman; but although an excellent debater, he is not a good linguist. In Romania they say, 'Rosetti thinks and Bratiano speaks,' but Bratiano thinks as well as speaks. So completely at one are the two statesmen that many of the uninformed poorer classes who have not seen them believe them to be one person, whom they call 'Bratiano-Rosetti,' and whilst we were in Bucharestwe saw a caricature (an art in which the Romanians take great delight) where the two statesmen were depicted as the Siamese twins.

The aim and policy of M. Bratiano are well expressed in one of his despatches on the question of the Danube, which were made public by that diplomatic phenomenon M. Callimaki-Catargi. 'Our attitude,' he says, 'like the whole policy of the ministry to which I belong, has always been, and ever should be, defensive, not offensive.'

Among the other leaders of political thought in Romania is Prince Demeter Ghika, President of the Senate, a fine burly good-natured gentleman of the old school; Prince Jon Ghika, at present the Romanian Ambassador in London, a patriot and a savant, whose sons were educated in England; M. Statesco, the Foreign Minister, a young and promising statesman; M. Stourdza, the director of the National Credit Association; and there are doubtless many others of whom we do not like to speak without a nearer acquaintance, or better information than we possess. One of these is M. Cogalniceanu, a deputy, who has written a good history of Romania, was a minister under Prince Couza, and we believe the author of the celebrated Act of 1864 which created the peasant proprietary of the country.

V.

From men to measures is a natural transition in politics. Although we have endeavored to show, and do not hesitate to repeat here, that some of the great principles laid down in the Constitution of Romania are only beginning to be carried out in practice, it is but just to add that the vigor and energy with which the party of progress has of late years developed the resources of the country is a matter of surprise and admiration even to foreigners resident there who are acquainted with our Western methods. The present *régime* began, as we have already said, in 1875, and since that time the foreign policy of the party in power first liberated the nation from the last vestige of foreign despotism; then firmly established it as a European kingdom. That they occasionally make mistakes no one can deny. For example, the recent announcement in the speech from the throne, that Romania was prepared in the present and future for every sacrifice which it might be necessary to make to ensure in all respects absolute facility of navigation of the Danube, appears to an outsider to have been an error in judgment, if the government were not prepared to hear with equanimity of the threatened departure of the ambassador of a neighboring State which had put the cap upon its head, and against whose unwarrantable pretensions the remark was directed. But it is easy to be wise after the event, and we admit that it is presumptuous for anyone to criticize hastily any matter that is being tossed about on the troubled sea of Oriental politics. Living as we do on a seagirt isle which is practically unapproachable to an external foe, and having for centuries enjoyed the blessings of freedom, we can have no conception of the difficult cards which Romanian statesmen have to play in the political game in which they are often compelled, much against their desire, to participate. From time to time they hear great international theories propounded for the benefit of their powerful neighbors, to which they are compelled to close their ears, however nearly those principles may apply to their own condition. Suppose, for example, some European Power claims new territory on the ground of geographical position. Why, ask the Romanians, should we be hemmed in as we are on every side? Why should not the plains on both sides of the Danube guarded by the Balkans and the Carpathians constitute a strong realm, one and indivisible, with the great river flowing as an artery through its center? The answer is, Russia! If an v of the Great Powers had insisted upon such a readjustment in the East, she would have opposed it, for is not Bulgaria her last stepping-stone to Constantinople? 'Skobeleff the First, King of Bulgaria' would suit her aims far better. This reminds one of 'Panslavism.' Who will deny the right of adjacent branches of the same race to live under one government? Admitted; but then why not also Panroumanism? In that case considerable portions of Austro-Hungary, Bessarabia, Bulgaria, Servia, would have to be added to the present dominions of King Charles of Romania; for there are almost as many Romanians in those countries as there are within the present boundaries of the kingdom.

But if Romanian statesmen are permitted to enjoy their *reflections* on these interesting political topics, they know that it would be unsafe to publish them, for, as we have seen, if they venture even, to cry too loudly 'Romania for the Romanians,' some hectoring neighbor instantly takes the alarm and threatens to withdraw its ambassador; and in case of a fracas between any two such neighboring States, even the rights which she at present enjoys would hardly be respected. Her policy is therefore tolerably well defined, and it was ably set forth in the royal speech which contained that dangerous reference to Austrian pretensions. Peace is requisite for her, in order that her Parliament may occupy itself in developing the riches of the soil and the economic interests of the country; but the organization of a strong defensive army is equally necessary to protect those interests from grasping and despotic States in her vicinity, and because, 'by the development of all the forces of the nation, Romania will become an element of order, peace, and progress in Eastern Europe.' In fact, she must make herself, by peaceful measures, what Michael the Brave succeeded for a very short time, and from motives of personal ambition, in making her by the sword in his day, the arbiter of surrounding nations, the Belgium of the East, which no aggressive despot would dare to assail; and she must become sufficiently strong to resist not only inimical but friendly foreign occupations, which have such a demoralizing effect upon her people.

On this undertaking her Government has already for some years past been embarked. It has secured railway property for the State which was in the hands of aliens, has begun to improve watercourses, created national credit institutions, reduced the interest upon the national debt, increased the value of Romanian securities, and has generally followed, as it still pursues, the ways of 'peace, retrenchment, and reform.'

We have no wish to patronize Romania even in words, for her best friend is he who tells her to depend entirely on her own resources and develop those herself; to carve her fortunes, and to shape her ends. But when we look upon her sufferings, reflecting how for ages she has lain beneath the claws of savage enemies, quailed under despots who sucked the lifeblood of the nation, and then compare her constitutional democracy with ours—nay, if alone from a material point of view we weigh the interest we have in her prosperity, we cannot fail to see that in the East is rising up a Power, in part of our creation, young and weak as yet, but full of hope and promise; and therefore, in concluding this imperfect record of her 'past and present,' we heartily commend her future to the earnest watchfulness of every English friend of liberty.

www.ingramcontent.com/pod-product-compliance
Lightning Source LLC
Chambersburg PA
CBHW070359120526
44590CB00014B/1181